Jury Nullification

The Jurisprudence of Jurors' Privilege

By

Travis Hreno

Jury Nullification: The Jurisprudence of Jurors' Privilege

By Travis Hreno

This book first published 2024

Ethics International Press Ltd, UK

British Library Cataloguing in Publication Data

A catalogue record for this book is available from the British Library

Print Book ISBN: 978-1-80441-090-5

eBook ISBN: 978-1-80441-091-2

Dedicated to My Beloved Wife, Tine

Your contributions, insights, and impeccable editing skills have been of immeasurable value to the quality and success of this book. The precision and clarity of my thoughts would not have found lucid expression were it not for your time and dedication in proofreading the (many different drafts of the) manuscript that I put in your capable editorial hands. Thank you for the tireless and benignant dedication you devoted towards wordsmithing my document into a readable and coherent form.

Yet, beyond the tangible elements of your assistance lies the intangible and priceless foundation upon which this project stands. Your support and countenance, offered unconditionally and with unmitigated devotion, made the successful completion of this manuscript possible. The consistent environment of encouragement you provided, both emotionally and practically, were instrumental to this endeavor. Your belief in me and in the importance of this work has been a guiding light, illuminating the path through countless hours of research, writing, and revisions. Without your presence, your wisdom, and your boundless love, this journey would not have been possible. For that, and for being my inspiration, my confidante, and my unwavering source of strength, I express my deepest gratitude and love.

Thank you for being my steadfast companion on this scholarly odyssey and in life.

With all my love,

Travis

Table of Contents

Acknowledgments

Financial support for this research was received from the *Faculty Research Committee* of The University of Akron.

I am deeply grateful to the following individuals and institutions whose support, guidance, and encouragement made this book possible:

The University of Akron: I would like to thank the University of Akron for its generous support during the research and writing of this manuscript. As a recipient of the University's Professional Development Leave (PDL) during the Fall 2023 semester, I was provided with invaluable time and resources that significantly contributed to the completion and quality of this work. I extend my sincere appreciation to The University of Akron for their patronage and for their commitment to the advancement of academic research.

The University of Akron School of Law: I extend my sincere gratitude to the University of Akron School of Law for the extraordinary privilege of being hosted as an *Affiliated Research Scholar* during the 2023-24 academic year. The conducive academic environment, coupled with the wealth of resources generously offered, played an instrumental role in the successful completion of this undertaking. The opportunity to engage with esteemed colleagues, access extensive library holdings, and participate in scholarly events profoundly contributed to the depth and quality of my research. I express my deepest appreciation for the collegial academic atmosphere and collaborative spirit that defines the School of Law at the University of Akron.

Dr. John Huss: I am deeply grateful for Dr. John Huss's encouragement and support throughout the writing of this book. His steadfast belief in the significance of this project has been a constant and motivating force. His insightful proofreading, editorial comments, and feedback were invaluable in refining the manuscript. Dr. Huss's commitment and dedication to this project has not only elevated the cogency and clarity of my work but has thereby made a lasting impact on its quality. It is no exaggeration to say that my achievements in this endeavor owe a great deal to his consistent backing, guidance, and support. Moreover, his mentorship has been instrumental to the overall success of this project, and I am profoundly grateful for the counsel and wisdom he has shared with me during this process. Finally, I would be remiss if I were not to mention how appreciative I am for John's continued friendship, advice, and collegiality.

Michael Gentithes: I express my sincere gratitude to Michael Gentithes, Associate Dean of Academic Affairs at The University of Akron School of Law. His instrumental role in facilitating my appointment as a *Visiting Research Scholar* at the School of Law was invaluable for this project's success. Moreover, he facilitated seamless access to crucial resources and research materials through the library, enabling me to delve into my project with comprehensive and relevant information. Michael also generously shared his time and expertise by answering my many questions related to doctrine and legal procedure. His guidance significantly enhanced the depth and accuracy of my research. Most notably, Michael's commitment to scholarly inquiry and investigation shone through when he graciously proofread my manuscript. His insightful feedback and comments were not only informative but also played a pivotal role in refining the content. I am truly appreciative of Michael Gentithes's dedication to the advancement of scholarship and his generosity in sharing knowledge.

Imre Huss: I would like to extend my appreciation and thanks to Imre Huss for his insightful and helpful comments and editing suggestions. I am grateful for his aid and assistance in polishing and clarifying my manuscript. His time and efforts are acknowledged with gratitude.

John Chaplin and Dr. Nathanial Blower: I would also like to thank my colleagues John Chaplin and Dr. Nathanial Blower for their helpful insight and feedback on earlier drafts of this manuscript. I am fortunate to have had the privilege of consulting with such dedicated and knowledgeable scholars.

This book is a reflection of the collective effort of these remarkable individuals and institutions. Thank you for being an integral part of this project.

Introduction

Jury nullification in the criminal law refers to that phenomenon whereby a jury returns a not guilty verdict for a defendant it believes to be factually and legally guilty of the crime charged. To put this explicitly, a jury nullifies when, despite believing both a) that the defendant did, beyond a reasonable doubt, commit the act/omission in question, and b) that such behavior is, in fact, prohibited by law, nevertheless returns a verdict of not guilty. That the jury can behave in such manner without fear of punishment, and without having its verdict impeached, overturned, or overruled, is beyond dispute, and case law overwhelmingly confirms as much.[1] The jury's absolute and unconditional power to conscientiously acquit a defendant when the law and facts would otherwise support a guilty verdict has been characterized as a "safety valve"[2] in the legal system, providing jurors with the authority to challenge laws they find objectionable or unjust. This creates an interesting tension in the law. Since jury verdicts of acquittal are, for the most part, binding (save for those cases involving legal or procedural errors), it would appear that built into the very legal system itself is a means for that legal system to be subverted. It is exactly because of this potential for jural self-subversion that jury nullification has been historically, and remains to this day, a highly contentious and controversial issue, both among legal scholars and the

---

[1] See, for example, *Horning v. District of Columbia,* 41 S.Ct. 53 (1920), where Holmes, J. stated: "[T]he jury has the power to bring in a verdict in the teeth of both law and facts;" *Morissette v. United States,* 342 U.S. 246, 275 (1952): "But juries are not bound by what seems inescapable logic to judges;" *United States v. Moylan,* 417 F.2d 1002, 1006 (4th Cir. 1969) (emphasis added): "If the jury feels the law is unjust, we recognize the undisputed power of the jury to acquit, even if its verdict is contrary to the law as given by a judge, and contrary to the evidence...If the jury feels that the law under which the defendant is accused is unjust, or that exigent circumstances justified the actions of the accused, or for any reason which appeals to their logic or passion, the jury has the power to acquit, *and the courts must abide by that decision;" U.S. v. Dougherty,* 473 F.2d 1113, 1130 (D.C. Cir., 1972): "The jury has an "unreviewable and irreversible power... to acquit in disregard of the instructions on the law given by the trial judge..."
[2] *U. S. v. Dougherty, supra* note 1, at 1134.

courts. As the Court in *State v. Hooks*[3] so articulately and eloquently explained the problem:

> Jury nullification, also called jury lenity, is the extraordinary power of the jury to issue a not-guilty verdict even if the law as applied to the proven facts establishes that the defendant is guilty. Jury nullification is a curious paradox: it is the jury's prerogative to disregard the law without actually committing an unlawful offense in doing so; its exercise is literally illegitimate (contrary to law) but practically legitimate (allowed by law). It is the physical power to disregard the law that has been laid down to [the jury] by the court. In that sense, the most accurate description of the jury's paradoxical authority to act on its own in disregard of the law even while it is charged with following the law is the raw power to bring in a verdict of acquittal in the teeth of the law and the facts.[4]

At a fundamental level, the nullification debate is in serious conceptual disarray. Even a cursory investigation of the extant literature will reveal that many of the arguments, objections, *ratio decidendi, obiter dicta,* perspectives on, and theories of, jury nullification are either predicated on an incomplete understanding of this legal phenomena, or rely on specious logic (or sometimes both) to reach conclusions that are, on deeper analysis, incompatible with sound jurisprudence and legal reasoning. Importantly, there are two central questions that currently surround the jury nullification debate. First, we can ask: "Is jury nullification a *right*?" Much time and energy has been spent discussing, deliberating, and reflecting on this question, and most of it, I contend, is wasted effort. My model of jury nullification as a *privilege* directly addresses this question and should, once and for all, settle the issue – jury nullification is not a *right* (at least not the legal sense). Nevertheless, I still maintain that jury nullification enjoys a legitimate, and *de jure,* status within the legal system. The other question often asked is: "Should juries be informed or instructed about jury nullification?" Again, the debate around this issue is often speculative, imprecise, conceptually unmotivated, and, on occasion, obviously contrary

---

[3] 752 N.W.2d 79 (Minn. Ct. App. 2008).

[4] *Id.* at 86.

to commonsense. It is my hope that the *bad-faith-juror* objection I put forward will show that the clear, unambiguous, and morally preferable answer to the *nullification instruction* question is that jurors ought *not* be informed of their *privilege* to nullify. Perhaps the biggest problem with the current discourse around jury nullification, however, is that, very often, these two questions, and the separate issues and consequences associated with them, are, in the extant literature, conflated, confused, or casually blended together to the detriment of a clear and lucid understanding of the topic. The focus and goal of this book, therefore, will be to examine each of these questions in turn in order to lend clarity to these two related, yet conceptually distinct, issues surrounding jury nullification. Such disambiguation and clarification is, of course, the purview of the philosopher.

Before we address and answer these central questions and associated controversies surrounding jury nullification, it is important to first identify as precisely as possible what exactly jury nullification actually is. As already mentioned, jury nullification occurs when a jury acquits a defendant it believes to be legally and factually guilty of the crime charged. In finding the defendant not guilty, the jury is refusing to be bound by the facts of the case or by the judge's instructions regarding the law. Thomas Green, in *Verdict According to Conscience,*[5] describes three ways in which a jury may nullify:

> Jury nullification in its strongest sense occurs when the jury recognizes that the defendant's act is proscribed by law but acquits because it does not believe that the act should be proscribed. The behavior, in other words, is not criminal in the eyes of the jury, and the jury is willing to assert its view in the face of what it is told by the judge [i.e., the jury is "judging the law"]. An intermediate form of nullification reflects the jury's view that although the act proved is properly classified as criminal, it is within a class of acts that do not deserve the punishment prescribed for them. Such nullification serves to protect defendants from punishments that are regarded as

[5] Green, Thomas A., *Verdict According to Conscience: Perspectives on the English Criminal Trial Jury, 1200-1800* (University of Chicago Press, 1985).

> excessive. A relatively weak form of nullification reflects the jury's view that although the act proved is criminal and falls in a class of acts that may well deserve the prescribed punishment, such punishment is inappropriate in the case at hand. When nullification is in this way ad hoc, a defendant, because of personal characteristics or the particular features of the case at hand, will escape the generally fair sanctions that a concededly just law prescribes.[6]

We can rephrase this as such: jury nullification occurs when the jury is of the opinion that, despite the law and evidence, it would be wrong to (and thus refuses to) sentence person *P* to punishment *y* for action *z*. The loci of *P*, *y*, and *z* map onto, respectively, Green's idea of weak, intermediate, and strong jury nullification. Green's analysis is generally considered the starting point for any discussion of nullification, and thus, will inform my investigation into this phenomenon as well.

One thing worth noting from the start, however, is that, despite the concerns voiced by some scholars and courts, there is no such thing as *reverse nullification*.[7] Jury nullification properly so-called, I contend, always, and can only, result in a verdict of *not guilty*. Simply put, it is not jury nullification otherwise. Consider the type of case referred to above where the jury returns a not guilty verdict for a defendant it believes to be both legally and factually guilty. Both case and statute law confirm that in such an instance, not only was the relevant law *not* put into effect, more importantly, the relevant law no longer *can* be put into effect, *vis-à-vis* that particular defendant, for that particular offense. Absent some independent legal error or some other form of juror malfeasance, the verdict must stand. In other words, we might say that in the situation so described, the effect and power of that law on that individual was nullified. However, *all* guilty verdicts are, in principle at least, open to review.[8] A jury who convicts a defendant it believes to be innocent has not thereby succeeded in

---

[6] *Id. at* xviii.

[7] See, for instance, *People v. Boyd*, 31 N.Y.3d 953 (N.Y. 2018); Eisen, Mitchell; Dotson, Brenna; and Olaguez, Alma, *Exploring the Prejudicial Effect of Gang Evidence: Under What Conditions Will Jurors Ignore Reasonable Doubt*, 2 Crim. L. Prac. 41 (2014); Finkel, Norman, *Common Sense Justice: Jurors' Notions of the Law* (Harvard University Press, 1995), where he discusses his worries regarding so-called "vengeful nullification."

[8] Though to be fair, such review is relatively rare.

necessarily nullifying the effect of the law on the defendant; the law still may be justly applied to the defendant at a later date after review by an appellate tribunal – an option not available when the jury returns a not guilty verdict. Thus, the law in such cases is not really nullified, though it may still be consciously misapplied by the jury deliberating upon a verdict. Moreover, we already have a name for so-called *reverse nullification*: an unjust conviction.[9]

It would be appropriate at this point to say a few words about the structure of this book before we begin our formal investigation into the jurisprudence of jury nullification and the *nullification instruction*. Chapter 1 traces the history and development of the criminal jury trial in Anglo-American law and the concomitant development of the doctrine of jury nullification until the late nineteenth century, by which point the jury pretty much resembles its modern counterpart. I also look at the doctrine, procedures, and law (both case and statute) surrounding the current right to a jury trial in criminal cases in American jurisprudence. In Chapter 2, I investigate why jury nullification is both derided but tolerated by the justice system. If it is such a pernicious element of the criminal jury trial, as its detractors suggest, why not try to rid the jury system of the ability to so behave altogether? The answer, I will show, turns out to be that there are overwhelming principled, practical, and policy considerations that recommend against any such move. Chapter 3, then, is the first place I really focus on the issue of whether jurors ought to receive the *nullification instruction*. In this chapter I look at the attempts to answer this question through analyzing the intrinsic legal nature or jural status of jury nullification. This method of resolving the question simply will not work, as I demonstrate through recourse to my *privilege*-based account of jury nullification, and so I turn, in Chapters 4 and 5, to an investigation of the *policy-based*, consequence-oriented arguments both for and against, respectively, giving the instruction. It is by looking to these consequences, and balancing them against the broader and more fundamental values we wish to see

[9] And the law has a long, rich history of (admittedly imperfect) procedures, doctrine, and legislation designed to prevent, ameliorate, and correct for, occurrences of such.

instantiated in the criminal justice system, that lead me to conclude that, all things being equal, the *nullification instruction* ought not to be given.

Finally, a note about the general focus of my research for this book. Jury nullification is an issue that has confronted the courts, legislatures, and jurists in nearly every legal regime and jurisdiction with a common law criminal jury tradition, particularly those whose legal systems were inherited from the British. These countries include Australia, Canada, Ireland, Jamaica, the United Kingdom, the United States, and New Zealand, to name but a few.[10] The keen reader will no doubt notice, however, that I confine my investigation of this widespread phenomenon to almost exclusively American cases and research. This was not done capriciously or accidentally, however. I am, after all, situated as a researcher and scholar within the American jural system. It has been my primary focus of study for over two decades; American jurisprudence and philosophy of law are my areas of expertise, specifically as regards jury nullification.

However, and significantly – and this is a point that should not be overlooked or lightly discounted – much of my analysis and critique regarding the nature of the contemporary jury nullification debate will, for the most part, transfer with little conceptual maneuvering to these other jural regimes. Certainly, some of my arguments and conclusions might very well be 'lost in translation,' as it were, or at least altered somewhat, due to differing jurisdictional specificities, including such things as constitutional law, legislation, case law, legal doctrine, and jural norms, traditions, and customs. But the overall texture of much of my analysis will be preserved for those jurisdictions and regimes whose criminal jury systems reflect, to a greater or lesser degree, the broader contours of the American experience in confronting jury nullification. In particular, I believe that my *bad-faith-juror* objection to the *nullification instruction* is jurisdictionally neutral, as is my *privilege* account of jury nullification. Whether these insights will prove useful in any practicable manner for resolving the debates and controversies around jury nullification in these other juridical systems is beyond the scope of this monograph; but I am

[10] This is a representative, but by no means exhaustive, list.

confident that the research and conclusions presented in these following pages will, in fact, be a valuable resource for everyone – including those members of the larger international community of legal scholars – interested in the jurisprudence and philosophy of jury nullification.

Part 1: Jury Nullification

Chapter 1
The Historical Development and Contemporary Law of Jury Nullification

The focus of this chapter is the history and development of the jury system, and the concomitant development of jury nullification, in Anglo-American criminal law. While such historical investigations may not be, in and of themselves, of the most important philosophical interest, they are nevertheless a valuable tool for understanding the context within which subsequent philosophical issues occur and have developed. Accordingly, we will begin this investigation in England, starting in the eleventh century, where the jury as we know it today first began to take shape and form.

1.1 The Early Development and Rise of the Jury System

It must be acknowledged from the start that any attempt to investigate the origin and growth of trial by jury in English jurisprudence is somewhat constrained by the fact that no record exists of its acceptance into English Law. No such records exist, of course, because trial by jury does not owe its existence to any positive law or legislation; it is not the creature of an act of Parliament or official decree. Instead, the jury trial arose gradually from forms and practices of justice whose own origins can only be guessed at. Those records that do exist of pre-Norman jurisprudence[1] do very little to clarify the situation. This has led one legal historian to state that the origin of the trial by jury "may be proved with as much certainty as that of the river whose well-head is a spring oozing out of a grassy bed, and which swells into a broad expanse of waters before it loses itself in the ocean."[2] The rise of the jury system is best seen, thus, as a gradual and natural

---

[1] Only gradually after the Norman conquest of 1066 did legal record keeping begin to become standardized and archived.

[2] William Forsyth, *History of Trial by Jury*, 5 (2nd ed., Frederick D. Linn, 1875).

sequence from the modes of trial in use amongst the Anglo-Saxons and Anglo-Normans.[3]

The jury as it is today – that is, as a body of persons apart from the court, but summoned to attend it in order to determine conclusively the facts of the case in dispute – was an institution unknown to the Anglo-Saxons.[4] Changes in the legal-political structure of England started to occur in earnest after the Conquest of 1066, and while by no means abrupt, these changes were significant as the Normans made their influence felt upon the laws and governance of England. Some of the more important changes made to the English judicial system by the Normans included the separation of the spiritual and temporal courts; the introduction, and addition of, the combat, or duel, to decide cases; and the appointment of justiciars (judges) to administer justice in the King's name throughout the realm. And, of course, the gradual introduction of the trial by jury. But perhaps the most significant influence on the English system of justice by the Normans was the establishment of a strong central court whose authority gradually began to be felt throughout the land. By the time of the reign of Henry II (1154-89), we can see the beginnings of a centralized judicial system which administered a law common to the whole country. It was this centralized judicial system which gradually reduced the local courts to insignificance and substituted one single common law system for the confused mass of local customs which the law of England had heretofore been.[5] By far, however, the two most important of these changes as regards the development of the criminal jury trial were the Assize of Clarendon in 1166, and the abolition of the ordeal by edict of the Roman church in 1215.[6] The later event removed the most common method of

[3] That is, both before and after the Conquest.

[4] Forsyth, *History of Trial by Jury, supra* note 2, at 4.

[5] *Id.* at 4-5.

[6] The two most common forms of ordeal at the time were the *ordeal of cold water,* and the *ordeal of hot iron*. The former required the accused to be plunged into water. Those who sank were considered guiltless and set free; those who floated were deemed guilty and punished according to their offense. The *ordeal of hot iron* required the accused to hold a hot iron in their hand while walking a number of paces. If after three days the resulting wound was clean, the accused was deemed innocent; otherwise, the verdict was guilty. For a more thorough account of the ordeal in early English criminal law, see Kerr, Margaret H.; Forsyth, Richard D.; and Plyley, Michael J., *Cold Water and Hot*

proof from the English criminal process and necessitated a search for its successor. The former event set up the institutional structures that ultimately led to the jury trial being settled upon as that successor.

Let us begin with the Assize of Clarendon. In the mid twelfth century, most criminal prosecutions were still privately initiated. In their simplest form, these prosecutions, called appeals, began with a formal complaint by the injured party. The accused – the appellee – denied the accusation, and the case was decided by combat. The form of publicly initiated prosecutions at this time is still a matter of some debate.[7] In 1166, Henry II reformed the public prosecution system with the Assize of Clarendon which ordained that twelve lawful men of each *hundred,* and four of each *vill,*[8] should report to the royal justices of the *eyre,*[9] or the local sheriff, those persons reputed to have committed certain serious crimes. This reporting body was called the *presenting jury*. When the justices arrived the *hundred* jurors were appraised of the articles of the *eyre* (the list of matters about which they were required to report to the justices). Felonies were always included. Thus, private actions began to be replaced by public prosecutions. This effectively eliminated combat as a method of proof for criminal cases, as private citizens were not permitted to engage in combat with the crown. This would be treason.

The *hundred* jurors reported felonies in their *hundred* by delivering to the justices their *veridicta,* their responses to the articles of the *eyre*. The *veridicta* reported felonies in two ways, either by a report of the crime itself (a presentment) or by a report that an appeal (a private prosecution) had been

---

Iron: Trial by Ordeal in England, Vol. 22, No. 4 The Journal of Interdisciplinary History 573 (Spring, 1992).

[7] See, for example, Groot, Roger D., *The Early-Thirteenth Century Criminal Jury,* 4 (Princeton University Press, 1988).

[8] In English history, the terms *hundred* and *vill* referred to administrative divisions or geographic units. A *hundred* was supposed to contain approximately 100 households or families, although the actual number could vary. Each *hundred* had its own local court, known as the *hundred court,* which dealt with local legal matters. A *vill* was a smaller area, usually a settlement or village, and was part of a *hundred*. Additionally, a *vill* sometimes could refer to a lord's *demesne* (manor and land holdings) and the lands worked by the *villeins* (serfs or peasants).

[9] An *eyre* was a periodic (or circuit) tour made by royal justices to various regions of the country to hear and decide legal cases.

made. Where the named defendant was actually present during a presentment, the trial could proceed directly to condemnation (sentencing) if the suspect had confessed or was manifestly guilty.[10] In all other cases, the defendant would deny the charge and proof would be sought by some form of the ordeal (excluding, of course, combat). In fact, not all presented defendants were awarded the ordeal. The *hundred* jury had the option of presenting someone and then stating that the person was "not suspected." There was no ordeal in such cases.[11] Thus, only when a *hundred* jury suspected and either produced evidence (or was joined in suspicion by the four *vills*), did the defendant go to the ordeal. By 1215, however, presenting juries had begun to evolve into more than just simply accusing juries. After accusing, the jurors decided which defendants should make proof by ordeal and which should not.

> This screening of defendants, ostensibly a statement about guilt or innocence, was just that when the hundredors produced evidence. When they did not, but were joined in suspicion by the vills, the verdict was probably as much a statement about the defendant's character…as about factual guilt or innocence. Nonetheless, an adverse verdict was medial only; it sent the defendant to the ordeal but it did not convict.[12]

Thus, between 1166 and 1215, the law in England developed such that every person who's liberty or life was put on peril by the justice system was spared the necessity of physical proof until a jury had first examined the case and found against him.

In 1215, the Church, at the Fourth Lateran Council, issued an edict forbidding any clerical participation in the ordeal. Given the central role the church played in all aspects of daily life at that time, this order effectively eliminated the ordeal as a method of proof in criminal cases. In

---

[10] Groot, *The Early-Thirteenth Century Criminal Jury, supra* note 7, at 6.

[11] For example, Groot offers the following account from the Lincolnshire Assize Rolls, 1202-1209: "Gilbert of Sausthorpe, accused of burglary, offers himself and is not suspected by the jurors and therefore let him be under pledge." *id.*

[12] As Groot points out, however, since a jury decision to send a defendant to ordeal almost always lead to either punishment or abjuration, such a decision did have a sort of convicting – a sanction imposing – quality. *id.* at 8, n.15.

1218 a major nationwide *eyre* commenced and soon after instructions were sent to the justices noting that, since the ordeal had been abolished, new methods of dealing with criminal cases had to be sought. Specifically, those accused of major crimes about which there was strong suspicion of guilt were to be committed to prison for safekeeping. Those defendants accused of less serious crimes, for which the ordeal would have been appropriate, were permitted to abjure the realm. And those accused of minor crimes about which there was no strong suspicion were to be placed under good-conduct pledges. This order was quite significant from the point of view of the development of the jury trial. In that it spoke of persons accused about whom there was or was not suspicion, it recognized and assumed the central adjudicative role that the jury was beginning to play in the administration of criminal justice. In effect, this type of jury was quasi-convicting; its verdicts had increasing effect on the lives of those accused of crimes.

With no other formal method of proof available, the judicial *eyres* of the thirteenth and early fourteenth centuries began to almost exclusively depend upon the jury to try criminal cases. It is not exactly clear why this is so, but it appears to be, at least in part, a matter of expedience; the institution of the presenting jury was already well entrenched, with its quasi-convicting role, and the people were by now familiar and comfortable with the convicting function of the jury. Most of those persons who were tried at the *eyre* in the thirteenth and early fourteenth centuries were brought forward after they had been named by the presenting jury and were asked how they pleaded. Virtually all pleaded not guilty and "put themselves on the country."[13] To go on the country meant, at least at first, to be tried by a body of persons that included some or all of the *hundredmen* who had comprised the jury of presentment. There were exceptions to this, with some defendants requesting an entirely different jury, or challenging some of the trial jurors who had been part of the presenting jury, but until

[13] A few refused to plead, exercising their right to do so. However, this right came at considerable cost; such defendants were subject to the *peine forte et dure*, wherein weights were laid upon them until they pleaded or expired. The reticent perished, but not having been convicted, they avoided forfeiture.

the end of the thirteenth century these two types of juries were not readily distinguishable.

This slowly began to change, and by the early Tudor period, the criminal jury trial had transformed in a few important respects. The trial jury, by this point, was a separate institution from the jury of presentment (the latter having come to resemble something akin to the modern grand jury). Having been selected and sworn, jurors heard the indictment against the accused. From the jury's perspective, the trial was a contest in which accuser and accused exchanged their stories in a heated give-and-take. The accuser might be prompted by the bench, which had in hand a written record of the charges he had laid before the justices or, in pretrial sessions, before assize clerks. The accuser's statement was supposed to correspond closely with the actual indictment upon which it had been based, lest the indictment be quashed for variance. Other witnesses for the Crown then spoke. It is not clear whether the jurors always heard the pre-trial examination of the accused; where it supported the Crown's case they almost certainly did, but probably in other cases they did not.[14] The case for the defense was put forth by the accused themselves. No one interceded on his or her behalf to influence the impression made upon the jurors. In rare cases, the accused had the assistance of counsel at the outset of the proceedings in order to make objections on matters of law as they arose from the indictment; but at trial, upon indictment, the accused was not allowed counsel (a rule that persisted in treason until 1696 and in all other capital cases until the eighteenth century). The defendant was forced to rebut evidence he had not seen beforehand. Moreover, the Crown employed sworn witnesses to aid private prosecutors, while only grudgingly allowing any witnesses, and never sworn ones, for the accused.[15]

By the late sixteenth century, we have the embryonic form of the jury as we now know it: a group of twelve persons assembled to hear evidence and render a verdict according to the evidence presented at trial. Of course, since that time the criminal jury trial has seen radical transformation, due

---

[14] Green, Thomas A., *Verdict According to Conscience: Perspectives on the English Criminal Trial Jury, 1200-1800*, 134-35 (University of Chicago Press, 1985).
[15] *Id.* at 135-36.

to such things as the increasing professionalization of the roles of the prosecution and the police, the introduction of defense counsel, the formalization of the rules of evidence, and a plethora of other such developments in the administration of the criminal law. However, I will mention these changes and transformations in subsequent chapters only insofar as they relate to the specific issue of jury nullification.

1.2 The Jury as Moral Arbiter

Jurors have always, to some degree or another, been concerned with some extra-legal notion of *desert*, and have not necessarily confined their deliberations to issues of legislative conformity. Their focus, we might say, is often with the *moral* nature of the verdict, and not necessarily the factual questions of the defendant's guilt. Seen as a predominantly moral investigation then, the history of the jury trial in many respects can be traced back to use of the ordeal in early English criminal justice. The ordeal, argues Robert Palmer, while ostensibly concerned with the factual question of the defendant's culpability, was probably viewed as an essentially moral device.[16] The issue addressed by the ordeal was not whether the accused had committed the act in question, but whether the prescribed punishment for such acts would be appropriate in a particular case. To be sure, such questions were often hard to distinguish; an affirmative answer to the former would often as a matter of course imply an affirmative answer to the latter. But, according to Palmer, the relationship between the defendant's actions and his failure at the ordeal was not that of antecedent to consequent, but rather the opposite. That is, a defendant who failed the ordeal was clearly guilty of the act in question; the failure of the ordeal was understood to mean that God wished the accused to be punished, and God would not punish the innocent. But God is merciful, and one who passed the ordeal might truly have been innocent of the crime charged, but might also have passed simply because of God's mercy; in either case, the passing of the ordeal simply meant that punishment would be inappropriate.

Palmer finds support for this interpretation of how the ordeal was understood in literary accounts, particularly in *La Mort le Roi Artu,* from the

[16] Palmer, Robert C., *Review - Conscience and the Law: The English Criminal Jury - Green's Verdict According to Conscience,* 84 Michigan Law Review 787 (1986).

early thirteenth century. At one point in this tale, Sir Lancelot kills Sir Gawain's brother, and Gawain is overcome with the desire to avenge his brother's death. Lancelot offers to make reparations: he abases himself; he offers to do homage to Gawain and to go on a pilgrimage alone. Gawain refuses this offer and demands instead to do battle. This refusal to accept Lancelot's offer was viewed with disapproval, and indeed, at battle Lancelot prevailed, proving his innocence.

> "Innocence" here, however, only concerned the present appropriateness of punishment. An offer of reparation, refused, reversed the appropriate result. This account of a trial by battle suggests strongly a similar conclusion about the ordeal. The question asked was not factual but moral, not about a past event but about present standing before God.[17]

In other words, Lancelot prevailed in battle, not because he was innocent of the crime he was charged with, but because of his genuine willingness to make reparations and accept responsibility for his wrongdoing. Gawain's desire for vengeance, in light of Lancelot's prostration, was therefore the greater wrong in God's eyes. If Palmer is correct about this, then it is hardly surprising that when the jury eventually replaced the ordeal this concern with the moral appropriateness of punishment would also be transferred. While Palmer's account of the ordeal is somewhat speculative, that the early juries were concerned with the moral appropriateness of punishment for felons is beyond doubt, and it is here that Thomas Green's scholarship is especially informative.

Green concerns himself primarily with early medieval jury behavior in homicide cases, and makes the following claim about the early English criminal jury: in homicide cases, juries systematically imposed the communities' concepts of liability upon the courts, drawing a distinction between cases of simple homicide and more malicious, stealthy homicide – a distinction that the formal legal rules of the time did not draw.[18] Because jurors of that era were both gatherers, as well as weighers of evidence, Green claims they used this gathering role to produce and present evidence

---

[17] *Id.* at 793.

[18] Green, *Verdict According to Conscience, supra* note 14, at 28-9.

to influence the outcome of trials in cases where strict adherence to the legal rules would have resulted in a verdict at odds with the community's sense of justice.

> [F]rom late Anglo-Saxon times to the end of the Middle Ages there existed a widespread societal distinction between "murder," i.e., homicide perpetrated through stealth, and "simple" homicide, roughly what a later legal age termed "manslaughter." This distinction, which was imposed upon the courts through the instrument of the trial jury, was fundamentally at odds with the letter of the law.[19]

In order to fully understand Green's reasons for this claim, it is necessary to first understand the law of homicide during this period. By the thirteenth century, all felonious homicides were capital offences. However, this had not always been the case. The distinction between slaying by stealth and slaying openly and of a sudden had been part of Anglo-Saxon law. The crown took interest only in the former, for which capital punishment awaited those found guilty. *Wergild*[20] was the remedy for the latter, and allegations of homicide of this type were prosecuted privately. This legal distinction survived the Conquest, and then was removed in the course of the legal reforms of Henry II. By the end of the twelfth century, the Crown took exclusive jurisdiction over all homicides and defined them as either: i) culpable and thus capital; ii) excusable and thereby pardonable; or iii) justifiable and therefore deserving of acquittal. Into this third category fell such things as the slaying of manifest felons and outlaws who resisted capture. Pardonable homicides were those committed by the insane, those done unintentionally, and those committed in self-defense. The rest, from deliberate, but sudden, homicides, to those homicides planned and stealthily perpetrated, were considered culpable. According to the law,

---

[19] *Id. at* 30.

[20] The *Wergild* system placed a monetary value on people according to rank, with categories ranging from king to freeman, and established a personal injury tariff schedule regulating payment by a perpetrator to a victim for injuries suffered through wrongdoing. See, Bothe, L.; Esders, S.; and Nijdam, J. A. (Eds.), *Wergild, Compensation and Penance. The Monetary Logic of Early Medieval Conflict Resolution*, 113 (Medieval Law and Its Practice; Vol. 31) (2021).

there were to be no distinctions made among them. All felonious homicide was thus considered capital.[21]

It is this second class of homicide, pardonable homicide, and in particular, the associated rules of self-defense, that is particularly relevant *vis-à-vis* nullification, according to Green. The rules of self-defense at this time were, from a modern point of view, incredibly strict. The slayer must have made every attempt to escape his attacker; he must have reached a point beyond which he could no longer retreat; and he must have retaliated out of vital necessity. Moreover, this test was objective; it was not enough for the jury to find only that the defendant genuinely *believed* that they had no other recourse. The jury must additionally find that there was, indeed, *actually* no other recourse.[22]

Green claims that the early English jury distinguished between those who committed simple homicide (roughly what we now refer to as manslaughter) and those who committed murder (homicide stealthily committed) when determining the fate of defendants brought before it – a distinction not recognized by the formal legal rules of the day. How does Green suggest that juries instantiated this distinction? Through the use of verdicts of self-defense. Up until the sixteenth century, claims Green, many who committed what we now refer to as manslaughter (a capital offense at that time), received unwarranted pardons, based on a jury finding of self-defense. Juries, it seems, if Green is to be believed, were loath to send to the gallows those whose crime was that of simple homicide.

> [M]any of those who received pardons for self-defense had in fact committed a felonious, simple homicide. The area of pardonable

[21] This tripartite classification of homicide remained intact until the late sixteenth century, when the legal distinction between murder and manslaughter finally emerged.

[22] Green, Thomas A., *The Jury and the English Law of Homicide, 1200-1600*, 74 Michigan Law Review 413, 428 (1976). Note that not only were pardons for self-defense formally very narrowly defined, they were also sanction imposing. A finding of excusable homicide resulted in the defendant's remand to gaol until he obtained a pardon from the king, a procedure that could take several months. Furthermore, originally, of those meriting pardons for excusable homicide, only persons who had tried to flee upon becoming a suspect suffered forfeiture of goods. After 1343, forfeiture of goods became automatic in all cases of excusable homicide.

> homicide, it appears, served as a possible way out in cases where the community did not believe the defendant deserved to be hanged.[23]

Green supports this claim through a detailed comparison of the trial roll with the corresponding coroner's rolls in those cases ending in a verdict of self-defense. In all homicide cases, the coroner, a Crown official at the county level, was required to hold an inquest as soon as possible, usually within a day or two of the discovery of the body.[24] There the coroner assembled an inquest jury, composed of representatives of the *vill* in which the slaying occurred and of several neighboring *vills*. At this inquest the coroner noted the cause of death, took down the names of suspects mentioned by the jurors, and ordered the arrest of those named suspects by the sheriff or *hundred* bailiff. A record of the coroner's inquest was available to the court at trial. However, such inquests were not conclusive, and the jurors took no oath when stating the facts of the deceased's death and those suspected. The coroner's enrollment was often far less formalistic than the trial rolls, according to Green, and represented a more candid reflection of the community's view as to who the assailant was, and how the homicide took place.

As we have seen, the rules of self-defense were quite strict, and since, at this time, the jury was the primary source of evidence in criminal trials, any verdict of self-defense had to be accompanied by a detailed accounting of the defendant's attempts to escape his alleged assailant. If juries used the category of excusable homicide to exculpate manslaughterers, as Green contends, they would have had to fabricate stories of retreat and last resort where in fact there had been neither. Such fabrications, continues Green, would be visible to us only by comparing the trial enrollments with the corresponding coroner's enrollments in those cases where the jury returned a finding of self-defense. Green did just such a comparison. In a number of cases in which the coroner reported sudden arguments that then escalated to violence, or attacks that could have been avoided without resort to deadly force, the jury at trial set forth a verdict that met the strict rules of self-defense.[25] By the end of the thirteenth century, the jury's statement in

---

[23] Green, *Verdict According to Conscience, supra* note 14, at 31.

[24] Green, *The Jury and the English Law of Homicide, supra* note 22, at 422.

[25] *Id. at* 430.

self-defense cases became very formulaic in order to meet the strict legal requirements. Nearly every act of self-defense, discovered Green, was said to have been undertaken by a cornered defendant, who was constrained from fleeing at every turn by ditches, walls, and hedges.

> In order to justify killing in self-defense, it will be recalled, the man attacked had to retreat until retreat was no longer possible. At the trial the jurors always alleged such a predicament, and though it was sometimes true, a comparison of the coroners' rolls and the trial rolls reveal that it often was not and that a petty jury had so altered the facts as to make pardonable what the law considered nonpardonable... A man whose life was threatened did not have to seek some means of escape; indeed, he need not do so though he was in no danger of losing his life. The court's concern with last resort indicates a concept of criminal liability clearly at odds with prevailing social norms.[26]

Green mentions many such cases where this is borne out through a comparison of the two rolls. For instance, there is the case of William Childerle, who returned home to find a burglar in his house. According to coroner's roll, a struggle ensued on the stairs and the intruder was slain.[27] At the trial, however, the jury found that upon seeing the intruder, William had fled to a wall near the door of the house where he was finally cornered and forced to strike back in self-defense.[28] More striking is the case of John Counte who, after quarreling with Robert Paunchard in Bishopsgate Ward, London, drew a knife and stabbed Paunchard to death.[29] The trial jury maintained that Paunchard had thrown rocks at Counte and driven him to a wall.[30] Green mentions many more such cases,[31] and finds that none of the cases evidencing transformation of the facts involved a defendant who had been described at the coroner's inquest as having slain through stealth or on account of a long-held grudge. The available evidence from cases ending

[26] Green, *Verdict According to Conscience, supra* note 14, at 38.
[27] JUST 2/18, m.41d/2: 1356.
[28] C 260/68, no. 20 (1357); Pardon: C.P.R., May 3, 1357, 530.
[29] *London Coroners' Rolls,* 242-43 Roll H, no. 9.
[30] C. 260/50, no. 61 (1339).
[31] See Green, *Verdict According to Conscience, supra* note 14, at Ch. 2.

in self-defense, concludes Green, suggests that "the frequent recourse to such findings resulted mainly from the jury's desire to save the lives of defendants who had committed simple homicide."[32] In none of the cases had the defendants acted out of true premeditation; they had neither ambushed the deceased, nor employed other means of stealth. But all were cases of felonious homicide according to the letter of the law, and thus were not pardonable. Had the true stories come out at trial, the defendants most certainly would have been sentenced to hang.

> In many, perhaps most, of the above cases the community surely believed the slaying was justified even though the official rules of self-defense had not been met. But in others there had been little or no element of self-defense, and the trial verdict appears to be an entire fiction devised for purposes of saving the defendant's neck.[33]

Regardless of why the jury behaved the way it did in these cases, if Green is correct, the various motives were united by one common feature; the jury felt that the law, if applied literally, would result in an injustice of sorts. "From the very onset of the common law period," concludes Green, "juries were inclined to structure evidence in such a way as to save the life of a manslaughterer."[34]

Later Tudor developments in criminal procedure, notably the emergence, around this time (the early 1500's), of the legally recognized distinction between culpable, but sudden homicide (which was not capital), and slaying with malice aforethought (which was capital) both reduced the number of cases involving court/jury tension and built into the fact-finding process more room for the kind of discretion that jurors had traditionally exercised.[35] "The flow of evidence provided some control, but in fact many cases lay so close to the legal line between capital and [non-capital] homicide that the bench had no grounds for second-guessing the jury."[36]

---

[32] Green, *The Jury and the English Law of Homicide, supra* note 22, at 431.

[33] Green, *Verdict According to Conscience, supra* note 14, at 45-6.

[34] *Id.* at 47.

[35] *Id.* at 126.

[36] *Id.* at 126-7.

This was not the situation, however, in cases involving theft, where the jury's role was quite different from its role in homicide cases. Because there was, in theft, little question regarding intent, there was little opportunity to conceal a merciful verdict. Juries were forced to acquit the defendant against sometimes substantial evidence to the contrary, or, at the very least, to undervalue the worth of the goods despite incontrovertible evidence of their real worth. Such tactics were, according to Green, quite common during this era,[37] and while still condemning the defendant to some form of punishment, at least spared them the gallows.

> Blackstone refers to the "pious perjury" under which jurors understated the value of articles stolen in order to avoid the capital charge... Lord Mansfield – a strict judge – advised a jury to find a gold trinket of less value than 40 shillings. When the prosecutor indignantly exclaimed that its fashion alone was worth double that, Lord Mansfield observed, "God forbid, gentlemen, we should hang a man for fashion's sake."[38]

1.3 The Rise of the Independent Jury

With the decline of the self-informing jury, and the concomitant rise in visibility of jury independence (and, with it, jury nullification), the bench began to take notice, and took steps to curb the practice. Juries had always been held liable, of course, for corruption, but the bench's understanding of corruption became substantively more inclusive around this time, and was no longer limited to cases of bribery and partisanship. One statute which addressed punishment for perjury specifically mandated fines for jurors who returned verdicts against "good and pregnant evidence."[39] Jury nullification – indeed, *any* verdict that the bench did not agree with – began to be equated with perjury.

The Crown also responded to this perceived threat of jury discretion in a number of ways. Most of the extant evidence regarding the management of the Tudor and early Stuart criminal prosecutions comes from the

---

[37] *Id.* at 127.

[38] *U. S. v. Dougherty*, 473 F.2d 1113, 1136-7, n. 53 (D.C. Cir., 1972).

[39] Stat. 26 Hen. 8, c. 4 (1534).

collections of state trials, most of which are composed predominantly of treason cases. The evidence suggests, according to Green,[40] that the Crown in such cases often hand-picked a jury sympathetic to its position. There is also evidence that the Crown coached the jurors before the trial got underway, and even an indication that the Star Chamber played a role in the pretrial preparation of jurors in especially important cases.[41] Conviction under these circumstances was nearly always a foregone conclusion.

However, jury-packing was but one of the ways the Crown sought to rein in the discretionary power of the jury. Where the bench believed that a jury had convicted a defendant against the evidence, it might reprieve the defendant and request that the Crown pardon him either freely or upon consideration. No sanctions were imposed upon the jury in such cases. Most cases of judge/jury disagreement, however, involved perceived *acquittals* against the facts, and here the bench often confronted the jury directly, using whatever pressure it could to influence the jury to return a verdict more in accordance with its view. Such coercion often involved the threats of fines and imprisonment. A mild form of coercion involved being sent back to deliberate until a satisfactory verdict was returned; it was a long-standing rule that jurors were not to eat, drink, consume tobacco, nor sleep until they rendered their verdict.[42]

By the 1660's the practice of fining and imprisoning jurors who refused to return verdicts consistent with the judge's view of the case had become commonplace. In part, the State's campaign against the Quakers in the mid-seventeenth century is responsible for the increase in jury discretion and the concomitant rise in judicial response to such.[43] Restoration persecution of the Quakers began with the 1662 Quaker Act[44] and reached its height in 1664, the year Parliament passed the Conventicles Act, which made non-Anglican religious meetings unlawful.[45] The purpose of this act was purportedly to prevent seditious meetings, "under pretence or colour of

---

[40] Green, *Verdict According to Conscience, supra* note 14, at 130-31.
[41] *Id.* at 131-32.
[42] *Id.* at 139-40.
[43] *Id.* at 209.
[44] Stat. 14 Chas. 2, c 1 (1662).
[45] Stat. 16 Chas. 2 c. 4 (1664).

religion," but the courts concluded that the jury must convict if there was manifest proof that the defendant had taken part in what appeared to be such a meeting. Conviction did not require proof of seditious purpose. That was to be presumed, the bench ruled, as a matter of law, and hence, was not within the purview of the jury to consider. Mere proof of presence at a Quaker meeting cast upon the defendant the burden of either proving that the meeting had not been for religious worship, or that the worship had been according to the Anglican form.[46] However, juries in such cases proved to be somewhat reluctant to return guilty verdicts,[47] and in several 1664 cases, including *Rex v. Selby*[48] and *Leech's Case,*[49] King's Bench ordered an information against the offending jurors and fined them substantial amounts. As always, jurors who refused to pay such fines were imprisoned until they relented. This practice finally came under scrutiny in *Wagstaffe's Case,*[50] tried before Lord Chief Justice Kelyng. The jury refused to convict the defendants, Quakers, for violating the Conventicles Act of 1664. Kelyng identified and fined the jurors he felt were responsible for the acquittal. The jurors came before the King's Bench on a writ of *habeas corpus*, arguing that the power to fine gave too much discretion to trial judges because their decisions would be essentially unreviewable; the natural result of which would be to impede and undermine the fact-finding role of the jury. The King's Bench did not agree. Fearing a failure of criminal justice, the court upheld the practice of fining, stating that "juries are not judges of fact so as to go clearly against it."[51] Thus, judges were given the sanction to fine and imprison jurors who reached verdicts contrary to the court's notions.

It was not until 1671 in the landmark *Bushel's Case*[52] that the principle of non-coercion of jurors was first established. *Bushel's Case* has been lauded as the case which first recognized the legitimacy of jury nullification in the common-law Anglo-American tradition.[53] Edward Bushel was a juror in

[46] Green, *Verdict According to Conscience, supra* note 14, at 205.
[47] See *id.* at Ch. 6.
[48] 1 Keble 769, 83 Eng. Rep. 1223 (1664).
[49] *Leech's Case,* 83 Eng. Rep. 53 (1664).
[50] *Rex. v. Wagstaffe,* 1 Keble 934, 1 Sid. 237, 82 Eng. Rep. 1101 (1665).
[51] As quoted in Green, *Verdict According to Conscience, supra* note 14, at 212, n. 43.
[52] *Bushel's Case,* 124 Eng. Rep. 1006 (1670).
[53] See, for instance, Scheflin, Alan W., *Jury Nullification: The Right to Say No,* 45 Southern California Law Review 168, 202-03 (1972).

the trial of the Quakers William Penn and William Mead.[54] After deliberations, eight jurors were ready to convict, but four, including Edward Bushel, refused. When the jury reported this to the court, the Recorder threatened that if the four continued to refuse to convict, "you shall be locked up, without meat, drink, fire, and tobacco; you shall not think thus to abuse the court; we will have a verdict by the help of God, or you shall starve for it."[55] The jury next returned with a verdict finding Penn guilty of speaking at Gracechurch Street, but not to an unlawful assembly. Mead was found not guilty. This was deemed unacceptable to the court, and the jury was sent back out. Finally, the jury returned a simple not guilty verdict.[56] In response to this, the court fined each juror forty pounds, and imprisonment until paid.

Two and a half months after Penn and Mead's trial, Edward Bushel, who had been imprisoned for refusing to pay his fine, sued a writ of *habeas corpus* out of the Court of Common Pleas. He claimed that the fine had no basis in law and that he was, therefore, being held without lawful cause. This suit was soon joined by three of the other jurors, and "brought to a head the recent political and legal ferment over the issue of fining jurors."[57] Five years had passed since *Wagstaffe's Case,* where the Court had ruled that such fining was, indeed, legal, although that case had been tried in front of the King's Bench, not, as *Bushel* was, in front of the Court of Common Pleas. Interestingly, Chief Justice John Vaughan, who wrote the decision in *Bushel,* had, three years previously, spoke in opposition to a bill introduced in Parliament outlawing the fining and imprisonment of jurors.

The charges facing Bushel were that his verdict was "*Contra plenum et manifestam evidentiam*" and "*Contra directionam cariae in materia legis.*"[58] Vaughan took up each in turn, and, holding that a trial judge is really in no position to evaluate how the jury views the evidence, noted that "the Court hath no knowledge by this return, whether the evidence given were full

[54] *Penn & Meads' Case,* (22 Charles II 1670).
[55] *Id.*
[56] Scott, Philip B., *Jury Nullification: An Historical Perspective on a Modern Debate,* 91 West Virginia Law Review 389, 395 (1989).
[57] Green, *Verdict According to Conscience, supra* note 14, at 236.
[58] "Against full and clear evidence," and, "Against the direction of the court in the matter of the law," respectively.

and manifest, or doubtful, lame and dark, or indeed evidence at all material to the issue."[59] Vaughan argued that men faced with the same facts often draw conflicting conclusions, and that even two judges frequently drew different conclusions after reading the same case.[60] Consequently, he reasoned that it made no sense to fine a juror for returning a verdict solely because it does not comport with the court's view of the case. "It is absurd that a jury should be fined by the judge for going against their evidence, when he who fineth know not what it is."[61] Vaughan concluded that a juror could only be fined if it be shown that he returned a verdict contrary to his own view of the evidence, which would make it, in Vaughan's view, an act of perjury, and therefore actionable.[62]

With this rationale as the main premise of the decision, Vaughan next dismissed the second charge:

> Without a fact agreed, it is impossible for a judge, or any other, to know the law relating to that fact or direct concerning it, as to know an accident that hath no subject. Hence it follows, that the judge in logic can never direct what the law is in any manner controverted, without first knowing the fact; and then it follows, that without his previous knowledge of the fact, the jury in logic cannot go against his direction for he could not direct.[63]

In discussing the respective roles of judge and juror, Vaughan continued:

> But upon all general issues… the jury find not (as in a special verdict) the fact of every case by itself, leaving the law to the court, but find for the plaintiff or defendant upon the issue to be tried, wherein they resolve both law and fact complicatedly, and not the fact by itself; so as though they answer not singly to the question what is law, yet they determine the law in all matters, where the issue is joined.[64]

---

[59] *Bushel's Case, supra* note 52, at 1016.
[60] *Id.* at 1006.
[61] *Id.* at 1012.
[62] *Id.*
[63] *Id.*
[64] As quoted in Scott, *supra* note 56, at 396-7, n. 42.

The return against Bushel, according to Vaughan, was deficient in showing that the jurors had found against their own view of the evidence, and hence, did not show actual perjury. Vaughan's ruling significantly limited a judge's ability to coerce jurors, or even to conclude that the jurors had committed perjury. Even if a judge questioned the jurors on their findings about certain facts, jurors would still be entitled to return a verdict at variance with the implications of such fact finding, ruled Vaughan, asserting that, after they gave their in-court answers, but before they pronounced their verdict, the jurors (or any one of them) might well have changed their minds regarding the sufficiency of the evidence given in court. The good faith of jurors, like that of judges, was to be assumed.

Vaughan's ultimate *ratio* for his decision was that the common law required trial by jury for criminal cases; in such trials, without the confessions of the jurors themselves, it could never be shown that the jurors had gone against the facts as they understood them, and/or had rejected judicial instructions on how the law ought to be applied. [65] No matter how wrong the jurors were in their sincere belief, the law guaranteed resolution of guilt or innocence according to *their* understanding. Although the King might pardon a defendant *convicted* against the evidence (and thus vitiate the jury's verdict of guilty), an *acquittal* by the jury so long as it was honestly motivated, was final. If a judge and jury disagreed on questions of fact, according to Vaughan, the jury prevailed, both because otherwise the institution would be ineffectual, and therefore pointless, and because it was unreasonable to compel jurors to swear to what they did not believe. "Preference for the jury's view was implicit in institutional arrangements; for Vaughan, historical usage *ipso facto* suggested correct practice."[66] With this powerful opinion, Chief Justice Vaughan put an end to the practice of fining criminal trial jurors. Although, technically, jurors could still be fined for finding against their own view of the case, this was almost impossible to prove, and the practice of fining ended.

What was the motivation behind the *Bushel* decision? Was it a vindication of the jury's ultimate control over matters of fact, or was it instead a

---

[65] Green, *Verdict According to Conscience, supra* note 14, at 245.

[66] *Id.* at 248.

vindication of the view that jurors are also judges of law as well as fact? Vaughan's decision has been interpreted to support either view.[67] However, it soon becomes clear that when we examine the *Bushel* decision for support of the pro-nullification view, we do so in vain. Vaughan certainly never explicitly addressed the issue of a legitimate (or otherwise) law-finding role for the jury;[68] his focus was exclusively on the powerful and unreviewable role of the jury to find facts. The thesis of his opinion is straightforward: the law of the case is dependent upon the facts; everyone draws different conclusions from the same facts; thus, it is impossible for a judge to say a given verdict is in conflict with the facts as the jury finds them. Consequently, neither can a judge rule that a given verdict is in contradiction of the law. However, it is difficult to believe that Vaughan intended his verdict to vindicate the jury as a *law*-finding institution. The theme of the jury as fact-finder is pervasive throughout his opinion, while the notion of the jury as law-finder is never expressed. In fact, Vaughan made his views on the division of labor between the judge and jury explicit:

> That Decantum in our books, '*ad quaestionem facti nonrespondent judices, ad quaestionem legis nonrespondent juratores,*' literally taken is true: for if it be demanded, what is the fact? the Judge cannot answer it: if it be asked, what is the law in the case, the jury cannot answer it.[69]

Seen in this light, the opinion in *Bushel* not only fails to support the nullification position, it actually undercuts it by explicitly reserving the role of law-finder for the judge.

---

[67] See, for instance, Simson, Gary J., *Jury Nullification in the American System: A Skeptical View,* 54 Texas Law Review 488 (1976), for the view that *Bushel's Case* establishes nothing more than that the jury is the sole judge of fact. See Scheflin, *Jury Nullification: The Right to Say No, supra* note 53, for the view that *Bushel's Case* establishes that the jury can also judge the law.

[68] Green, *Verdict According to Conscience, supra* note 14, at 242.

[69] As quoted in Scott, *Jury Nullification: An Historical Perspective, supra* note 56, at 406, n. 107.

1.4 Jury Independence in Early Colonial America

After *Bushel*, the English courts conceded that a jury's determination of fact, and application of law to fact, was unreviewable and final in criminal trials. However, the English courts never recognized the jury as having a law-finding – in addition to its fact finding – role. The American tradition, on the other hand, building upon the outcome of the trial of John Peter Zenger, developed along slightly different lines – at least at first.

A bit of background on the law of seditious libel in the eighteenth century is needed to fully understand the trial of John Zenger and its implications. By the early 1700's, the King's Bench had obtained jurisdiction of seditious libel cases. The common law crime of seditious libel was characterized as the intentional publication of a writing that "scandalized" the government – i.e., tended to bring it into disesteem. Although indictments for seditious libel generally alleged that the accused had acted falsely and maliciously, the law did not recognize truth as a defense. Moreover, the court itself decided as matters of law two questions that had the appearance of questions of fact: whether the act was done with criminal intent, and whether the writing was seditious or defamatory.[70] Consequently, the only questions left for the jury were the fact of publication and whether the publication referred to the particular people of the government body as charged. The jury, in seditious libel cases, "had been reduced to a mere formality, used only to rubber stamp the fact of publication."[71] The trial of John Zenger unfolded against this background when, in 1735, in the American colony of New York, a jury for the first time refused to accept its diluted role and found a publication non-libelous.[72]

John Zenger was a printer in New York who made a modest living printing Dutch works and theological tracts. In 1733 he was approached to print *The New York Weekly Journal*, a mouthpiece for two New York politicians, Lewis Morris and Rip Van Dam, political opponents of the then Governor of New

[70] *Id.* at 408-09.

[71] *Id.* at 409.

[72] As Scott explains, the trial of Zenger occurred well before the onset of legal reporters. The only report of the trial is a near-verbatim account by James Alexander, Zenger's attorney in the case. *id.* at 409, n. 122.

York, William Cosby. In 1734 Cosby convened a grand jury to return an indictment against Zenger for seditious libel. On three different occasions the grand jury refused to indict. Finally, in January of 1735, Cosby prevailed upon Attorney General Richard Bradely to bring an information against Zenger, thereby bypassing the grand jury process. Zenger's trial began in August of 1735, with Andrew Hamilton, a prominent Pennsylvania lawyer, serving as Zenger's counsel. At trial, Hamilton essentially conceded the fact of publication and instead argued the appropriateness of the law of seditious libel to the jury. Reading from Vaughan's opinion in *Bushel* at length to the jury, Hamilton argued that by making the question of libel one of law, the King's Bench had deprived the jury of their right to apply the law to the facts.[73]

> [Juries] have the right beyond all dispute to determine both the law and the facts, and where they do not doubt of the law, they ought to do so. This of leaving it to the judgment of the Court whether the words are libelous or not in effect renders juries useless (to say no worse) in many cases.[74]

Despite the fact that the trial judge stressed to the jury that he, and only he, was to give the law of the case, the jury quickly returned a not guilty verdict and Zenger was set free. Since the defense had conceded the fact of publication, the jury's verdict could only plausibly be interpreted as a rejection of the law of seditious libel as it then stood.

After news of Zenger's acquittal spread to England, acquittals in seditious libel cases became relatively frequent, with juries on occasion refusing to return general guilty verdicts and instead returning special verdicts of guilty of publication only.[75] The result in *Zenger*, combined with already widespread dissatisfaction with the law of seditious libel[76] resulted, finally, in 1792, with the English Parliament passing Fox's Libel Act[77] which declared, among other things, that in seditious libel cases, questions as to

---

[73] *Id.* at 414.
[74] *Id.*
[75] *Id.* at 415.
[76] See, Green, *Verdict According to Conscience, supra* note 14, at Ch. 5.
[77] 32 Geo. 3, ch. 60 § 1 at 627.

the libelous nature of the publication and criminal intent were questions of fact, not law, and hence, were within the purview of the jury. Nowhere in the statute, however, was it either stated or implied that the jury possessed any more right in libel cases than in other cases to reject the law as stated by the bench.

However, according to Scott, Zenger's victory was seen by the American colonists as a vindication of the jury's right to decide both law and fact in criminal trials.[78] The political realities of the time may help to explain the American perspective on the outcome of the Zenger trial. The jury in colonial America was seen, claims Scott, as "a shield between the people and a despotic undemocratic government."[79] Moreover,

> [t]he American people were eager to try out their newly-won democratic freedoms. Their political philosophy demanded popular control of every facet of government. The colonists had a basic distrust of legal experts and a profound belief in the ability of the common man… Consequently, each juror was just as qualified as each judge to determine the true law.[80]

Zenger became the cornerstone of the early American tradition of the jury's right to decide the law. The 1794 Supreme Court case, *State of Georgia v. Brailsford*,[81] (the only Supreme Court case to seat a jury), strikingly demonstrates the then-contemporary view of the jury's discretionary role in criminal trials. Jay, C.J., in issuing instructions to the jury, stated, in part, that "you have nevertheless a right to take upon yourselves to… determine the law as well as the fact in controversy."[82] In every jurisdiction that addressed the issue, state and federal, American juries were affirmed to have the right to decide the law.[83]

However, this American perspective on the jury as law-finder as well as fact finder was relatively short lived, and increasingly, the American bench

---

[78] Scott, *Jury Nullification: An Historical Perspective*, *supra* note 56, at 416ff.
[79] *Id.* at 417.
[80] *Id.*
[81] 3 U.S. 1 (1794).
[82] *Id.* at 4.
[83] *Id.* at 416.

began to express concern at the prospect of jurors deciding and deliberating upon matters of law. A typical expression of this concern was voiced by Justice Story in *U.S. v. Battiste*:[84]

> If the jury were at liberty to settle the law for themselves, the effect would be not only that the law itself would be most uncertain... but in case of error there would be no remedy or redress to the injured party, for the court would not have any right to review the law as it had been settled by the jury. Every person accused as a criminal has a right to be tried according to the law of the land, and not by the law as a jury may understand it, or choose, from wantonness, or ignorance or accidental mistake, to interpret it.[85]

The final nail in the coffin for judicial and political support for the notion of jury nullification came just over half a century later when *Battiste* was cited with approval by the U.S. Supreme Court in *Sparf & Hansen v. United States*.[86] Here Harlan J., speaking for the majority, stated that juries:

> have the physical power to disregard the law, as laid down to them by the court. But, I deny that...they have the moral right to decide the law according to their own notions or pleasure. On the contrary, I hold it the most sacred constitutional right of every party accused of a crime that the jury should respond as to the facts, and the court as to the law... This is the right of every citizen, and it is his only protection.[87]

And later,

> Public and private safety alike would be in peril, if the principle to be established that juries in criminal cases may, of right, disregard the law unto themselves... [T]he result would be that the enforcement of law against criminals and the protection of citizens

[84] 24 F. Cas. 1042 (C.C.D. Mass., 1835).
[85] *Id.* at 1043.
[86] *Sparf and Hansen v. United States*, 156 U.S. 51 (1895).
[87] *Id.* at 74.

> against unjust and groundless prosecutions would depend entirely upon juries uncontrolled by any settled, fixed, legal principles.[88]

Since 1895 the United States Supreme Court has held firm in its conviction that jury nullification is fraught with danger and in no way, shape, or form, ought to be encouraged or endorsed. This is the situation we find ourselves in today, with, on the one hand, jury nullification still a very real possibility, and, on the other, widespread, if almost complete, judicial disapproval of the practice in all Anglo-American legal systems.

1.5 The Current Right to a Jury in American Criminal Trials

The right to a trial by jury has been a foundational feature of the American criminal justice system since the very beginning of the nation. In fact, the American *Declaration of Independence* explicitly mentions the denial of this right as one the main grievances against the British Crown.[89] The fundamental nature of this right was perhaps best captured in *Duncan v. Louisiana*[90] where the Court stated: "Our conclusion is that in the American States, as in the federal judicial system, a general grant of jury trial for serious offenses is a fundamental right, essential for preventing miscarriages of justice and for assuring that fair trials are provided for all defendants."[91] While many reasons and justifications have been offered by the courts over the years as to why the jury is necessary for just and fair trials in the criminal context, the four main reasons most often appealed to are: i) the jury is necessary as safeguard against Government oppression;[92] ii) the jury is a necessary means to instill public confidence in the administration of the law;[93] iii) the jury is necessary in order to instantiate

---

[88] *Id.* at 101-02.
[89] "**Grievance 18**: For depriving us in many cases, of the benefit of trial by jury," *Declaration of Independence of the United States*, Grievance 18 (1776).
[90] 391 U.S. 145 (1968).
[91] *Id.* at 157-58.
[92] *Baldwin v. New York*, 399 U.S. 66, 72 (1970): "But the primary purpose of the jury is to prevent the possibility of oppression by the Government."
[93] *Taylor v. Louisiana*, 419 U.S. 522, 530 (1975): "Community participation in the administration of the criminal law… is also critical to public confidence in the fairness of the criminal justice system."

the ideals of Democracy in the administration of the law;[94] and, iv) the jury is necessary in order to add an element of mercy/justice into the otherwise strict application of the law.[95] Regardless of the reasons offered, the courts have been unanimous and consentient that granting a criminal defendant the right to trial by jury is a necessary and essential component to preserving justice in the administration of the law.

Currently, the right to a trial by jury in American criminal law is governed by, at the federal level, the *U.S. Constitution*,[96] and at the state-level, various State Constitutions.[97] Moreover, in *Duncan*,[98] the U.S. Supreme Court ruled that in all state criminal trials, the defendant must be granted a jury trial in cases in which a jury trial would be granted were the case to be tried at the federal level. However, these constitutional provisions do not a guarantee that a defendant will always receive a trial by jury in *every* case, as the U.S. Supreme Court has, over a number of cases, over a number of years, somewhat narrowed the scope and limited and the applicability of this right to a subset of criminal cases – all crimes except those deemed to be "petty offences."[99] To be fair, and given the trend over recent decades towards more and more severe penalties in the criminal code, it is a rare

[94] *State v. LaMere*, 298 Mont. 358, 372 (Mont. 2000): "Our jury system, no less than our system of representative government, is based upon a democratic ideal: that justice is best served by a broadly representative group of individuals 'drawn from the various walks of life.'"

[95] *United States v. Folse*, No. CR 15-2485 JB, *9 (D.N.M. Nov. 9, 2015): "The criminal jury's role at the Founders' time was primarily that of a factfinder, but also included as a secondary role acting as the community's conscience to determine whether the law, or the application of law to the facts, was conscionable."

[96] This includes both Article III, §2, cl. 3 of the *U.S. Constitution* ("the Trial of all Crimes, except in Cases of Impeachment, shall be by Jury"), and the Sixth Amendment of the *U.S. Constitution* ("in all criminal prosecutions the accused shall enjoy the right to a speedy and public trial, by an impartial jury…").

[97] "All states, in some form and to some degree, have protection in their constitutions for the right to jury trial in criminal cases," Gertner, Nancy; Mizner, Judith H.; and Dubin, Joshua, *The Law of Juries*, 6 (Thomson Reuters, 2018).

[98] *Supra* note 90, at 149.

[99] In the US, 18 U.S.C.A. §19 currently defines a petty offense as a misdemeanor, the penalty for which is imprisonment for no longer than 6 months, or a fine no greater than $5000.

federal criminal prosecution for which a jury trial would be, in principle, unavailable.

In the U.S., the Federal Rules of Criminal Procedure require a jury of 12 persons for federal criminal cases, although both parties may stipulate to a lower number of jurors, as long as such stipulation is in writing and meets with court approval.[100] While juries with as little as six members have been deemed to be consistent with the Constitution,[101] the Court, in *Ballew v. Georgia*,[102] ruled that a jury of five jurors was not "of sufficient size to promote group deliberation, to insulate members from outside intimidation and to provide a representative cross-section of the community."[103]

A typical criminal jury trial in the American justice system consists of several different stages. While the exact number of stages and their specific names vary according to jurisdiction and even the crime charged, there are several common stages to all such trials shared by nearly every jurisdiction within the United States.

1.5.1 Jury Selection or Voir Dire

This is the stage where potential jurors are questioned and selected to serve on the trial jury. While the trial judge usually conducts these proceedings, the prosecution and defense attorneys may also be involved in this process. The scope of questioning allowed of potential jurors is reflected by the dual goals of *voir dire* – to illicit evidence of potential bias, and "to obtain information to guide the exercise of peremptory challenges."[104] During *voir dire*, both the defense and prosecution have the opportunity to argue that certain jurors, due to their biases, may be unable to remain impartial and should be removed for cause; it remains the judge's discretion whether to grant such a request. Furthermore, both parties have the opportunity to exercise peremptory challenges to remove potential jurors they deem unfavorable. In exercising their limited number of peremptory

---

[100] Fed. R. Crim. P. 23(b).

[101] See, for instance: *Williams v. Florida*, 399 U.S. 78 (1970).

[102] 435 U.S. 223 (1978).

[103] *Id.* at 230.

[104] Gertner; Mizner; and Dubin, *The Law of Juries, supra* note 97, at 58-9.

challenges,[105] however, counsel are prohibited from discriminating against protected groups.[106] Otherwise, counsel have very wide discretion on when and where to use peremptory challenges to remove potentially hostile jurors.

This *voir dire* process is designed primarily to defend and instantiate the defendants' Sixth Amendment constitutional guarantee of a trial by an impartial jury of their peers. This right to an *impartial* jury, however, does not extend to the right to a *nullifying* jury.[107] The courts have been very clear in this regard; the explicit standards in this respect as regards the *voir dire* process are that:

1. Jurors are not to be questioned, informed, or otherwise made aware of its existence during the *voir dire* process. "Defendant and Defense counsel may not raise jury nullification or possible sentencing consequences to the jury during trial or during *voir dire* and may not encourage the jury to ignore the Court's instructions."[108]
2. If, during *voir dire*, a potential juror expresses an unwillingness to follow the law as given by the judge, or otherwise intimates or reveals a knowledge and approval of, or likelihood of engaging in, jury nullification in any way, the court is both empowered and perhaps even obligated to remove the recalcitrant juror from the panel.[109] "Trial courts have the duty to forestall or prevent jurors

[105] The exact number of which varies depending on jurisdiction and the nature of the crime charged, among other factors.
[106] See, for instance, *Batson v. Kentucky*, 476 U.S. 79 (1986): holding that the discriminatory use of peremptory challenges to exclude potential jurors on the basis of race is unconstitutional.
[107] See, for instance: *United States v. Roy*, 855 F.3d 1133, 1188 (11th Cir. 2017): "A defendant has no entitlement to the luck of a lawless decisionmaker, even if a lawless decision cannot be reviewed;" *Lee v. State*, 743 P.2d 296, 300 (Wyo. 1987): "As this court previously has noted, the possibility of jury nullification is not a right enjoyed by a defendant in a criminal case."
[108] *United States v. Kirk*, 1:20-cr-0079 KWR, *4 (D.N.M. May 27, 2020).
[109] See, for instance: *Poyner v. Commonwealth*, 229 Va. 401, 414 (Va. 1985): "A juror opposed to the imposition of the death penalty is not impartial. This is so because he or she would be unwilling or unable to follow the law. Such a juror might attempt to undermine the proper functioning of the courts by engaging in jury nullification. Thus, such a juror can be excluded from a jury panel without violating the defendant's right

> from engaging in nullification ...by dismissal of an offending juror from the venire."[110]

While the courts may not be able to prevent a seated jury from engaging in jury nullification, they are more than willing to employ the *voir dire* process to prevent a jury so-inclined to be seated in the first place.

1.5.2 The Trial

The trial itself consists of many individual steps and stages, the number, names, and specific procedures of which can and do depend greatly upon both the jurisdiction the trial takes place within, and the nature of the crime charged – but for the purposes of this monograph, the specifics are not particularly germane. Relevantly, and much like the *voir dire* process, the jury is not to be informed, or otherwise made aware of, the existence of jury nullification during the trial process;[111] moreover, any and all issues of law or legal interpretation that might arise during the trial are also not to be presented to, or argued in front of, the jury, lest this lead the jury down the path of deliberating on issues of law and, hence, nullifying. Put explicitly,

---

to a fair and impartial jury;" *U.S. v. Thomas*, 116 F.3d 606, 616-17 (2d Cir. 1997): "Indeed, one of the principal purposes of voir dire is to ensure that the jurors ultimately selected for service are unbiased and willing and able to apply the law as instructed by the court to the evidence presented by the parties."

[110] *Merced v. McGrath*, No. C 03-1904 CRB, at *9 (N.D. Cal. Feb. 10, 2004).

[111] See, for example: *U.S. v. Moloian*, No. 10-CR-20666, at *2 (E.D. Mich. Aug. 19, 2011): "The Court concludes that insofar as Defendants seek to introduce the concept of 'jury nullification' in this trial, legal precedent dictates that 'jury nullification' will not be raised in this trial;" *United States v. Diaz*, 820 F. Supp. 2d 301, 306 (D.P.R. 2011) (citations omitted): "Other circuit courts have similarly held that a district court has the authority to prevent a party from raising jury nullification arguments at trial… Thus, the government's motion is GRANTED and the defendants are precluded from raising jury nullification arguments at trial;" *United States v. Little*, CASE NO.: 2:19-cr-43, at *2-3 (S.D. Ga. May 7, 2020) (citations omitted): "It is well- established that parties and their counsel may not seek jury nullification at any time during trial, including through the introduction of irrelevant evidence or through argument. Consequently, no party or counsel will be permitted to encourage jurors to violate their oath by encouraging disregard of the law or the evidence;" *United States v. Penn*, 969 F.3d 450 (5th Cir. 2020) (citations omitted): "Evidence admitted solely to encourage nullification is by definition irrelevant, and thus inadmissible, regardless of what other evidence might be introduced at trial."

the standard is that the law itself is not to be considered as evidence to be judged or evaluated by the jury.[112]

1.5.3 Jury Instructions

Once the trial process has finished, and before the jury retires to deliberate, the trial judge provides the jury with instructions on the laws that apply to the case, outlining the legal principles and concepts the jury should consider and use while deliberating. These principles include such things as the presumption of innocence, the burden of proof, the elements of the crime, the concept of reasonable doubt, and many others, depending on the jurisdiction and crimes charged.

Perhaps the most important judicial instruction, at least from the perspective of this project, is the judge's description and explanation of the ***adjudicative division of labor*** between judge and jury. It is the function of the judge in a criminal jury trial to determine the relevant law for the case, and it is the function of the jury to determine the salient facts and then reach a verdict by applying the former to the latter: "Questions of credibility and weight to be attached to testimony are matters clearly for the jury. *The province of the jury as the exclusive arbiters of fact is holy ground, not to be approached by a trial court and the trial court should remain totally aloof on contested questions of fact.*"[113] To put this succinctly, judges judge law, juries

---

[112] See, for example, *Cooley v. United States*, 501 F.2d 1249, 1253-54 (9th Cir. 1974): "[T]he law is given to the jury by the court and not introduced as evidence… Obviously, it would be most confusing to a jury to have legal material introduced as evidence and then argued as to what the law is or ought to be;" *U.S. v. Unruh*, 855 F.2d 1363, 1376 (9th Cir. 1987): "We have condemned the practice of attempting to introduce law as evidence;" *United States v. Zipkin*, 729 F.2d 384, 387 (6th Cir. 1984) (citations omitted): "It is the function of the trial judge to determine the law of the case. It is impermissible to delegate that function to a jury through the submission of testimony on controlling legal principles …In the orderly trial of a case, the law is given to the jury by the court and not introduced as evidence. It would be most confusing to a jury to have legal material introduced as evidence;" *United States v. Warwick*, No. 16-CR-4572 MCA, at *6 (D.N.M. Oct. 30, 2017): "[A]llowing such evidence [about the nature of the law] would undermine protections built into the jury trial process to ensure the jury applies the law as instructed by the Court. Such prejudicial testimony will not be admitted into evidence."

[113] *Johnson v. State*, 150 Ga. App. 405, 406 (Ga. Ct. App. 1979) (emphasis added). See, also *Richardson v. State*, 403 So. 2d 293, 295 (Ala. Crim. App. 1981): "The weight to be

find fact.[114] There is to be, ideally, no conflation of these two roles.[115] Case law is rife with judgements affirming as much.[116] The U.S. Supreme Court,

given to evidence is wholly within the province of the jury, and any invasion of this province by the court in its orders is error; and any statement by the court, however unintentional, made in the presence of the jury, calculated to control the jury in its consideration of the weight to be given to testimony, will work a reversal;" *Mitchell v. Harmony*, 54 U.S. 115, 144 (1851): ""*Et sicut ad quæstionem juris non respondent juratores sed judices; sic ad quæstionem facti, non respondent judices sed juratores*." For jurors are to try the fact, and the judges ought to judge according to the law that ariseth upon the fact, for *ex facto jus oritur*… Thus, literally translated, his annunciation is "And as with respect to the questions of law, the jury must not respond, but only the judges; so, or in like manner, or under like restriction, the judges must not respond to questions of fact, but only the jury.""

[114] Except for very rare cases such as, for instance, directed verdicts of acquittal, where judges in jury trials are allowed to enter a verdict of not guilty before the issue goes to jury, simply on the grounds of insufficient evidence to support a reasonable prosecution. See, for example: *Jackson v. Virginia*, 443 U.S. 307 (1979).

[115] See, however, the Appendix at the end of this chapter for a discussion of the constitutional provisions in Maryland, Georgia, Indiana, and Oregon that purportedly grant juries the right in criminal trials to judge both law and fact in criminal trials.

[116] See, for instance: *United States v. Burton*, 575 F. Supp. 1320, 1323 (E.D. Tex. 1983): "[I]t is the judge's duty to instruct the jury as to the law applicable in each case;" *Cooley v. United States*, *supra* note 112, at 1253-54: "In the orderly trial of a case… [i]t is the function of the jury to determine the facts from the evidence and apply the law as given by the court to the facts as found by them from the evidence;" *Berra v. United States*, 351 U.S. 131, 134 (1956): "The role of the jury in a federal criminal case is to decide only the issues of fact, taking the law as given by the court;" *United States v. Gleason*, 726 F.2d 385, 388 (8th Cir. 1984): "it is the district court's duty to instruct the jury on the law applicable to the case, and not the jury's duty to interpret the law;" *Babson v. United States*, 330 F.2d 662, 666 (9th Cir. 1964): "It is essential to the administration of justice that a jury scrupulously follow the law as given to it by the judge;" *United States v. Renfroe*, 634 F. Supp. 1536, 1549 (W.D. Pa. 1986): referring to the "the now familiar rule that juries are obliged to follow the law as given by the court;" *United States v. West Coast News Company*, 228 F. Supp. 171, 182 (W.D. Mich. 1964): affirming "the rule which requires the jury to take the law as given to them by the Judge, and from no other source;" *Corson v. United States*, 147 F.2d 437, 438 (9th Cir. 1945): Affirming that the jury must accept the "law as given to you by the Judge in these instructions. It would be a violation of your duty to attempt to determine the law or to base a verdict upon any other view of the law than that given you by the court;" *U.S. v. Lucero*, 895 F. Supp. 1421, 1426 (D. Kan. 1995): "As for jury nullification, the court should not encourage the jurors to violate their oath by refusing to apply the law as given in the court's instructions;" *United States v. Trujillo*, 714 F.2d 102, 105 (11th Cir. 1983): "its [the jury's] duty is to apply the law as interpreted and instructed by the court."

in *United States v. Martin Linens Supply Co.*,[117] for instance, issued a strongly worded ruling affirming both the fundamental nature of this adjudicative division within the criminal law, as well as its value as a mechanism for preserving and promoting just and fair trials:

> [I]n a jury trial the primary finders of fact are the jurors. Their overriding responsibility is to stand between the accused and a potentially arbitrary or abusive Government that is in command of the criminal sanction. For this reason, a trial judge is prohibited from entering a judgment of conviction or directing the jury to come forward with such a verdict regardless of how overwhelmingly the evidence may point in that direction. The trial judge is thereby barred from attempting to override or interfere with the jurors' independent judgment.[118]

The other dimension of this instruction – that issues of law are the sole and exclusive purview of the trial judge – is clearly seen in the Criminal Pattern Jury Instructions provided by the United States Court of Appeals for the Eleventh Circuit:

> Your decision must be based only on the evidence presented here. You must not be influenced in any way by either sympathy for or prejudice against the Defendant or the Government. *You must follow the law as I explain it – even if you do not agree with the law – and you must follow all of my instructions as a whole.. You must not single out or disregard any of the Court's instructions on the law.*[119]

The singular importance of this adjudicative division of labor instruction is vividly demonstrated here by the priority the Eleventh Circuit Court of

---

[117] 430 U.S. 564 (1977).

[118] *Id.* at 572-73. See, also *Sparf and Hansen v. United States*, *supra* note 86, at 106: "The duty of the court to expound the law, and that of the jury to apply the law as thus declared to the facts as ascertained by them. In this separation of the functions of court and jury is found the chief value, as well as safety, of the jury system. Those functions cannot be confounded or disregarded without endangering the stability of public justice, as well as the security of private and personal rights."

[119] *Criminal Pattern Jury Instructions* (March 2022) §B2.1, The United States Court of Appeals for the Eleventh Circuit (emphasis added).

Appeals accords it; this instruction, or some form of it, is one of the very first instructions the jury hears regarding its expected role and responsibilities before the trial commences; it, or some form of it, is also among the very first instructions given to the jury at the end of trial, right before the jury retires to deliberate.[120]

While this adjudicative division of labor is justified on the policy considerations mentioned by the Supreme Court in *Martin Linens Supply Co.* and other cases[121] – protecting the accused from arbitrary and abusive Government action, and preserving the security of personal and private rights – it also has important limiting implications vis-à-vis the controversy surrounding jury nullification. Despite the near universal recognition by the judiciary that juries have the unreviewable power to nullify, such behavior is seen by the courts as incompatible with the adjudicative division of labor – the jury, in judging the law, is attempting to supplant and arrogate the authority and role of the trial judge. Today, therefore, the dominant and prevailing approach among the courts that have directly considered this issue heretofore is that the jury has no right to nullify, the defendant has no right to a nullifying jury, and, hence, the court has no duty to inform or otherwise instruct the jury regarding the existence of its nullification power during trial; in fact some courts have gone so far as to assert that there is a positive duty to keep such information from the jurors.[122] This issue of the *nullification instruction*, and the central role it

---

[120] In some jurisdictions this is referred to as the 'Duty to Convict' Instruction. See, for instance, *State v. Nicholas*, 185 Wash. App. 298, 300 (Wash. Ct. App. 2014): "If you find from the evidence that each of these elements has been proved beyond a reasonable doubt, then it will be your duty to return a verdict of guilty."

[121] See note 113.

[122] See, for instance: *State v. Sayles*, 2021 WL 302807 (Md. 2021); *Davis v. State*, 520 So. 2d 493, 494 (Miss. 1988); *Lee v. State, supra* note 107; *State v. Cote*, 129 N.H. 358, 530 A.2d 775 (1987); *Commonwealth v. Fernette*, 398 Mass. 658, 500 N.E.2d 1290 (1986); *Annas v. State*, 726 P.2d 552 (Alaska App. 1986); *Walker v. State*, 723 P.2d 273 (Okla. 1986); *State v. Allie*, 147 Ariz. 320, 710 P.2d 430 (1985); *State v. Perkins*, 353 N.W.2d 557 (Minn. 1984); *Walker v. State*, 445 N.E.2d 571 (Ind. 1983); *Williams v. Commonwealth*, 644 S.W.2d 335 (Ky. 1983); *State v. Lang*, 46 N.C. App. 138, 264 S.E.2d 821 (1980); *Keenan v. State*, 379 So.2d 147 (Fla.App. 1980); *State v. Hunter*, 586 S.W.2d 345 (Mo. 1979); *State v. Vigna*, 260 N.W.2d 506 (S.D. 1977); *State v. Willis*, 218 N.W.2d 921 (Iowa 1974). For federal decisions, see: *United States v. Wiley*, 503 F.2d 106 (8th Cir. 1974) citing *United States v. Dellinger*, 472 F.2d 340 (7th Cir. 1972); 410 U.S. 970, 93 S.Ct. 1443, 35 L.Ed.2d 706 (1973); *United States v. Simpson*, 460 F.2d 515 (9th Cir. 1972); *United States v. Moylan*, 417 F.2d

plays in the larger jury nullification debate, will be taken up in subsequent chapters.

1.5.4 Jury Deliberations

Once the trial stage has ended, the jury retires to discuss the case, deliberate, and reach a verdict. The length of deliberations can vary widely, and there is no set time limit on how long or short deliberations can be – the court will allow the jury as much time as needed to reach a unanimous verdict. American criminal juries deliberate and decide cases in secret, and these deliberations are not disclosed nor part of the trial record. Interestingly, this prohibition against juror deliberative transparency is not legislatively mandated, nor does the *U.S. Constitution* compel the secrecy of jury deliberations; rather, this constraint is a matter of case law.[123] The American courts have been unanimous, unambiguous, and clear that, (except for cases where substantive and significant juror malfeasance is alleged),[124] it is improper for a trial judge to pierce the veil of juror secrecy and inquire into how a jury arrived at its verdict:

> As a general rule, no one — including the judge presiding at a trial — has a "right to know" how a jury, or any individual juror, has deliberated or how a decision was reached by a jury or juror. The secrecy of deliberations is the cornerstone of the modern Anglo-American jury system. Courts and commentators alike recognize

---

1002 (4th Cir. 1969); *Washington v. Watkins*, 655 F.2d 1346, 1374 n. 54 (5th Cir. 1981); *U. S. v. Krzyske*, 836 F.2d 1013 (6th Cir. 1988).

[123] See, for example, *United States v. Patterson*, 587 F. App'x 878, 24 (6th Cir. 2014) (citations omitted): "The District of Columbia and Second Circuits have placed a premium on the secrecy of jury deliberations by limiting the trial courts' ability to inquire into allegations of jury bias, jury nullification, or a failure to follow the court's instructions… As the Second Circuit aptly recognized, this standard might leave open the possibility that jurors will engage in irresponsible activity that will remain outside the court's power to investigate, but to open the door to the deliberation room any more widely and provide opportunities for broad-ranging judicial inquisitions into the thought processes of jurors would… destroy the jury system itself."

[124] See, for instance, *Pena-Rodriguez v. Colorado*, 137 S. Ct. 855 (2017). Here, the Court held that the jury secrecy rule must yield to the constitutional right to a fair trial.

that the secrecy of deliberations is essential to the proper functioning of juries.[125]

Specifically, the U.S. Supreme Court provided four reasons or rationales that justify this policy of jury deliberative secrecy. According to the Court, preserving the secrecy of jury deliberations: i) protects jurors from possible post-verdict harassment;[126] ii) facilitates freedom of debate amongst the jurors;[127] iii) promotes and preserves community confidence in the jury system;[128] and, iv) preserve the finality of verdicts.[129] Moreover, in *Tanner v. United States*,[130] the Court explicitly emphasized the important principles that ground this need to protect the secrecy of juror deliberations, stating: "This Rule is supported by substantial policy considerations, including the need to assure full and frank discussion in the privacy of the jury room, to prevent the harassment of jurors by losing parties, and to preserve the community's trust in a system that relies on the decisions of laypeople."[131] Other courts have also emphasized the importance of maintaining and preserving the finality of verdicts as a justification for maintaining the secrecy of jury room deliberations.[132]

1.5.5 The Verdict

Once the jury reaches a verdict, the jurors return to the courtroom, and the verdict is read aloud. The defendant is either found guilty or not guilty –

---

[125] *U.S. v. Thomas, supra* note 109, at 618. See, also *Tanner v. United States*, 483 U.S. 107, 120 S. Ct. 2739 (1987): "There is little doubt that postverdict investigation into juror misconduct would in some instances lead to the invalidation of verdicts reached after irresponsible or improper juror behavior. It is not at all clear, however, that the jury system could survive such efforts to perfect it… [and would] seriously disrupt the finality of the process;" and at 127: "[L]ong-recognized and very substantial concerns support the protection of jury deliberations from intrusive inquiry."

[126] *McDonald v. Pless*, 238 U.S. 264 (1915).

[127] *Clark v. United States*, 289 U.S. 1, (1933).

[128] *Tanner v. United States, supra* note 125.

[129] *McDonald v. Pless, supra* note 126, at 267-68.

[130] *Supra* note 125.

[131] *Id.* at 107.

[132] See, for instance, *United States v. Moten*, 582 F.2d 654, 664 (2d Cir. 1978) (citations omitted): "In addition, certain limits on post-trial inquiry into jury verdicts are necessary in the interest of finality lest judges become Penelopes, forever engaged in unravelling the webs they wove."

this is referred to as a *general verdict*.[133] The jury's verdict must be unanimous to sustain juridical legitimacy and avoid the declaration of a mistrial.[134] Verdicts of not guilty are final, and, for the most part, unappealable by the prosecution. This is in great part because the Fifth Amendment of the *U.S. Constitution*, through the operation of the *Double Jeopardy Clause*, forbids the State from pursuing multiple prosecutions against an individual for the same crime. The pertinent section of the Fifth Amendment reads, "No individual can be twice placed in jeopardy of life or limb for the same offense."[135] This essentially means that once an individual has been acquitted or convicted of a specific crime at trial, they are thereafter immune from any and all subsequent prosecution for the same offense, irrespective of the verdict in the initial trial.[136] "Perhaps the most fundamental rule in the history of double jeopardy jurisprudence has been that '[a] verdict of acquittal... could not be reviewed, on error or otherwise, without putting [a defendant] twice in jeopardy, and thereby violating the Constitution.'"[137] Moreover, and perhaps surprisingly, the scope of this amendment has been interpreted to extend even so far as to include not guilty verdicts subsequently judged to be entered erroneously.[138]

While nothing in this amendment speaks specifically and directly to the status of *jury* verdicts in criminal trials, the courts have traditionally interpreted the double jeopardy clause to mean that, in the absence of some

---

[133] The jury's verdict in criminal cases, for the most part, speaks only to the guilt or innocence of the accused, and does not usually include particulars as to how the verdict was reached. This is known as a *general* verdict. This idea of a general verdict of guilt or innocence *simpliciter* is contrasted with a *special* verdict, where a finding of fact is made and the legal conclusion to be drawn thereby is left to the Court to decide.
[134] See, *Ramos v. Louisiana*, 140 S. Ct. 1390 (2020).
[135] *U.S. Constitution*, Amendment V.
[136] As with all Amendments to the *U.S. Constitution*, the Double Jeopardy Clause originally applied only to the federal government. However, in *Benton v. Maryland*, 395 U.S. 784 (1969), the Supreme Court ruled that the Double Jeopardy Clause applied to state prosecutions as well.
[137] *United States* v. *Ball*, 163 U.S. 662, 671 (1896).
[138] See, for instance: *Fong Foo v. United States*, 369 U.S. 141, 143 (1962) (citations omitted): "The Court of Appeals thought, not without reason, that the acquittal was based upon an egregiously erroneous foundation. Nevertheless, the verdict of acquittal was final, and could not be reviewed... without putting [the petitioners] twice in jeopardy, and thereby violating the Constitution."

actionable (and *very* narrowly defined) malfeasance on the part of the jury,[139] jury verdicts of not guilty in criminal trials are final, unreviewable, and immune to any and all impeachment and appeal.[140] A defendant freed by such a verdict need never fear subsequent prosecution for the same crime. Of particular note, this unreviewability and finality of not guilty verdicts by the jury has been held to specifically encompass those arrived at through jury nullification. The Court in *U.S. v. Siegelman,*[141] for instance, stated this principle explicitly: "For example, we permit logically inconsistent jury verdicts as to different counts, and even as to different co-defendants. *We permit jury nullification*. We do not inquire whether a verdict is the result of compromise, mistake or even carelessness."[142] The principle of double jeopardy serves as a bulwark against the government's continued and repeated prosecution of an individual for the same alleged offense, and thereby ensures both an individual's right to fair and just treatment at the hands of the State, as well as the conclusive resolution of, and finality to, legal proceedings. The courts have repeatedly stressed the value of this last principle:

> [T]o speculate whether the jury really meant to acquit when it wrote "Not Guilty," would create an unwarranted exception to the "fundamental" and "absolute" rule of double jeopardy that a jury's verdict of acquittal is final — an exception that would inevitably undermine the rule's "absolute" nature. *See Burks v. United States,*437 U.S. 1, 16, 98 S.Ct. 2141, 57 L.Ed.2d 1 (1978) ("[W]e necessarily afford absolute finality to a jury's *verdict* of acquittal.").[143]

---

139 See *Pena-Rodriguez v. Colorado, supra* note 124.

140 See, for example, *United States v. Scott,* 437 U.S. 82, 91 (1978): "A judgment of acquittal, whether based on a jury verdict of not guilty or on a ruling by the court that the evidence is insufficient to convict, may not be appealed and terminates the prosecution."

141 640 F.3d 1159 (11th Cir. 2011).

142 *Id* at 1185 n. 36 (emphasis added). See, also, *State v. Grey,* 147 N.J. 4, 9 (N.J. 1996) (emphasis added): "The Court [*Dunn v. United States,* 284 U.S. 390 (1932)] held that the inconsistency in the verdicts did not necessarily indicate that the jury was unconvinced of the defendant's guilt, but that such a verdict might indicate only an [allowable] exercise of leniency or *nullification*."

143 *Stow v. Murashige,* 389 F.3d 880, 883 (9th Cir. 2004). See also, *Losey v. Frank,* No. 02-C-1252, at *1 (E.D. Wis. June 16, 2003): "Under double jeopardy principles, an unreversed

1.6 The Modern 'Independent' Jury

Taken together, the five stages of the criminal jury trial process, and the role carved out for the jury in each of these stages through case law and legislation, have combined to form the modern notion of, not just an impartial jury, but, as so many courts have noted, an *independent jury*.[144] And while the appropriate depth and breadth of this concept of jury independence is still a living and active debate in legal circles and the judiciary, the received view amongst the courts who have confronted the issue specifically is that an 'independent' jury means, not a jury that is free to act *however* it wishes, *whenever* it wishes, during any and all stages of the trial process, but, rather, that jury independence is best understood as the principle that *the jury is at liberty to deliberate and return a verdict free from any and all external coercion and influence, including that from the bench*.[145] This notion of an independent jury, free from all judicial control and oversight in its deliberations and verdict has now been firmly established by case law.[146] Perhaps the strongest articulation of this view that the right to a fair

---

verdict results in finality. This is so because a verdict constitutes a determination of a defendant's culpability. Thus, acquittals are an absolute bar to appeal or to a new trial;" *United States v. Scott, supra* note 140, at 91 (1978) "To permit a second trial after an acquittal, however mistaken the acquittal may have been, would present an unacceptably high risk that the Government, with its vastly superior resources, might wear down the defendant so that 'even though innocent he may be found guilty.'" (quoting *Green*, 355 U.S., at 188).

[144] See, for instance, *Martinez v. Court of Appeal of Cal.*, Fourth App. Dist, 528 U.S. 152 (2000); *Reid v. Covert*, 354 U.S. 1 (1956); *People v. Nicolas*, G054672 (Cal. Ct. App. Oct. 5, 2018); *People v. Mina*, No. F074901 (Cal. Ct. App. Dec. 13, 2018).

[145] See, for example, *State v. Simon*, 79 N.J. 199, 199 (N.J. 1979), where the Court asserted that "a jury in a criminal case has the paramount, exclusive and independent responsibility for making the final adjudication of guilt or innocence and cannot be compelled by the court to return a guilty verdict even though evidence of guilt is overwhelming."

[146] See, for example: *State v. Kirkman*, 159 Wn. 2d 918, 941 (Wash. 2007): "One element of this [Sixth Amendment] guaranty is the right to trial by a free and independent jury;" *State v. Carlin*, 40 Wn. App. 698, 701 (Wash. Ct. App. 1985): referencing a defendant's "constitutional right to a jury trial, including the independent determination of the facts by the jury;" *Stepney v. Lopes*, 592 F. Supp. 1538, 1547 (D. Conn. 1984): referencing a defendant's "federal constitutional rights to a trial by a jury which must be permitted to exercise the independent judgment of its members;" *State v. Lang*, 458 P.3d 791, 795 (Wash. Ct. App. 2020): describing a defendant's "constitutional right to an independent jury determination of guilt;" *State v. Revey*, 134 Wn. App. 1028 (Wash. Ct. App. 2006):

trial necessarily implies a corresponding right to an independent jury comes from the Court in *State v. Silcox*:[147] "To impinge upon the independent determination of guilt or innocence by any juror [jeopardizes] the defendant's right to a fair trial, which all courts recognize as a fundamental right, and… cannot be tolerated."[148]

In the following chapter, I next explore how this contemporary model of jury independence and the concept of jury nullification are necessarily and inextricably intertwined, both at the conceptual and practical levels. Jury nullification is, fundamentally, a necessary element of the criminal jury trial process as it now stands.

Appendix – State Constitutions and the Independent Jury

Despite the near ubiquitous nature of the adjudicative division of labor between judge and jury found in American criminal jurisprudence, the state constitutions of Georgia,[149] Indiana,[150] Maryland,[151] and Oregon,[152] all currently have provisions guaranteeing the right of jurors to "judge" or

---

referencing a defendant's "right to an independent determination of guilt by the jury;" *People v. Frazier*, 123 Ill. App. 3d 563, 573 (Ill. App. Ct. 1984): here the Court asserted that the jury's "particular duty it is to provide an independent determination of guilt or innocence;" *State v. Steenhard*, 9 Wn. App. 2d 1072 (Wash. Ct. App. 2019): equating a defendant's right to a fair trial to "the jury's ability to critically assess the State's evidence and make an independent determination of guilt;" *State v. Ragland*, 105 N.J. 189, 222 (N.J. 1986) (citation omitted) (emphasis added): "I am comfortable with the prevailing view, which recognizes that tacit toleration of jury verdicts of innocence, in apparent contradiction to clear proof of guilt, affords adequate protection of *a defendant's entitlement to a trial by an impartial and independent jury*."

[147] 103 Idaho 483 (Idaho 1982).

[148] *Id* at 490.

[149] Article 1, § 1, of the *Constitution of the State of Georgia* states, in part: "In criminal cases, the defendant shall have a public and speedy trial by an impartial jury; and the jury shall be the judges of the law and the facts."

[150] Article 1, § 19, of the *Constitution of Indiana* states, in part: "In all criminal cases whatever, the jury shall have the right to determine the law and the facts."

[151] Article 23 of the *Declaration of Rights in the Constitution of Maryland* states, in part: "In the trial of all criminal cases, the Jury shall be the Judges of Law, as well as of fact, except that the Court may pass upon the sufficiency of the evidence to sustain a conviction."

[152] Article 1, § 16 of the *Constitution of Oregon* states, in part: "In all criminal cases whatever, the jury shall have the right to determine the law, and the facts under the direction of the Court as to the law."

"determine" the law in all state-level criminal cases, seemingly endorsing, at the constitutional level, the jury's right to nullify. However, in practice, this has turned out not to be the case. The courts in all of these states have interpreted these constitutional provisions very narrowly so as to limit any meaningful role for the jury to play in actually 'judging the law' in practice. Often the logical gymnastics employed to parse this distinction between constitutional mandate and actual court practice border on the Mad-Hatter-esque. For example, the Court in *Meeks v. State*[153] asserted the following claim: "The court has carefully scrutinized... Article I, Section 19, and [holds] that the constitutional right of the jury to determine the law in criminal cases does not include the right to disregard or ignore the law as it exists."[154] The Court did not, however, elaborate on, or otherwise explain or elucidate the nature of this conceptual distinction between 'determining' and 'ignoring' when it comes to applying rules to action; no doubt because such a distinction is entirely specious. If jurors genuinely have the right to judge or determine what the law, in fact, is for a particular situation (does the law, for instance, say x or $\sim x$ given fact constellation y), then, presumably, the jury is operating well within its purview when it judges a particular law not to apply to a specific set of facts – when it concludes $\sim x$ in other words. Equally, a judgement of x would similarly be within its purview. The *Meeks* Court, however, seems to have interpreted Article 1, Section 19, of the *Constitution of Indiana* to mean: 'In all criminal cases whatever, the jury shall have the right to determine the law *(as long as the courts agrees with said determination)* and the facts.' Of course, the right to agree with the State is not really a right at all.

This hostility to meaningful jury independence in general, and jury nullification in particular, has been echoed in judgements and constitutional interpretations across all four mentioned states,[155] effectively

[153] 759 N.E.2d 1126 (Ind. Ct. App. 2001).

[154] *Id.* at 1131.

[155] See, for instance: *Walker v. State, supra* note 122, at 575 (emphasis added): "As you will recall, the Constitution of the State of Indiana makes you the judges of both the law and the facts. Though this means that you are to determine the law for yourself, *it does not mean that you have the right to make, repeal, disregard, or ignore the law as it exists;" Hamilton and Fletcher v. State,* 12 Md. App. 91, 98 (Md. Ct. Spec. App. 1971): "Article XV, § 5, of the Constitution of Maryland... does not confer upon [the jury] untrammeled discretion to enact new law or to repeal or ignore clearly existing law as whim, fancy,

eliminating any nullificatory jury rights including, centrally, the right to be informed.[156] Despite Maryland's constitutional provision, for instance, the Court in *State v. Sayles*[157] nevertheless ruled:

> We hold that, despite the circumstance that jury nullification occurs, jury nullification is not authorized in Maryland and a jury does not have a right to engage in jury nullification. No case, statute, or rule in Maryland authorizes or gives juries the right to engage in jury nullification, *i.e.* , there is no grant of authority permitting a jury to nullify. Rather, Maryland case law makes clear that it is improper for an attorney to argue jury nullification to a jury, and that jury instructions on the law are binding and trial courts must advise juries as much.[158]

As stated by the Court in *Pyburn v. State*:[159] "A defendant has no entitlement to the luck of a lawless decisionmaker."[160] Whatever might be implied by

---

compassion or malevolence should dictate;" *Fauvre v. Roberts*, 309 Or. 691, 696 (Or. 1990) (emphasis in original): "It is not the law in this state that a jury has the "right" — as opposed to the undoubted *power* — to acquit a defendant whose guilt had been proved beyond a reasonable doubt;" *Bryant v. State*, 163 Ga. App. 872, 873 (Ga. Ct. App. 1982) (citations omitted): "It is now accepted that the province of the court [is] to construe the law applicable in the trial of a criminal case, and of the jury to apply the law so construed to the facts in evidence. While the impaneled jurors are made absolutely and exclusively judges of the facts in the case, they are, in this sense only, judges of the law." *Cargill v. State*, 255 Ga. 616, 642 (Ga. 1986): "the jury does possess a de facto power of nullification, i.e., a power to acquit the defendant regardless of the strength of the evidence against him. However, it nonetheless is true that if the evidence proves the defendant guilty beyond a reasonable doubt it is the jury's duty to convict;" *Bivins v. State*, 642 N.E.2d 928, 946 (Ind. 1995) (citation omitted): "[I]t is improper for a court to instruct a jury that they have a right to disregard the law. Notwithstanding Article 1, Section 19 of the Indiana Constitution, a jury has no more right to ignore the law than it has to ignore the facts in a case."

[156] See, for example, *Watkins v. State*, 265 Ga. App. 54, 56 (Ga. Ct. App. 2004): "Thus, we have found no error when a trial court declines to give such charge on jury nullification;" *McCullough v. State*, 351 Ga. App. 385, 388 (Ga. Ct. App. 2019): "This does not mean, however, that courts should *encourage* juries to disregard the law. The Supreme Court of Georgia previously held that a jury is properly charged to focus solely on the guilt or innocence of the defendant."

[157] *Supra* note 122.

[158] *Id.* at 216.

[159] 301 Ga. App. 372, (Ga. Ct. App. 2009).

[160] *Id.* at 376-77 (citation omitted).

the jury's apparent constitutional right to judge or determine the law in these states, it most decidedly does not include, so far as the courts are concerned, the right to nullify.

Chapter 2
The 'Necessity' of Nullification[1]

It would no doubt be an understatement to suggest that the courts view instances of jury nullification rather unfavorably; overt animosity might perhaps be a more accurate description. Leventhal, J., for instance, passionately condemned the practice in *U. S. v. Dougherty*,[2] stating that "[t]his so-called right of jury nullification is put forward in the name of democracy, but its explicit avowal *risks the ultimate logic of anarchy*."[3] A similar objection was voiced by the U.S. Court of Appeals for the Second Circuit in *U. S. v. Thomas*:[4]

> We categorically reject the idea that, in a society committed to the rule of law, jury nullification is desirable or that courts may permit it to occur when it is within their authority to prevent.[5]

And again, in *State v. McClanahan*,[6] where the court stated that "the administration of justice cannot be left to community standards or community conscience but must depend upon the protections afforded by the rule of law."[7] Such an objection also found voice in *State v. Willis*,[8] where the court asserted:

---

[1] Some of the thoughts and ideas expressed in this chapter have been previously explored in Hreno, Travis, *Necessity and Jury Nullification*, vol. 20, no. 20 Can. J. L. & Juris. 351 (2007). However, it is important to note that the substantive content and conclusions drawn have undergone substantial revisions, developments, expansions, and updates to reflect current jurisprudence, as well as the specific focus and tenor of this project. The author acknowledges this earlier publication as a foundation for the present work.

[2] 473 F.2d 1113 (D.C. Cir. 1972).

[3] *Id.* at 1133 (emphasis added).

[4] 116 F.3d 606 (2nd Cir. 1997).

[5] *Id.* at 614.

[6] 212 Kan. 208, 510 P.2d 153 (1973).

[7] *Id.* at 153.

[8] 218 N.W.2d 921, 924-25 (Iowa 1974).

> [j]ury nullification exalts the goal of particularized justice above the ideal rule of law. We are persuaded the rule of law should not be subverted. A central theme in our constitutional system is that no [person] is above the law and all are equally accountable to it. The people are sovereign, but they exercise their sovereignty through government rather than juries.[9]

In *United States v. Moylan*,[10] Sobeloff, J., commenting on jury nullification, made the following claim:

> To encourage individuals to make their own determinations as to which laws they will obey and which they will permit themselves as a matter of conscience to disobey is to invite chaos. No legal system could long survive if it gave every individual the option of disregarding with impunity any law which by his personal standard was judged morally untenable. Toleration of such conduct would not be democratic, as appellants claim, but inevitably anarchic.[11]

This view was also echoed by the Kansas Supreme Court, which, in commenting on jury nullification stated that "[d]isregard for the principles of established law creates anarchy and destroys the very protections which the law affords."[12] In short, the judiciary "view jury nullification as a pernicious element in the criminal justice system… the jury's official role in court proceedings is limited solely to judging the facts of the case and applying the law as given by the judge to those facts."[13] There are many more examples of this type of thinking,[14] but all that it is important here to note is that, particularly amongst the judiciary, there is widespread condemnation of the practice and promotion of jury nullification.

---

[9] *Id.* at 924.

[10] 417 F.2d 1002 (4th Cir. 1969).

[11] *Id.* at 1009.

[12] *State v. McClanahan*, *supra* note 6, at 159.

[13] Hreno, Travis, *Necessity and Jury Nullification*, 20 Can. J. L. & Juris. 351, 352 (2007).

[14] See Scheflin, Alan W. and Van Dyke, Jon M., *Jury Nullification: The Contours of a Controversy*, 43 Law & Contemp. Probs. 51, 85-90 (1980), for an in-depth discussion of such objections.

Nevertheless, and despite such widespread condemnation, case law is also replete with judgments affirming that the jury can, in fact, behave in such manner without fear of censure, and without having its verdict impeached, over-ruled, or vitiated. Consider, for instance, *Horning v. District of Columbia,*[15] where the court affirmed that: "the jury has the power to bring in a verdict in the teeth of both law and facts." A more striking statement of this view can be found in Chief Justice Jay's instructions to the jury in *Brailsford,*[16] the United States Supreme Court's only jury trial:

> It may not be amiss, here, Gentlemen, to remind you of the good old rule that on questions of fact, it is the province of the jury; on questions of law it is the province of the court to decide. But it must be observed that by the same law which recognizes this reasonable distribution of jurisdiction, you have nevertheless a right to take upon yourselves to judge of both, and to determine the law as well as the fact in controversy. On this and on every other occasion, however, we have no doubt you will pay that respect which is due to the opinion of the court: for, as on the one hand, it is presumed, that juries are the best judges of facts, it is, on the other hand, presumable that the court is the best judge of law. But still both objects are lawfully, within your power of decision.[17]

Many other cases have asserted and affirmed the same principle.[18] As it stands, under current Anglo-American criminal law, nothing is done to

---

[15] 41 S. Ct. 53 (1920).

[16] *Georgia v. Brailsford,* 3 U.S. 1 (1794).

[17] *Id.* at para. 4.

[18] *Morissette v. United States,* 342 U.S. 246, 275 (1952): "But juries are not bound by what seems inescapable logic to judges;" *United States v. Moylan, supra* note 10, at 1006: "If the jury feels the law is unjust, we recognize the undisputed power of the jury to acquit, even if its verdict is contrary to the law as given by a judge, and contrary to the evidence...If the jury feels that the law under which the defendant is accused is unjust, or that exigent circumstances justified the actions of the accused, or for any reason which appeals to their logic or passion, the jury has the power to acquit, and the courts must abide by that decision;" *U.S. v. Dougherty, supra* note 2, at 1130: "The jury has an "unreviewable and irreversible power... to acquit in disregard of the instructions on the law given by the trial judge;" *R. v. Krieger,* [2006] 2 S.C.R. 501, 2006 SCC 47: "It has since then been well established that under the system of justice we have inherited from England juries are not entitled *as a matter of right* to refuse to apply the law — but they do have the *power* to do so when their consciences permit of no other course."

prevent or correct for instances of suspected jury nullification. So long as no other form of impropriety is alleged (such as jury tampering, or, perhaps, overtly racist behavior on the part of jurors),[19] the jury's verdict remains unimpeachable.

In fact, most of the current debate about jury nullification, both in the courtroom and in academic circles, for the most part does not even address the issue as to whether juries *ought* to have the ability to nullify. The only contentious issue in the contemporary debate around jury nullification is whether the jury ought to be *informed* or *instructed* of this ability (this issue will be the focus of later chapters). This might seem surprising; yet even those opponents of jury nullification who view it as inimical to the goals and ends of the jury system do not go so far as to advocate for the wholesale *removal* of a jury's ability to so act;[20] rather, such opponents focus on how to best *minimize* instances of jury nullification.

2.1 Jury Nullification and Legal Redress

It must be asked: if jury nullification is seen as unsanctioned and unwelcome behavior (which, as we saw above, is clearly how the courts see it), how come the courts do not treat nullification like any other form of jury malfeasance (overt bias, for example) – as something to be prevented and, where such prevention fails, as something to be corrected for? In other words, why not seek to remove this ability from the jury through some *method of legal redress* (MLR)?[21] In examining the possibility of an MLR for jury nullification, we need to be careful as to just what it is that we are inquiring into. Our question cannot be understood as asking whether it is possible to *always* prevent or correct for instances of jury nullification. If we

---

[19] See, for instance, *Pena-Rodriguez v. Colorado*, 137 S. Ct. 855 (2017).

[20] For instance, Simson, Gary J., *Jury Nullification in the American System: A Skeptical View*, 54 Texas Law Review 488, 524 (1976), who, while arguing that jury nullification does more harm than good to the promotion of a just legal system, nevertheless states that "any measures calculated to diminish significantly the scope of the jury's current power to nullify bear unacceptable repercussions for the system as a whole."

[21] I will use the term 'method of legal redress' to refer to procedures involving both statute and/or the common law designed to prevent, and where such prevention fails, to correct, legally unsanctioned and unwelcome behavior. The varieties, means, methods, and procedures for doing so are vast and varied, so the use of this generic umbrella term is for the sake of concision and rhetorical focus.

frame the question that way, then, obviously, the answer will be "no." But, of course, in a free and just society there are many things that can neither be prevented nor corrected for with complete success, not least among them such violent crimes as assault and murder. However, we still have MLR's for assault and murder. Thus, we cannot be tempted to conclude from the fact that a particular action cannot always be prevented or punished that it is therefore futile to try to do so. On the other hand, such a line of reasoning is attractive if it turns out that a particular action can *never* be prevented or corrected. This is what must be looked into: not the possibility of complete success, but the possibility of complete failure. If it turns out that it is simply not possible, even in principle, to prevent instances of jury nullification, then it is, of course, hardly surprising that we have no MLR regarding jury nullification.

2.2 The Impossibility Argument

But what would it mean to claim that it is never possible to prevent, or correct for, instances of jury nullification? Essentially, this claim can best be understood as asserting that we have no MLR for jury nullification because the jury, *qua* jury, must have the ability to nullify. The objections to jury nullification are, after all, fundamentally about the manner in which a jury arrives at its verdict. Therefore, if we wish to avoid instances where the jury returns a verdict through an unsanctioned deliberative process, we could simply do away with jury verdicts altogether. If the jury cannot return a verdict, it cannot nullify. So, in a very real sense, we *do* have an MLR for jury nullification. Of course, this would be akin to solving the problem of drunk drivers by getting rid of all vehicular traffic. To further the analogy, the problem with drunk drivers isn't simply that they are drivers, but that they are the wrong *type* of drivers. We want to eliminate drivers of that kind while still allowing for drivers of the approved kind (i.e., sober). Similarly, we might claim that the problem with juries that nullify isn't so much that they are returning a verdict, but rather that they are returning a verdict through an unsanctioned and unapproved deliberative process. We want to eliminate verdicts of this kind while still allowing for verdicts of the proper kind. So, the claim that no MLR is possible for jury nullification, if it is to be understood as the sort of thing a *reasonable* person might argue for, must be understood as the somewhat more modest assertion that no effective MLR for jury nullification is possible that would still allow the jury to perform its current function.

So, let us take a look then at this claim: jury nullification cannot be prevented without subverting the fundamental function of the jury – to render independent verdicts free from coercion from the bench. Let's call this *the impossibility argument*. At first glance this view might seem plausible – indeed, it is the basis for one of the fundamental arguments in favor of jury independence. After all, the jury returns a general verdict of guilty or not guilty, and is not required to justify or give any reasons for its verdict. We, as outside observers, have no way of knowing why a particular jury might vote to acquit. While we might suspect in a particular case that a verdict of not guilty was the result of jury nullification, we cannot be sure that, instead, the jury simply was not convinced of the defendant's guilt to the requisite degree. A properly instructed and obedient jury, after all, will still vote to acquit a defendant it *believes* to be guilty if that belief is *not* beyond a reasonable doubt. Thus, the *impossibility argument* claims, evidence of jury nullification will always be under-determined by any particular verdict.

Given that a not guilty verdict is, from the perspective of the bench, equally consistent with the jury nullifying as it is with the jury not being convinced of the defendant's guilt to the requisite degree, the verdict itself, one might argue, cannot be regarded as evidence that the jury has nullified. Yet the verdict is the only thing the court has access to. We can call this the *identification problem* for any MLR for jury nullification: since we cannot distinguish instances of nullification from instances of proper jury behavior, we cannot prevent, or correct for, jury nullification, at least without also preventing the jury from performing its properly sanctioned function. This seems to be exactly what Lord Chief Justice Vaughan reasoned in *Bushel* when he stated that the court could never know whether the jury had nullified, for the court could never know what facts the jury found: "A man cannot see by another's eye, nor hear by another's ear, nor more can a man conclude or infer the thing to be resolved by another's understanding or reasoning."[22]

Vaughan went on to argue that, at most, the trial judge was only in a position to say whether he approved of the verdict or not. Because the jury could legitimately disagree with the court over the trustworthiness of witnesses, the court, argued Vaughan, was in no position to say that the jury decided the case contrary to the trial judge's legal instructions.[23] Admittedly, this appears to be a persuasive argument, at least initially. To see where it goes wrong, however, it might be helpful to give a formalized version of it.

The Impossibility Argument:

1. To prevent, or correct for, instances of jury nullification while still allowing for proper verdicts[24] to be rendered, we must have at the very least, some way of distinguishing between the two.
2. We have no way to distinguish between the two (the *identification problem*).
3. We wish to allow for proper jury verdicts to rendered.

therefore,

4. We cannot prevent, or correct for, instances of nullification/No method of legal redress is available for jury nullification.

Let us examine this argument in some detail. The first premise seems to be rather uncontroversial. Let us grant, for the sake of argument, that it is true. Let us also make the same concession regarding premise three. The key, then, to this argument is premise two – *the identification problem* – and it is this premise that we will investigate.

---

[22] *Bushel's Case,* 124 Eng. Rep. 1006, 1012 (1670).

[23] *Id.* at 1006.

[24] That is, verdicts reached through an officially sanctioned deliberative process – in other words, verdicts based solely on an evaluation of the evidence admitted at trial and the law as given by the judge.

Is it possible to know when a jury has nullified? To proponents of the *impossibility argument* (such as Vaughan) this is akin to asking if we can know what the jurors were actually thinking – what their motivations, reasoning-processes, and/or mental states were. Since we can never really know what another person is thinking – never really know, in Vaughan's words "the thing to be resolved by another's understanding or reasoning"[25] – we can, the reasoning goes, never know when a jury has nullified. From the outside, we might claim, a jury's behavior appears identical whether it nullifies or behaves appropriately. The only difference is the jury's motivations/intentions/reasons for choosing to acquit – and the court has no direct access to those.

Interestingly, and conveniently, however, and contrary to what Vaughan seems to assert, the criminal law already provides a framework for distinguishing between behavior and motivation. In legal terms, this division between behavior and motivation is referred to, respectively, as the division between *actus reus* and *mens rea*. If the *identification problem* is to support the *impossibility argument*, we must have some reason to believe that there can be no corrective jurisprudence for situations where the *only* difference between legally sanctioned behavior and that which is not is the *mens rea* element – the motive behind the action, the very thing Vaughan asserted was beyond knowing. But, of course, the criminal law is replete with distinctions based solely on *mens rea*. Take, for instance, the crimes of manslaughter and second degree murder. Both refer to a type of culpable homicide. However, in many circumstances, the only distinction between these two crimes is the *mens rea* element; otherwise, in such cases, there is nothing to distinguish one from the other. This is hardly the only example of the importance of *mens rea* in the criminal law. It is, for instance, a defense to many criminal charges that, though the *actus reus* occurred, there was nevertheless an absence of the relevant *mens rea*. Judgments of a defendant's mental states are made constantly in the criminal law.[26]

Now, of course, we can never really know to a certainty what someone was actually thinking at a particular time; we can only infer mental states from

[25] *Supra* note 22.

[26] Such judgments also play a large role in private law, particularly regarding accusations of intentionally tortuous behavior.

actions. But are such inferences unwarranted? If so, then the *identification problem* might very well prove fatal to the possibility of an MLR for jury nullification. Let's assume then, for the moment, that such inferences are not warranted. To begin with, nearly the whole of the criminal justice system would be thrown in complete disarray. As the Supreme Court asserted: "Although there are exceptions, the "general rule" is that a guilty mind is a necessary element in the indictment and proof of every crime."[27] Given that it rests with the prosecution to prove the elements of a crime, and given that a defendant's mental state at the time the alleged crime occurred is one of those elements, if we adopt Vaughan's view that we can never know another's mental state then we are faced with the possibility of either giving up trying to obtain criminal convictions altogether, or making the vast majority of criminal offences into absolute liability offences in order to obtain such convictions. Neither of these options are attractive, for obvious reasons.

The fact of the matter is, Vaughan may have been correct about the difficulty involved in *knowing* the mental states of another, but he was wrong in thinking that the law requires such knowledge – or at least knowledge to the degree that Vaughan seems to be implying. In fact, the strictest epistemic standard demanded by the criminal law is that of '*beyond a reasonable doubt*.' Even giving credence to the questions raised by the possibility of solipsism, the reasonable doubt standard can often be met in regard to a defendant's state of mind. That is, a particular jury might well be extremely confident, beyond a reasonable doubt, that the defendant's actions are a reliable indicator, on the whole, as to what her mental state was at the time in question. Such inferences from behavior to intention are clearly sanctioned by the criminal justice system. As the Court in *Hudyih v. Smith*[28] put it: "The jury may infer intent from the criminal act itself, or from the defendant's conduct and the surrounding circumstances."[29] If

---

[27] *Elonis v. United States*, 135 S. Ct. 2001, 2009 (2014) (citation omitted).

[28] 12-CV-1761 (SAS) (S.D.N.Y. July 1, 2015).

[29] *Id.* at *14 (citation omitted). See, for also, *U.S. v. Monea*, 376 F. App'x 531, 539 (6th Cir. 2010): "A court can infer intent based on a defendant's conduct;" *In re Zuhone*, 88 F.3d 469, 473 (7th Cir. 1996): "As we noted above, *mens rea* can be inferred from conduct;" *People v. Smith*, 79 N.Y.2d 309, 315 (N.Y. 1992): "Often there is no direct evidence of a defendant's mental state and the jury must infer the *mens rea* circumstantially from the surrounding facts;" *United States v. Jones*, No. 3:16-cr-059, at *7 (S.D. Ohio Jan. 30, 2021):

Vaughan's claim is to have any purchase, then, it cannot depend on the general claim that inferences from behavior to intention are (for the purposes of the law, anyway) always unwarranted; there must be something specific about the jury that makes such inferences unwarranted.

It might be argued, in support of Vaughan, that there *is* something specific about the jury that does render such inferences unwarranted. It might be claimed, for instance, that because, from the outside, the jury's behavior is *identical* whether it nullified or deliberated properly, any evidence that might support the inference to nullifying behavior would *equally* support the inference to proper jury behavior. The key to this argument is not the claim that we can *never* adduce intention from behavior, but, rather it is the claim that if a particular behavior is *equally* consistent with two mutually exclusive mental states then we can never be in a position to make a warranted or reasoned inference to one over the other. This claim does appear unimpeachable. However, this underdetermination assertion can only support the impossibility argument if we assume, as we have been heretofore (provisionally, and for the sake of argument), that the jury's behavior is, in fact, *identical* from the outside whether it nullified or deliberated properly. But is this really true? There is, I argue, reason to suspect not.

To begin with, jury verdicts are not rendered in a vacuum, but rather against the backdrop of the evidence heard at trial. Thus, we might speculate, it could be possible to gain indirect insight into the jury's deliberative process by evaluating its verdict against the evidence heard at trial. Not only might it be possible to do this, but, in fact, this is *exactly* what appellate tribunals are, in certain circumstances, authorized to do.[30] If an

---

"A jury may also infer that *mens rea* element from circumstantial evidence;" *U.S. v. Buffington*, 815 F.2d 1292, 1302 (9th Cir. 1987): "It is permissible to infer intent from a defendant's conduct and the surrounding circumstances."

[30] See, for instance, *The Federal Rules of Appellate Procedure*, Rule 52(a)(6) (2023): "Findings of fact, whether based on oral or other evidence, must not be set aside unless clearly erroneous, and the reviewing court must give due regard to the trial court's opportunity to judge the witnesses' credibility," allowing for an appellate tribunal to review findings of fact – the purview of the jury trial; or, *Jackson v. Virginia*, 443, U.S. 307, 307 (1979), where the court stated that an appellate tribunal must "consider not whether there was any evidence to support a state court conviction, but whether there

appellate tribunal can evaluate the reasonableness of a verdict based on the evidence heard at trial, then, for all intents and purposes, the claim *cannot* be made that the jury's behavior is always identical whether it nullified or deliberated properly. Clearly, the courts feel capable and warranted in evaluating the jury's verdict against the evidence presented at trial – at least in some cases. There are, thus, seemingly no obvious conceptual barriers to the identification of nullifying verdicts, *pace* Vaughan. While not all nullifying verdicts will necessarily be obvious to outside observation and scrutiny, it does seem likely that at least *some* will be transparent. To summarize: if we can infer a jury's deliberative process by comparing its verdict to the evidence, and if such inferences are, on the whole, considered warranted for the purposes of the law (at last in some contexts), then the *identification problem* does not prove to be a barrier to the possibility of some method of legal redress for jury nullification. In other words, the main premise on which the *impossibility* argument is predicated upon cannot be defended. Thus, there is no reason to believe that, if we so desired, we could not – at least in principle – identify at least some instances of jury nullification (even if we could only do so for the very obvious cases).

2.3 Practical Constraints

Even if, conceptually speaking, there is no reason why we couldn't identify at least some instances of jury nullification, the courts have traditionally resisted any temptation to prevent it or strip the ability to so act from the jury. Why is this? To properly address this question, we need to understand what an MLR for jury nullification might look like. As mentioned earlier, an MLR is designed to either prevent, or correct for, legally proscribed behavior. In regard to jury nullification, three (non-exclusive) options immediately present themselves as possible candidates. We could declare a mistrial in those cases where nullification is proven, and thus correct for it. We could criminalize nullifying behavior on the part of jurors (treating it like some other form of juror malfeasance, such as bribery), and thus prevent nullification through deterrence. Thirdly, we could require that jurors in criminal cases give special verdicts as opposed to general verdicts.

---

was sufficient evidence to justify a rational trier of fact to find guilt beyond a reasonable doubt."

This would function to prevent jury nullification by allowing the judge to render the final verdict based on the factual issues resolved by the jury. I will look at each of these options in some detail and show how, from a practical perspective, none of them can succeed as effective MLR's for jury nullification.

2.4 The Division of Labor Instruction

Before we look at these three options, however, there is potentially a fourth MLR for jury nullification that needs to be addressed. This MLR is particularly important to discuss as it is one that is already in place: judicial instructions to the jurors to the effect that they are to take the law as given to them by the trial judge and limit their deliberations on the verdict exclusively to questions of fact. This, it could be argued, is obviously a MLR designed to prevent jury nullification. While this does seem, *prima facie,* to be a plausible view, a closer examination exposes its inherent flaws. This instruction is, as it stands, really more like a suggestion or a request than an order. No sanction attaches to those jurors who disregard/disobey the judge's instructions regarding this division of labor and instead choose to nullify. This lack of sanction attached to jury nullification is significant; it is, in a formal sense, legally unpunishable behavior. However, it must be admitted that, to the degree that such judicial instructions to the jury *are* action guiding, they appear to be a form of legal redress. Surely this instruction will prevent *some* juries from evaluating questions of law when deliberating on the verdict and thus prevent *some* cases of what would otherwise be jury nullification. The authority and respect accorded the judge at trial, this argument asserts, will act as a strong deterrent against those jurors tempted to overstep the proper adjudicative boundaries carved out for them.

But to understand exactly why the division of labor instruction fails as a MLR for jury nullification, we need only look to the intended audience for that instruction – the jury. Recall, when a jury nullifies, it is returning a verdict of not guilty *despite* believing that, on the facts as resolved, the law requires a guilty verdict. It simply is not an example of jury nullification if the jury merely thinks the defendant is not guilty according to the law, regardless of whether this belief is mistaken. The actions of a jury that nullifies are the actions of a jury therefore, that is prepared to disregard instructions from the bench in the interests of a more deeply held principle than mere fidelity to the law. Put another way, a juror who obediently obeys the division of labor instruction merely because the judge issued it was hardly a potentially nullifying juror to begin with. Such an instruction, therefore, does not speak to those who might be inclined to reject judicial instructions, and thus has no real, practical effect as a method of nullificatory redress.

2.5 Special Verdicts

As mentioned, one possible MLR for jury nullification is the special verdict. But would such an MLR actually work? The verdict that a jury returns can be either general or special. A general verdict is one by which the jury pronounces generally upon all or any of the issues, either in favor of the prosecution or the defense. That is, the jury returns simply a verdict of guilty or not guilty for each of the counts of the indictment. No explanation as to why the jury reached the particular verdict it did is required. A special verdict, by contrast, is one by which the jury finds the facts only, and communicates its factual findings to the court, leaving the verdict to the judge to pronounce. The practice of requiring the jury in criminal trials to return a special verdict, while not specifically proscribed by statute, has nevertheless been condemned by the courts.[31]

Amongst those who discuss the nullification doctrine, there are some who endorse the view that the jury's ability to render a general verdict is the key to understanding jury nullification. John Adams noted in his February 12, 1771, diary that:

> the jury power to nullify the judge's instructions derives from the general verdict itself, but if a judge's instructions run counter to fundamental constitutional principles, "is a juror obliged to give his verdict generally, according to his direction or even to the fact specially, and submit the law to the court? Every man, of any feeling

---

[31] See, for instance, *United States v. Gaudin*, 515 U.S. 506, 510 (1995); also: Nepveu, Kate H., *Beyond 'Guilty' or 'Not Guilty': Giving Special Verdicts in Criminal Jury Trials*, vol. 21, no. 1 Yale Law & Policy Review 263 (2003).

> or conscience, will answer, no. It is not only his right, but his duty, in that case to find the verdict according to his own best understanding, judgment, and conscience, though in direct opposition to the direction of the court .... [T]he common people ... should have as complete a control, as decisive a negative, in every judgment of a court of judicature" as they have in other decisions of government.[32]

The view that jury nullification and the general verdict are fundamentally connected is repeatedly asserted in the contemporary literature on the issue as well. Clay Conrad, for instance, states that:

> [t]he basis of the doctrine [of jury nullification] is the fundamental power of criminal trial juries to deliver a general verdict of "guilty" or "not guilty." Jurors are not obliged to justify their conclusion to the court. The verdict in a criminal case does not rest on certain "findings of fact" by the jury, as it may in civil cases; there is no need for the jury to elaborate on or justify their verdict in any way.[33]

Alan Scheflin and Jon Van-Dyke make a similar claim:

> If juries were restricted to finding facts, cases with no disputed factual issues would be withheld from the jury. But such cases are presented to the jury. By its general verdict of innocence, the jury may free a person without its verdict being subject to challenge. The judge cannot ask jurors to explain their verdict, nor may the judge punish the jurors for it. Although judges now generally tell jurors they must obey the judge's instructions on the law, the jurors may not be compelled to do so.[34]

The central idea behind this view is that by requiring the jury to return a special verdict – to answer factual questions only – and leave the final

---

[32] As quoted in Scheflin, Alan W., *Jury Nullification: The Right to Say No*, 45 Southern California Law Review 168, 174-175 (1972).

[33] Conrad, Clay S., *Jury Nullification: Evolution of a Doctrine*, 7 (Carolina Academic Press, 1998).

[34] Scheflin and Van Dyke, *Jury Nullification: The Contours of a Controversy*, *supra* note 14, at 71.

determination of guilt or innocence up to the judge, the jury's ability to judge the law will be removed. Conrad puts it this way:

> A series of questions, posed so as to lead inexorably to a pre-determined result, would completely deprive the defendant of the reasoned moral judgment of the community, by forcing the jury to follow the path of reasoning the judge felt appropriate.[35]

A few things ought to be said about this line of reasoning. To begin with, the sole problem with special verdicts it is claimed, is that they are incompatible with jury nullification. But given the adjudicative division of labor between judge and jury, it is difficult to see what is bad about this, at least from the perspective of the judiciary. A defendant in a criminal trial has a right to a jury properly instructed to evaluate issues of fact, but she decidedly does *not* have the right to a jury with the purview to make judgements of law.[36] In other words, it is not enough to simply state that special verdicts are incompatible with jury nullification and from that conclude that special verdicts are therefore undesirable. Some independent reason must be given for why a system that allows for jury nullification is preferable to one that doesn't, or why a system that allows for special verdicts in criminal cases is, on its own merits (or lack thereof), undesirable.

Conrad hints at what such a reason might be when he describes special verdicts as involving "a pre-determined result" reached by a "path of reasoning the judge felt appropriate."[37] A pre-determined verdict based on the whims of a particular judge is, of course, the antithesis of a fair and impartial trial. However, this is somewhat of a misrepresentation of special verdicts. The factual questions to be decided are still left to the jury. Until the jury resolves such factual questions, no result is pre-determined. The jury is free to draw whatever conclusions it wishes regarding the evidence presented at trial. This fundamentally constrains the final verdict. A trial

---

[35] Conrad, *Jury Nullification: Evolution of a Doctrine, supra* note 33, at 128-29.

[36] See, for instance: See, for instance, *Strickland v. Washington*, 466 U.S. 668, 695 (1984): "An assessment of the likelihood of a result more favorable to the defendant must exclude the possibility of arbitrariness, whimsy, caprice, "nullification," and the like. A defendant has no entitlement to the luck of a lawless decisionmaker, even if a lawless decision cannot be reviewed."

[37] Conrad, *Jury Nullification: Evolution of a Doctrine, supra* note 33, at 129.

judge is free to rely upon a path of reasoning she deems appropriate, but a conviction is always, at least in principle, subject to appellate review; the verdict must not be deemed unreasonable.[38] An unreasonable verdict (that is, a verdict that cannot reasonably be supported based on the factual issues as resolved by the jury) will not survive appellate review. Moreover, leaving the final determination of guilt or innocence to the trial judge in no way violates the legal division of labor between judge and jury. It is, in many situations, a *legal* question as to whether a certain collection of facts can or cannot support a guilty verdict. As such, it would seem to be well within the trial judge's purview to make such a determination.

There are, of course, many reasons to favor a criminal jury system predicated on the general verdict over one which is not. However, an in-depth examination of this topic is beyond the scope of this project.[39] For now, we can occupy ourselves with a more practical question: are special verdicts actually incompatible with jury nullification? In other words, would requiring special verdicts for criminal jury trials actually work as an MLR for jury nullification? I do not believe so. By requiring special verdicts instead of general verdicts, this merely pushes the issue back one level, as it were. To think that special verdicts would be an effective MLR for jury nullification assumes that jurors are either incapable of reasoning for themselves what verdict their answers will reasonably support, or that they will always honestly report their factual findings to the court. There is little reason to assume the former, and the very idea of nullification suggests that the latter is also not likely: a jury that wanted to secure an acquittal for a particular defendant need only report its factual determinations in such a fashion as to render a guilty verdict unreasonable.[40] Such factual determinations are not subject to judicial oversight, nor to appellate review. It cannot be overstated just how much power this gives the jury. A jury may, for example, determine that a particular defendant was not at a

---

[38] See, for example, *Sapir v. United States*, 216 F.2d 722 (10th Cir. 1954).

[39] See, for cases that directly address this issue, *United States v. Shelton*, 588 F.2d 1242 (9th Cir. 1978); *U.S. v. Robertson*, 74 F.3d 1247 (9th Cir. 1996); *United States v. Gonzales*, 841 F.3d 339 (5th Cir. 2016); *United States v. Spock*, 416 F.2d 165 (1st Cir. 1969); *State v. Lawson*, 144 Ariz. 547 (Ariz. 1985).

[40] See, for instance, my discussion of the early medieval jury and the law of self-defense in **CHAPTER 1**.

particular location where and when the alleged crime took place, despite a confession to the police that she was, as well as an admission on the witness stand to that effect. It is, after all, a *question of fact* as to whether the accused's testimony is credible.[41] While this is an extreme, and perhaps far-fetched, example, it is nonetheless illustrative of how much latitude a jury still has in determining the final verdict even when it is limited to returning a special verdict: a jury wanting to nullify would find little to no barrier to doing so via the special verdict.[42]

2.6 Evidentiary Constraints

An effective method of legal redress, as discussed above, must prevent, or correct for, jury nullification in those who are prepared to undertake unsanctioned behavior. As mentioned earlier, two obvious candidates for such a method are: i) criminalizing jury nullification; and/or, ii) declaring a mistrial when jury nullification has taken place and ordering the accused to be re-tried. However, implementing either of these MLR's raises the issue of evidence. Neither option - a mistrial nor criminal proceedings against nullifying jurors - can be pursued in the absence of some evidence that a jury has nullified. Indeed, there must be more than just *some*

---

[41] See, for example, *Britt v. State*, 334 Ark. 142, 164 (Ark. 1998): "In all trials the judge should preside with impartiality. In jury trials especially, he ought to be cautious and circumspect in his language and conduct before the jury. He should not express or intimate an opinion as to the credibility of a witness, or as to controverted facts. For the jury are the sole judges of fact, and the credibility of witnesses; and the constitution expressly prohibits the judge from charging them as to the facts;" *Kimbrell v. State*, 148 Ga. App. 302, 305 (Ga. Ct. App. 1978) (citation omitted): "[J]urors are the exclusive finders of fact and judges of credibility of witnesses. A trial judge invades the province of the jury when he withdraws an accused's sole or principal defense from the jury by his determination that it is unbelievable."

[42] Admittedly, jurors with limited legal knowledge or expertise may not necessarily be able to strategically nullify in the way that I suggest. To that degree, special verdicts might serve as a *practical* limiting constraint on some potential instances of jury nullification. My own view on the issue, however, is that there is something rather duplicitous, unseemly, and substantively antithetical to the foundational principles of a fair and unbiased jury for the State to predicate the practical success of a nullification MLR on juror naïveté and/or ignorance. I extend my sincere thanks to Michael Gentithes for his valuable insight in initially bringing this point to my attention.

evidence; such evidence must be substantial.[43] It is here where the aforementioned *identification problem* has some purchase. While there may be no specific *conceptual* bars to knowing to the requisite legal degree that a jury has nullified, there are, I believe, significant *practical* and *policy* barriers to obtaining the necessary evidence to support such a conclusion.

We must first ask ourselves what could possibly count as evidence that a jury has nullified. The simplest and most obvious answer would be the verdict itself. By comparing the evidence presented at trial with the verdict returned by the jury, we ought to be in a position to say whether the jury behaved in a reasonable manner. Appellate tribunals already have the power to order a new trial in cases where the evidence could not reasonably support a guilty verdict. All that would be necessary to address jury nullification would be to expand the scope of this power to include evaluations of not guilty verdicts as well. Of course, such an evaluation might only reveal that *some* sort of juror malfeasance has occurred without specifically identifying that malfeasance as jury nullification. However, to the degree that any and all unwarranted not guilty verdicts were identified and addressed, this approach would certainly be a possible method for identifying some instances jury nullification.

As promising a course of action as this might initially seem, there are practical constraints as to its applicability. To begin with, cases where the reasonableness of a verdict is at issue are extremely rare. An appellate tribunal is limited to evaluating only legal issues, and cannot second guess the jury regarding the resolution of factual issues. This is a substantially limiting constraint on an appellate court's power to evaluate a verdict. Recall that even such things as witness credibility are factual issues, and thus the sole purview of the jury and not subject to judicial review or oversight. A jury is therefore free (though perhaps not likely) to reject a particular piece of evidence despite substantial and seemingly overwhelming proof of its veracity.

---

[43] Appellate courts are reluctant to order a new trial in the absence of clear proof that a miscarriage of justice likely occurred, and criminal convictions cannot be supported if the evidence of guilt is less than that of beyond a reasonable doubt.

Secondly, it must be remembered that convictions are, in the criminal justice system, entirely different beasts than acquittals. This has to do with the burden of proof required for a conviction – that of beyond a reasonable doubt. A conviction requires that there be some compelling reason to believe that the accused is, in fact, guilty. An acquittal, on the other hand, requires no such corresponding proof. No evidence of the accused's innocence is necessary. All that is required to obtain an acquittal is that the evidence adduced by the prosecution be less than necessary to meet the requisite burden of proof for a conviction. While most often this does entail some positive proof of the accused's innocence, this is by no means a necessary condition. Even if no proof of the accused's innocence is presented at trial, a properly instructed jury will still acquit if it believes the accused to be only *probably* guilty. This *asymmetry of evidentiary burden* means that it is much easier to determine whether a conviction is reasonable than it is to make the same judgment for an acquittal. For example, the court can ask itself whether, if believed, the prosecution's case could possibly support a reasonable verdict of guilty. On the other hand, the court cannot ask itself the same question regarding the defendant's case, as the answer is, in fact, irrelevant. Even if the defendant's case is not believed (or not believable), this does not entail that the prosecution's case is proven or that a guilty verdict is thereby the only reasonable outcome. The facts as presented by the opposing parties in an adversarial system of criminal justice do not represent an exhaustive description of what may or may not have occurred. Thus, even if the accused's version of events, if believed, could not reasonably support an acquittal, a verdict of not guilty is still warranted and appropriate if the jury remains unconvinced by the prosecution's case. This point is important, and bears emphasis. If the prosecution's case cannot reasonably support a guilty verdict, then it is clear that a verdict of not guilty is the only appropriate verdict. If, however, the accused's case cannot reasonably support a not guilty verdict, it is not at all clear that, therefore, a guilty verdict is appropriate. This is the abovementioned asymmetry at play. While the jury cannot accept two inconsistent accounts of the same event as true, it can reject both accounts as false. Given this possibility, an appellate tribunal will often find itself confronting an insurmountable epistemic barrier regarding a jury's motive for acquittal – and not for the quasi-solipsistic reasons suggested by Lord Vaughan, but rather because, in the end, and in a very real sense, a verdict of not-guilty is a judgement on the strength of the prosecution's case, and not the defendant's innocence.

2.7 Monitoring the Jury Room

If conclusive evidence is required that a jury did, in fact, nullify, perhaps one way to acquire such evidence could be to monitor the jury deliberations either overtly (e.g., by having someone in the jury room with the jurors) or covertly (e.g., through hidden monitoring equipment). Thus, if the jury strayed from deliberating solely upon questions of fact, this information would become available to the court which would then be in a position to declare a mistrial and/or initiate criminal proceedings against the jurors.

How would such an MLR work? Let us take a look at the most extreme example: the overt monitoring of jury deliberations with nullifying jurors subject to criminal sanctions. Certainly, arguments could be made in favor of such an MLR. For one thing, it most decidedly would reduce instances of jury nullification. Moreover, such obvious instances of juror malfeasance such as bribery, for example, or juror interference, might also be curtailed. It is not difficult, however, to see problems with this approach. The Sixth Amendment of the *U.S. Constitution*, for instance, guarantees the right to an impartial jury in criminal trials.[44] Impartial in this context refers to (in addition to 'independent of the State'), the fact that the jury is not to be guided or directed towards a particular resolution of the factual questions at issue. Placing a court observer in the jury room with the jurors would compromise jury impartiality and independence: after all, in a criminal jury trial the prosecutor represents the State,[45] and their job is to convince the jury to return a guilty verdict. Let us suppose that upon entering the jury room to deliberate upon the verdict, the jurors find yet another representative of the State there – someone whose job it is to monitor their deliberations and to report back to the court any and all improprieties. In effect, the jurors would be sent the message that if they do not conform their deliberative process so as to meet with the State's approval, they

---

[44] Such provisions can be found in the constitutions of many constitutional democracies.

[45] In the U.S., prosecutors are typically members of the executive branch.

themselves might be charged with a criminal offence and have to face the possibility of a criminal record and criminal sanctions.

Perhaps it might not appear to be such a bad thing to insist that jurors behave in the properly prescribed manner when deliberating upon their verdict. However, in politically sensitive trials where the State might appear to have a vested interest in obtaining a guilty verdict, the presence of a state representative overseeing the jury's deliberations most certainly conflicts with, if not actual jury independence and impartiality, then, at the very least, the appearance of such independence. It is precisely those trials where the State might appear to have a vested interest in the outcome that the independence of the jury is of particular importance, and thus ought not to be compromised. The jury in such a case, if subject to deliberative observation, might well feel subtle (or not) pressure to return a guilty verdict, lest a not guilty verdict displease the State. Again, this would be the very antithesis of an independent jury.

Of course, if the jurors have behaved properly in returning a not guilty verdict, one might argue that they have no reason to fear retribution from the State. However, the State's retributive powers are far reaching, and historically have sometimes been over-indulged. Let us grant in such cases that those jurors who faced trial for their (appropriate) actions would not be convicted. Nevertheless, those jurors would still go through the experience of being arrested, finger-printed and photographed, and put on trial, along with incurring the concomitant legal fees such a process entails. Such an experience is emotionally, as well as financially draining, and being found not guilty is often a rather bitter-sweet experience for those who have wrongfully been put on trial. Thus, the threat of such an experience, even if a not guilty verdict is what awaits the accused at its end, could be, nonetheless, a very coercive factor. To the degree that such an MLR would be successful in reducing instances of jury nullification, it's success would supervene upon an overall reduction in not guilty verdicts; this overall reduction in not guilty verdicts would be caused, not by more accurate and conscientious deliberations on the part of the jury (though, that might be one of the positive side effects of such an MLR), but (also) by the potentially coercive presence of a state representative observing the jury's deliberative process.

As it now stands, when the jury returns a verdict, that verdict must stand (subject to a possible appeal, of course), and the jurors are free from criminal liability for their verdict if it simply displeases the State. The State, if it wishes to pursue criminal charges against the jury, must have some proof of actionable juror malfeasance. Allowing the State into the jury room during the deliberation stage would, of course, provide the State with a heretofore unavailable opportunity to obtain such evidence. While on the surface this may appear to be a good thing, it would also allow the State a heretofore unavailable ability to abuse its prosecutorial powers. While we should remain optimistic that such abuse would not actually occur were the State to be afforded such an opportunity, the fact remains that in politically sensitive trials, the jury may have reason (justified or not) to abandon such optimism. The liberty jurors currently enjoy to freely and openly debate the merits of a case against the defendant would be significantly constrained by the knowledge that 'anything they say in the jury room may be used against them in a court of law,' to paraphrase the well-known right to remain silent (presumably a right we do not wish to encourage jurors to exercise while deliberating).

An observed jury is a coerced jury.[46] A coerced jury is not an impartial jury. When the need arises to balance the value of jury impartiality against the value of limiting instances of jury nullification, it seems clear that the constitutionally mandated guarantees of jury independence and impartiality must win out. The value placed on an impartial jury is clear, and as such, any obvert observation of the jury must be rejected. While the courts may not approve of certain forms of juror impropriety, they are willing to tolerate such behavior in order to preserve jury independence:

> We recognize that this standard — buttressing the core principle of the secrecy of jury deliberations — leaves open the possibility that jurors will engage in irrational activity that will remain outside the

[46] See, *Babson v. United States*, 330 F.2d 662, 665-66 (9th Cir. 1964) (citations omitted): "A juror must be insulated against influences and protected from pressures that would tend to fetter him in the free exercise of his own judgment. To this end the law requires that all deliberations by a jury must be conducted in the utmost privacy;" *Remmer v. United States*, 350 U.S. 377, 382 (1956): "[F]or it is the law's objective to guard jealously the sanctity of the jury's right to operate as freely as possible from outside unauthorized intrusions purposefully made."

> court's powers to investigate or correct. It is an imperfect rule, no doubt, but one fully consistent with our history and traditions, in which the judge's duty and authority to prevent nullification and the need for jury secrecy co-exist uneasily.[47]

To quote the Court in *United States v. Laffitte*,[48] "disclosure of the substance of jury deliberations poses a threat to adjudicatory finality and would undermine the free exchange of ideas that is *essential to the functioning of the jury system*."[49] Indeed, the Constitution demands such tolerance, with all of the procedural constraints implied therein.

Perhaps the problem with this MLR is that the observation is overt. The coercive nature of the observation, one might argue, could be mitigated or even eliminated if such observation were instead covert so that the jurors were not aware of the scrutiny they were under. Instead of having a representative of the State in the jury room with the jurors during their deliberations, perhaps such deliberations could be monitored for impropriety through surreptitious means, and without the jurors' knowledge. Thus, whatever pressures the jurors might feel to return a guilty verdict – pressures caused by the presence of a court observer – could be avoided; the jurors, after all, would be unaware that they were being observed and would not feel pressure to conform their verdict to what they perceived to be the State's wishes. Such a line of reasoning, however, is, for obvious reasons, a non-starter. Remember that the only reason for monitoring jury deliberations (covertly or otherwise) would be to obtain sufficient evidence to support an MLR for jury nullification. If such covertly gathered evidence were to actually be used in court proceedings, the fact that such deliberations were monitored would not long remain secret. With rare exception, criminal trials are public events; it would be reasonable to assume that the general public would soon become aware that jury deliberations were being monitored if the transcripts of such began to appear as evidence in criminal prosecutions. Thus, for the same reason that

---

[47] *U.S. v. Thomas*, *supra* note 4, at 622.
[48] CRIMINAL ACTION 9:22-00658-RMG (D.S.C. Mar. 6, 2023).
[49] *Id.* at *12.

overt observation of jury deliberations must be rejected, so too must covert observation.

Perhaps the real problem with the last two approaches discussed is that the jurors would be subject to prosecution were nullification suspected. As I argued, the fear of such might well motivate jurors to conform their verdict with what they believe the State desires, and not necessarily with what they believe the evidence supports. To that degree, we might claim that it is the possibility of *criminal* sanctions for nullification that is inconsistent with an independent jury. Thus, we might further reason, if we remove the fear of criminal sanction, we remove the possibility of bias in favor of the State. Under this proposed MLR for jury nullification, juries that nullify (when this is proven) would simply have their verdicts vitiated. The accused would face retrial, this time by a jury that (hopefully) conformed itself to the adjudicative division of labor. On the surface, this seems to avoid the problems that beset the other mentioned MLR's for jury nullification. Juries are not supposed to nullify, after all, so unless it can be shown that the very idea of preventing nullification is anathema to some fundamental principle of criminal justice, this approach appears to be an acceptable remedy for jury nullification. The advantage of this MLR is that the jurors would not be threatened by the possibility of criminal sanctions.

However, this approach would be antithetical to the very idea of a fair trial with an independent and impartial jury.[50] If the jury's deliberations were to be scrutinized by the State, with those verdicts rejected via mistrial that were reached via a deliberative process that the State did not approve of, then, for all intents and purposes, it would be the State, not the jury, that would have final say over the verdict – a direct conflict with the constitutional guarantees of independent and impartial juries. Under this approach, if the State approved of the way the jury has deliberated and reasoned, the verdict would stand; if the State disapproved of the way the jury has deliberated and reasoned, the case would simply be re-tried, this time by a different jury. Again, this might not initially appear to be such a bad thing. After all, the jury is only supposed to consider the factual questions put to it, and there does not seem to be anything wrong – at least

[50] Not to mention the *double jeopardy* clause.

in principle – with declaring a mistrial in those cases where the jury oversteps its evaluative authority. The jury's verdict will still be heeded, except for those cases where it fails to act in accordance with its legal responsibilities, duties, and limits.

Crucially, however, in the administration of the criminal justice system it is not only important that justice *be* done, but also that justice *be seen to be* done. Put another way, just as it is important that the State not abuse its authority, it is equally important that the State not *appear* to abuse its authority. As long as the State has the final authority to reject jury verdicts, the jury's verdict is never truly free from state oversight and, hence, never truly independent. While the State might use this power responsibly, the possibility exists that it will not. In trials where the State might appear to have a vested interest in a guilty verdict, the power to veto a jury's verdict of not guilty makes vivid this tension between the concept of an independent jury and an MLR that gives the State the ability to over-rule the jury's verdict. As mentioned above, the right to an independent jury is constitutionally mandated; if respecting this right somehow conflicts with our desire to have the jury behave in accordance with the adjudicative division of labor, the constitutionally enshrined independence of the jury is the value must be preserved:

> We recognize the important competing interests that are implicated in a judge's intrusion into jury deliberations to investigate allegations of jury misconduct. It is beyond question that the secrecy of deliberations is critical to the success of the jury system. *We must bear in mind that the confidentiality of the thought processes of jurors, their privileged exchange of views, and the freedom to be candid in their deliberations are the soul of the jury system.*[51]

The problem with this MLR then, has to do exclusively with the idea of state oversight of the jury's verdict based on the jury's deliberative process. It matters not at all, therefore, whether the State responds with criminal sanctions, or by vitiating the jury's verdict.

---

[51] *U.S. v. Boone*, 458 F.3d 321, 329 (3d Cir. 2006) (citations omitted) (emphasis added).

To sum up: the problem with the last three MLR's is not that the State *will* abuse the power to oversee the jury's verdict. Rather, these MLR's open up the possibility that the State *could* abuse its power to do so. As such, they are incompatible with the notion of an impartial and independent jury. The impartiality of the jury is at once a practical and an abstract ideal. So long as the possibility exists for the State to interfere with the jury's verdict, then jury independence no longer exists, regardless of whether the State actually ever does so interfere. The State would be always 'allowing' the jury to have its say, but, of course, it need not. Whether jury monitoring leads to a mistrial or criminal sanctions, such an approach would be entirely inconsistent with, and antithetical to, the very idea of an independent and impartial jury.[52]

2.8 Juror Testimony

There is one final source of evidence that needs to be examined: juror testimony as to whether nullification occurred. Jurors could, perhaps, be required to testify at an inquiry into their verdict if nullification (or even some other form of juror malfeasance) is suspected.[53] However, this does not seem to be a likely candidate for a successful MLR for jury nullification. In the first place, if the jurors have, in fact, nullified, then by this very act they have demonstrated their willingness to disregard the adjudicative division of labor and/or misrepresent their factual findings as to the accused's culpability. There is no reason to believe that, simply because the question is put to them directly, the jurors will thereby admit that they believe that the facts as presented at trial actually support a verdict of guilty. Jurors that nullify do so precisely (and only) because they do not

[52] See, for instance, *United States v. Miller*, 284 F. Supp. 220, 225 (D. Conn. 1968) (emphasis added): "A jury is not required to elaborate its answer, and its ratiocination may not be probed, *either secretly by recording or listening to them while they are deliberating*."

[53] Given the right against self-incrimination, such an inquiry, if jurors were legally required to give their testimony, could not give rise to criminal charges against the jurors. Even if there were not such a right, one can hardly imagine what incentive there would be to testify honestly if admitting to nullification left one subject to criminal prosecution. As such, an MLR for jury nullification that depends upon juror testimony as its source of evidence most likely would simply involve the declaration of a mistrial as its corrective feature.

believe that the accused ought to be found guilty. Admitting that they behaved in this manner would therefore be obviously self-defeating. So long as the jurors deny that they have nullified (and, on the face of it, we can expect that they would), such an inquiry would produce no positive evidence of jury nullification.

Let us suppose, however, that some of the jurors have a change of heart and admit to nullifying. Would this constitute evidence of nullification? If it were simply one or two jurors, certainly not. Remember, appellate courts are loathe to order new trials unless the evidence of impropriety leading to a miscarriage of justice is significant. So long as the majority of jurors declare that they acquitted the defendant solely on how they resolved questions of fact, there would not appear to be adequate proof to support the declaration of a mistrial. We might suspect that this would change, however, if an equal number, or a majority, of the jurors admitted to nullifying. This, it must be admitted, certainly appears to be *prima facie* evidence that the jury nullified. However, the courts have found good reason to disregard such evidence as being incompatible with the idea of a fair trial:

> A similar choice — to protect deliberative secrecy at the risk of leaving some juror misconduct beyond the court's power to remedy — underlies the long-standing common law rule that "a juror may not impeach his own verdict…" The Supreme Court has expressly recognized the choice that is the basis of the rule: The rule is based upon controlling considerations of a public policy which in these cases chooses the lesser of two evils. When the affidavit of a juror, as to the misconduct of himself or the other members of the jury, is made the basis of a motion for a new trial, the court must choose between redressing the injury of the private litigant and inflicting the public injury which would result if jurors were permitted to testify as to what had happened in the jury room.[54]

Once a jury has been dismissed, the jurors once again become ordinary members of the community, and are free to come in contact with evidence

---

[54] *U.S. v. Thomas, supra* note 4, at 623.

that, for one reason or another, was declared inadmissible at trial and hence was not available to them while they were jurors. If jurors were free to retract their verdicts simply by stating that they had nullified, we would need to ensure that this claim was genuine, and not motivated by exposure to inadmissible evidence prejudicial to the accused. Even in cases where there were no issues of admissibility over evidence, juror testimony alone would still be a problematic source of proof that the jury did, in fact, nullify; we would want to protect against the possibility that the jurors simply had a change of heart – perhaps because of public displeasure with the verdict, or any other number of reasons – and were using the nullification claim to give effect to this change. For this reason, among others,[55] the courts are therefore reluctant to rely on juror evidence to impeach a verdict; juror testimony simply cannot be considered a reliable source of evidence for jury nullification:

> Public policy forbids that a matter resting in the personal consciousness of one juror should be received to overthrow the verdict, because being personal it is not accessible to other testimony; it gives to the secret thought of one the power to disturb the expressed conclusions of twelve; its tendency is to produce bad faith on the part of a minority, to induce an apparent acquiescence with the purpose of subsequent dissent; to induce tampering with individual jurors subsequent to the verdict.[56]

2.9 Lord Mansfield's Rule

All of the MLR's so far discussed share one common feature – they all require that the statutory and common law rules regarding the secrecy of jury deliberations be abandoned or substantially weakened so as to allow for more reviewability of the verdict. There is, obviously, an advantage to having some form of review of jury verdicts, but whatever the gains might

---

[55] See, for example, *State v. Peeler*, 2007 Ct. Sup. 12157, 12159 (Conn. Super. Ct. 2007) (citation omitted): "A second concern, at least when a jury has been dismissed years ago, is epistemological. Our Supreme Court has appreciated the difficulty that all twelve jurors could have in recalling the various included offenses on which they had been instructed… years ago."

[56] *Mattox v. United States*, 146 U.S. 140, 148-49 (1892) (citation omitted).

be, we must be wary lest the price be too high. As the Court in *U.S. v. Thomas*[57] stated:

> Where the duty and authority to prevent defiant disregard of the law or evidence comes into conflict with the principle of secret jury deliberations, we are compelled to select the lesser of two evils. *Achieving a more perfect system for monitoring the conduct of jurors in the intense environment of a jury deliberation room entails an unacceptable breach of the secrecy that is essential to the work of juries in the American system of justice.* To open the door to the deliberation room any more widely and provide opportunities for broad-ranging judicial inquisitions into the thought processes of jurors would, in our view, destroy the jury system itself.[58]

To fully grasp the importance of the principles regarding jury room secrecy, and their relevance to the larger question of jury nullification, it is necessary to first understand the statutory and common law rules of jury secrecy. This common law rule (often referred to as Lord Mansfield's rule)[59] prohibits the court from receiving evidence of jury deliberations for the purposes of impeaching the verdict, and can be traced back to the case of *Vaise v. Delaval*[60], in which Lord Mansfield ruled that the court could not receive affidavits from jurors attesting to their own misconduct. In the United States, Federal Rule of Evidence 606(b), governs the secrecy of jury deliberations at the federal level. It states that after a verdict has been rendered, jurors may not testify about what occurred during deliberations, except in very limited circumstances. Specifically, jurors are generally prohibited from testifying about any statements made by themselves or other jurors, the mental processes involved in reaching their verdict, or any factors that influenced their decision-making. The American courts have been unanimous and clear that it is improper (except for cases where substantive and significant juror malfeasance is alleged)[61] for a trial judge

---

[57] *Supra* note 4.

[58] *Id.* at 623 (emphasis added).

[59] *Nemo turpitudinem suam allegans audietur* (Latin: "No one will be heard who alleges his own turpitude").

[60] *Vaise v. Delaval*, (1785).

[61] See, for instance, *Pena-Rodriguez v. Colorado, supra* note 19. Here, the Court held that the jury secrecy rule must yield to the constitutional right to a fair trial.

to inquire as to how the jury reached its verdict. In *Tanner v. United States*,[62] the Supreme Court emphasized this, stating: "[L]egislative history demonstrates with uncommon clarity that Congress specifically understood, considered, and rejected a version of Rule 606(b) that would have allowed jurors to testify on juror conduct during deliberations."[63] As Thomas, J. asserted in his dissenting opinion in *Pena*: "By the time the Fourteenth Amendment was ratified, Lord Mansfield's no-impeachment rule had become firmly entrenched in American law."[64]

The original rationale for Lord Mansfield's rule was that because the violation of the jurors' oath was, at the time, a high misdemeanor, affidavits of jurors themselves were self-incriminatory, and thereby inadmissible. While this rationale no longer has purchase, the courts on many occasions have asserted the continued importance and centrality of this policy for the effective functioning of the jury system. Indeed, this seems to be the very conclusion reached in *Garcia v. State*,[65] where the Court asserted: "the secrecy of [jury] deliberations is the cornerstone of the modern-day American judicial system, and, generally, nobody, including the trial judge, has a 'right to know' how a jury, or any individual juror, has deliberated or how a decision was reached by a jury or juror."[66]

Maintaining the secrecy of the jury room deliberations has traditionally been supported by five distinct rationales: i) to prevent tampering with the jury by outside influences;[67] ii) to protect the jury from post-verdict harassment;[68] iii) to preserve the finality of jury verdicts;[69] iv) to protect and

---

62 483 U.S. 107 (1987).

63 *Id.* at 125.

64 *Pena-Rodriguez v. Colorado, supra* note 19, at 873.

65 480 Md. 467, 486 (Md. 2022).

66 *Id.* at 486.

67 See, for example, *Tanner, supra* note 62, at 117-23, noting that the courts have not "favored any public or private post-trial inquisition of jurors as to how they reasoned, lest it operate to intimidate, beset and harass them."

68 See, for example, *McDonald v. Pless*, 238 U.S. 264, 267-68 (1915): noting that permitting jurors to attempt to impeach their jury deliberations post-trial would encourage juror harassment by the defeated party "to the destruction of all frankness and freedom of discussion and conference."

69 See, for example, *United States v. Moten*, 582 F.2d 654, 664 (2d Cir. 1978): stating that unlimited attack on juror deliberations and verdicts, were it allowed, would

promote robust freedom of debate during deliberations;[70] and, v) to promote and preserve community trust in the jury.[71] By preserving the confidentiality of jury deliberations, this rule promotes and protects the integrity of the jury system. The principle of jury room secrecy ensures that jurors can freely and candidly discuss the evidence presented during the trial and reach their verdict without fear of external influence or repercussions. While substantially limiting such rules might allow for the possibility of correcting some jury verdicts arrived at via an unapproved deliberative process (such as nullification), the cost of doing so would, according to the courts that have confronted the issue, be too high.[72] Once again, this reasoning seems to be correct.

Finally, Lord Mansfield's Rule is fundamental to the notion of a fair trial. The idea of a fair trial includes, not only an independent and effective jury, but also an unbiased and impartial jury. Many steps are taken to ensure juror impartiality, including court control of the evidence the jury is exposed to. This is why the jury is dismissed from the courtroom when issues of admissibility are argued, why jurors are told to refrain from discussing the case with anyone, why they are prohibited from social interaction with any of the principal players in the trial, why a mistrial can be declared if the jury is inadvertently exposed to especially prejudicial inadmissible evidence, and why jurors are sometimes sequestered during the entire length of the trial. This desire to prevent inadmissible evidence from influencing the jury is also why jury verdicts are considered, with few

---

undermine public interest in finality and cast judges as "Penelopes, forever engaged in unravelling the webs they wove."

[70] *Clark v. United States*, 289 U.S. 1, 13 (1933): "Freedom of debate might be stifled and independence of thought checked if jurors were made to feel that their arguments and ballots were to be freely published to the world. The force of these considerations is not to be gainsaid;" *U.S. v. Thomas, supra* note 4, at 618: "[j]uror privacy is a prerequisite of free debate, without which the decision-making process would be crippled;"; *re Globe Newspaper Co.*, 920 F.2d 88, 94 (1st Cir. 1990): "It is undisputed that the secrecy of jury deliberations fosters free, open and candid debate in reaching a decision."

[71] See, for example, *U.S. v. Thomas, id.* at 618: "disclosure of the substance of jury deliberations may undermine public confidence in the jury system."

[72] See, for instance, *People v. Rendon*, G054006, at *43 (Cal. Ct. App. June 26, 2018): "Nevertheless, the tension between preserving the secrecy of jury deliberations and investigating whether good cause exists for dismissing a deliberating juror has been struck in favor of keeping secret the substance of jury deliberations."

exceptions, to be final, and why, after the verdict is delivered, the jury is considered to be *functus officio*.[73] Post-trial investigations into jury deliberations cannot be allowed to retroactively impeach the jury's verdict if the standards of a fair trial by an unbiased and impartial jury are to be preserved.[74] The possibility of juror bias due to post-trial exposure to inadmissible evidence simply cannot be discounted or dismissed.[75]

Most importantly, the courts have concluded that the idea of a fair trial is coextensive with the principle of juror secrecy.[76] This view make sense for at least three reasons. First, requiring jurors to explain how they reached a particular verdict may well be inconsistent with the principle that jurors are to be free from coercion from the bench when deliberating upon the verdict. Jurors so compelled might thereby feel that they must justify themselves to the trial judge, who may view their reasoning with disapproval. It's one thing to be told that your decision is final and quite another to be told that you must explain to the court how and why you reached a particular decision.[77] Secondly, since the determination of facts is the sole and exclusive purview of the jury, the trial judge simply does not have the authority to review how those facts were arrived at. Even if the trial judge was in fundamental disagreement with the jury as to what the facts of the case actually were, she would be powerless to do anything about it; it is contrary to the adjudicative division of labor between judge and jury for the judge to ask the jury to explain how a particular verdict

---

[73] Latin: *Out of Office*. In legal parlance, that a case is closed, no longer a matter before the court.

[74] *United States v. Pimentel*, 654 F.2d 538, 542 (9th Cir. 1981): "Testimony of a juror concerning the motives of individual jurors and conduct during deliberation is not admissible. Juror testimony is admissible only concerning facts bearing on extraneous influences on the deliberation, in the sense of over acts of jury tampering."

[75] See, for instance, *People v. Senter*, B225495 (Cal. Ct. App. Feb. 21, 2012).

[76] See, for instance, *U.S. v. Thomas, supra* note 4, at 618-19: "Juror privacy is a prerequisite of free debate, without which the decision-making process would be crippled… For the process to work according to theory, the participants must feel completely free to dissect the credibility, motivations, and just deserts of other people. Sensitive jurors will not engage in such a dialogue without some assurance that it will never reach a larger audience."

[77] See, for instance, *United States v. Olano*, 507 U.S. 725, 726 (1993), stating that it is a "cardinal principle that jury deliberations shall remain private and secret, the purpose of such privacy is to protect deliberations from improper influence."

was reached. And last, if jurors knew that the views they expressed in the jury room might eventually come to light, they may be less inclined to argue for a verdict that could be perceived as unpopular, regardless of their actual determination of the defendant's guilt or innocence.[78]

So far, I sought to show that even though it may be, in principle, possible to prevent or limit jury nullification, there remain overwhelming jural and policy-based barriers to successfully implementing an MLR designed to do so. Continuing along these lines, I shall now illustrate how the very idea of the jury itself, and the role we wish it to play in the criminal justice system, precludes the possibility of an MLR for jury nullification. Let's begin by first asking: "what role is it that we wish the jury to play in the criminal justice system?" The answer to this question, I contend, will demonstrate quite clearly why the jury's *de facto* ability to nullify must not be interfered with, regardless of whether we see nullification as a positive or negative aspect of the jury system.

2.10 The Role of the Jury

The jury, throughout its history, has played many different roles and functioned in many different ways. Like all such legal institutions, it is best seen as something that continues to evolve and grow in response to the demands put on it by a continually changing society. Moreover, at any one time, the jury functions in many different respects. In defending the continued role of the jury in the criminal law, the American courts have offered a number of explanations and justifications. At least two of these rationales touch directly on the issue of jury nullification. The jury system, it is said, serves to protect individuals from government oppression,[79] and

[78] See, for example, *Tanner, supra* note 62, at 120-2 (citations omitted): "Allegations of juror misconduct, incompetency, or inattentiveness… seriously disrupt the finality of the process. Moreover, full and frank discussion in the jury room, jurors' willingness to return an unpopular verdict, and the community's trust in a system that relies on the decisions of laypeople would all be undermined by a barrage of postverdict scrutiny of juror conduct."

[79] *Duncan v. Louisiana*, 391 U.S. 145, 155-56 (1968): "The guarantees of jury trial in the Federal and State Constitutions reflect a profound judgment about the way in which law should be enforced and justice administered. A right to jury trial is granted to criminal defendants in order to prevent oppression by the Government. Those who wrote our constitutions knew from history and experience that it was necessary to

injects community values into the administration of the criminal law.[80] The jury's role in reflecting community values and protecting against government oppression has been a fundamental aspect of the American criminal justice system from the beginning. For instance, Thomas Jefferson stated, in 1789, "I consider [trial by jury] as the only anchor ever yet imagined by man, by which a government can be held to the principles of its constitution."[81] This view was re-affirmed a few years later by the Court in *Taylor v. Louisiana*,[82] which, seeing these two functions as intrinsically inter-related, stated:

> The purpose of a jury is to guard against the exercise of arbitrary power - to make available the commonsense judgment of the community as a hedge against the overzealous or mistaken prosecutor and in preference to the professional or perhaps over-conditioned or biased response of a judge.[83]

Indeed, the American courts have traditionally been quite effusive in their praise of the jury system in this respect. Consider, for instance, what the court had to say in *Duncan*:[84]

> A right to jury trial is granted to criminal defendants in order to prevent oppression by the Government... Providing the accused with

---

protect against unfounded criminal charges brought to eliminate enemies and against judges too responsive to the voice of higher authority."

[80] See, for example, *State v. Lankford*, 116 Idaho 860, 883 (Idaho 1989) (citations omitted): "By definition, juries, not judges, are the cross-section of the community, reflecting community values. Only a representative jury assures meaningful community participation. Jurors, unlike judges, are selected to enhance the likelihood that they represent the whole range of community beliefs and backgrounds; the different segments of the community bring to the representative jury perspectives and values that influence both jury deliberation and result;" *Witherspoon v. Illinois*, 391 U.S. 510, 520 n.15 (1968) (citations omitted): "[O]ne of the most important functions any jury can perform in making such a selection is to maintain a link between contemporary community values and the penal system – a link without which the determination of punishment could hardly reflect the evolving standards of decency that mark the progress of a maturing society."

[81] Jefferson, Thomas, *Letter to Thomas Paine*, ME 7:408, Papers 15:269 (1789).

[82] 419 U.S. 522 (1975).

[83] *Id.* at 530.

[84] *Supra* note 79, at 145.

> the right to be tried by a jury of his peers gave him an inestimable safeguard against... corrupt or overzealous [state action]... Fear of unchecked power... found expression in the criminal law in this insistence upon community participation in the determination of guilt or innocence.[85]

This view was referenced with approval in *Batson v. Kentucky*,[86] where the court stated that for "a jury to perform *its intended function as a check on official power*, it must be a body drawn from the community."[87] The role of the jury as guardian of liberty and protector of community values has been asserted by the courts in many cases, as well as by many legal theorists and historians.[88] It is, perhaps, one of the most uncontroversial elements of the institution of trial by jury. Suffice to say, it is settled law in Anglo-American jurisprudence that, among its many roles and functions, the jury serves to protect the citizens of the State against government oppression, as well as to allow the law in its application to reflect the values of the community.

If we start then with the premise that the jury functions as a guardian of liberty and protector of community values, the argument that any move to prevent the jury from nullifying is, fundamentally, contrary to the purpose of the jury becomes rather straightforward. To quote Wiseman D.C.J., in the Middle District of Tennessee:

> [T]he essential feature of a jury obviously lies in the interposition between the accused and his accuser of the commonsense judgment of a group of laymen, and in the community participation and shared

---

[85] *Id.* at 156.

[86] 476 U.S. 79 (1986).

[87] *Id.* at 86 n.8 (emphasis added).

[88] See, for example, *R. v. Bryant*, 42 C.R. (3d) 312 (1984); *Williams v. Florida*, 399 U.S. 78 (1970); *Beckwith v. State*, 386 So. 2d 836 (Fla. Dist. Ct. App. 1980); *Mills v. State*, 310 Md. 33 (Md. 1987); *U.S. v. Gilliam*, 994 F.2d 97 (2d Cir. 1993); *State v. Lankford*, 116 Idaho 860 (Idaho 1989); *State v. Kills on Top*, 241 Mont. 378 (Mont. 1990). These are but a few of the many cases that refer to the jury's role as that of, among other things, the guardian of liberty and protector of community values. For more on this, including references to English cases where this same role is affirmed for the jury see, generally: P. Devlin, *Trial by Jury* (3rd ed., Stevens, London, 1966); William Forsyth, *History of Trial by Jury*, Ch. 3 (2nd ed., Frederick D. Linn, 1875); and, Conrad, *Jury Nullification: Evolution of a Doctrine*, *supra* note 33, at Ch. 2.

> responsibility that results from that group's determination of guilt or innocence... If community oversight of a criminal prosecution is the primary purpose of a jury trial, then... *to deny a defendant the possibility of jury nullification would be to defeat the central purpose of the jury system.*[89]

The reasoning here is very straightforward. If a jury is to function so as to protect the citizens of the State from government oppression, it must have the ability to refuse to enforce those laws that are oppressive. If the jury is to function so as to ensure that the law reflects, or does not contradict, the community's values, it must have the ability to refuse to enforce those laws that do not reflect, or directly conflict with, the community's values. In other words, the very function of the jury – its role in the criminal justice system – demands that it not be prevented from nullifying. There are, of course, many ways the State can oppress its citizens. One of these ways is through the criminal justice system. The State can pass laws that serve to oppress, or it can simply choose to enforce seemingly non-oppressive laws in such an arbitrary or biased manner (for example, by targeting a specific racial or religious group) so as to amount to a form of oppression. Examples of either approach abound. A jury prevented from nullifying in some manner simply becomes a passive participant in such oppression.[90] A jury free to nullify the law, on the other hand, is a jury free to prevent such oppression from continuing by refusing to return a guilty verdict in spite of sufficient evidence of the defendant's guilt. This has a two-fold effect. First, the individual defendant is spared the imposition of a criminal sanction under an oppressive law. Secondly, laws that are routinely nullified (such as the prohibition laws in the U.S. during the early twentieth century), soon cease to exist.[91] Thus, the ability to nullify allows the jury to

---

[89] *United States v. Datcher*, 830 F. Supp. 411, 412 (M.D. Tenn. 1993) (emphasis added).

[90] "When jurors feel they have been coerced into returning an unjust conviction. ...the jury has not been empowered to truly perform the function for which juries are intended: to protect the accused against an oppressive act of government." Conrad, *Jury Nullification: Evolution of a Doctrine, supra* note 33, at 156-57.

[91] See, for a detailed discussion of this phenomenon, generally, Conrad, Clay S., *Jury Nullification: Evolution of a Doctrine, id.* at 108-115; Green, Thomas A. *Verdict According to Conscience: Perspectives on the English Criminal Trial Jury, 1200-1800*, Ch. 2-5 (University of Chicago Press, 1985).

prevent the government from oppressing its citizens through the law both on the micro and macro levels.

A final consideration: if the jury is supposed to ensure that the law is reflective of the community's values, this is an acknowledgement that the law as written and promulgated may not always reflect the values of the community. This may puzzle us, for, in a free and democratic society, the criminal law is supposed to reflect what the people want it to be.[92] The reality of the situation is, however, often quite different. Changes to the criminal law do not occur overnight, while corresponding social values can and do change much more rapidly. Thus, laws that seems reasonable a generation, or even a decade ago, might now strike us as unreasonable encroachments on liberty, and their enforcement unconscionable. The Supreme Court's endorsement of the jury's role as protector of community values seems to be an acknowledgment of this fact. While laws that no longer reflect (or go so far as to contradict) prevailing social norms might fall into disuse and eventually be struck from the books, the problem remains with what to do with those who are charged under such laws. Clearly the jury, as a representative of the community is in an ideal position to ensure that the enforcement of the criminal law does not violate community standards. To the degree that the jury is to play that role, they must be free to nullify. This seems to be Justice Learned Hand's reasoning when he asserted that the jury "introduces a slack into the enforcement of law, tempering its rigor by the mollifying influence of current ethical conventions."[93]

2.11 The Necessity of Nullification

From this point, the question as to whether the jury has, and ought to have, the ability to nullify will be taken as settled. While there are, in principle, seemingly no real barriers to identifying at least some instances of jury nullification, in practice adducing sufficient evidence to legally redress nullification presents insurmountable challenges. Moreover, even if such challenges could somehow be met, there remain substantial and fundamental legislative, precedential, and policy considerations that

---

[92] Consistent, of course, with relevant Constitutional provisions.

[93] *United States v. Adams*, 126 F.2d 774, 776 (2d Cir. 1942).

would disallow the vitiation of any jury verdict of not guilty on the grounds of nullification.[94] To the degree that we wish to both have an impartial and independent jury, as well as preserve the principle of double jeopardy, we must accept the reality that jury nullification is an intrinsic and necessary part of the criminal jury system as it currently exists.

However, it is one thing to argue that the jury should have the power to nullify, and quite another thing altogether to argue that the jury ought to *use* this power. As mentioned earlier, jury nullification is still viewed with great disdain by the courts, even if they are loathe to attempt to redress it. Thus, the central debate being played out in the courts and in the academy tends to focus on whether the jury ought to be *informed* of its nullifying powers. To those who object to the idea of jury nullification in practice, keeping the jury in the dark about the existence of such is a way of both ensure jury independence while preserving the integrity of the justice system *vis-à-vis* the adjudicative division of labor. To those who see jury nullification as "a mechanism that permits a jury, as community conscience, to disregard the strict requirements of law where it finds that those requirements cannot justly be applied,"[95] giving the *nullification instruction* is a way to ensure that the jury can best fulfill that role. One of the central areas of focus in this debate turns on whether the jury's nullifying ability is perceived to be a *right* or a mere *power*. Accordingly, it is to this issue that we will turn to in the next chapter.

---

[94] See, for example, *United States v. Moylan, supra* note 10, at 1006 (emphasis added): "If the jury feels the law is unjust, we recognize the undisputed power of the jury to acquit, even if its verdict is contrary to the law as given by a judge, and contrary to the evidence...If the jury feels that the law under which the defendant is accused is unjust, or that exigent circumstances justified the actions of the accused, or for any reason which appeals to their logic or passion, the jury has the power to acquit, *and the courts must abide by that decision.*"

[95] *U.S. v. Dougherty* (dissent), *supra* note 2, at 42.

Part 2: The Nullification Instruction

Chapter 3
The Failure of the *Rights/Power* Approach[1]

Jury Nullification in the criminal law context occurs when a jury returns a not guilty verdict for a defendant it believes to be guilty (factually and legally) of the crime charged. That the jury can behave in such manner without fear of censure, and without having its verdict impeached, is beyond dispute, and case law is replete with judgments affirming this fact.[2] As the Court in *United States v. Moylan*[3] stated:

> If the jury feels the law is unjust, we recognize the undisputed power of the jury to acquit, even if its verdict is contrary to the law as given by a judge, and contrary to the evidence...If the jury feels that the law under which the defendant is accused is unjust, or that exigent circumstances justified the actions of the accused, or for any reason which appeals to their logic or passion, the jury has the power to acquit, *and the courts must abide by that decision.*[4]

3.1 The Nullification Instruction

While it is fairly well established that the jury *has* the ability to nullify and *ought* to have this ability, it nevertheless remains, for many, an open question as to whether the jury ought to actually *engage* or *use* its

---

[1] Some of the thoughts and ideas expressed in this chapter have been previously explored in Hreno, Travis, *The Jury Nullification Instruction and the De Jure / De Facto Debate: A Hohfeldian Analysis*, vol. 22, no. 3 Public Affairs Quarterly 231 (July 2008). However, it is important to note that the substantive content and conclusions drawn have undergone substantial revisions, developments, expansions, and updates to reflect current jurisprudence, as well as the specific focus and tenor of this project. The author acknowledges this earlier publication as a foundation for the present work.
[2] See, for example, *Horning v. District of Columbia*, 254 U.S. 135, 138 (1920), where Holmes, J. stated: "[T]he jury has the power to bring in a verdict in the teeth of both law and facts;" *Morissette v. United States*, 342 U.S. 246, 275 (1952): "But juries are not bound by what seems inescapable logic to judges;" *U. S. v. Dougherty*, 473 F.2d 1113, 1132 (D.C. Cir. 1972): "The jury has an unreviewable and irreversible power... to acquit in disregard of the instructions on the law given by the trial judge."
[3] 417 F.2d 1002 (4th Cir. 1969).
[4] *Id.* at 1006 (emphasis added).

nullification abilities. It is, after all, one thing to have the ability to do *x*, and quite another thing altogether to actually exercise that ability – at least from a normative standpoint. For example, we can be opposed to a law prohibiting adultery and still say without fear of contradiction that one ought not to commit adultery. Similarly, we can endorse the idea of the jury's *privilege* to nullify without necessarily endorsing its use. Indeed, the majority of the current controversy regarding jury nullification tends to center on whether the practice of jury nullification is to be discouraged or encouraged. This debate is almost entirely focused on the issue of whether the jury ought to be *informed* that it has this ability. Informing the jury that they can nullify is sometimes referred to as 'giving a *nullification instruction*,' as it is an instruction (one among many) that the jury would receive from the trial judge before trial proceedings or jury deliberations.[5] Such an instruction might look something like this:

> Although you are a public body bound to give respectful attention to the laws, you have the final authority to decide whether or not to apply a given law to the acts of the defendant on trial before you; you represent the community, and it is appropriate to bring into your deliberations the feelings of the community and your own feelings based on conscience. Nothing will bar you from acquitting the

[5] The jury could, of course, also learn of jury nullification from counsel during the trial proceedings. However, the courts have been clear that the *source* of the *nullification instruction* is not a substantive consideration for the purposes of law. See, for example, *United States v. Manzano (In re United States)*, 945 F.3d 616, 626 (2d Cir. 2019) (citations omitted) (emphasis added): "Here, the district court in fact recognized that our case law preclude[d] it from encouraging the jury to nullify… but then proceeded to draw an arbitrary distinction between encouraging the jury via jury instructions – which it properly deemed impermissible – and granting defense counsel's motion to argue nullification. *This distinction is unsupported by our case law;*" *U.S. v. Sepulveda*, 15 F.3d 1161, 1190 (1st Cir. 1993) (citation omitted): "Though jury nullification has a long and sometimes storied past, the case law makes plain that a judge may not instruct the jury anent its history, vitality, or use… [I]t makes no difference that the jury inquired, or that an aggressive lawyer managed to pique a particular jury's curiosity by mentioning the subject in closing argument, or that a napping prosecutor failed to raise a timely objection to that allusion;" *U.S. v. Manning*, 79 F.3d 212, 219 (1st Cir. 1996) (citations omitted): "We have consistently held that a district court may not instruct the jury as to its power to nullify. An attorney's attempt to achieve the same end indirectly, by arguing the severity of the punishment to the jury, is equally impermissible."

defendant if you feel that the law, as applied to the fact situation before you, would produce an inequitable or unjust result.[6]

The thinking here is fairly straightforward: informing jurors about jury nullification, the reasoning goes, will result in increased occurrences of such.[7] Depending on your view of the merits (or lack thereof) of the practice of jury nullification, you will therefore either advocate for, or object to, a jury *nullification instruction*. As a matter of doctrine, however, the courts have, with almost complete unanimity, adopted the view that juries are not to receive the *nullification instruction*.[8] Nevertheless, and despite hundreds of cases affirming this anti-instruction policy, the jury *nullification instruction* continues to be a controversial and contentious issue in the American criminal justice system to this day.[9]

3.2 The Rights/Power View

While attempts to resolve this debate take many forms, one popular approach adopted by the courts and scholars involves inquiring into the fundamental nature and legal status of nullification: is jury nullification a mere power that the jury possesses (that is, does it have a strictly *de facto* status) or is it also a legal right (that is, does it also have *de jure* status)?[10] The difference between a freedom/liberty/power that is strictly *de facto* and one that is *de jure* is straightforward: A *de jure* power is one that is recognized by law; a mere *de facto* power has no such recognition. To put

---

[6] As adapted from Horowitz, I. A., *The Effect of Jury Nullification Instruction on Verdicts and Jury Functioning in Criminal Trials*, Law and Human Behavior 9.1, 25, 30-31 (1985).

[7] Or, conversely, not informing jurors about jury nullification will result in less instances of it.

[8] See CHAPTER 1, note 122 for a representative sample of relevant cases. As I indicated in the previous chapter, the courts, for the most part, view jury nullification as a pernicious element in the criminal justice system. The objections to nullification range from the claim that it violates the rule of law (see, for instance, *U.S. v. Thomas*, 116 F.3d 606 (2d Cir. 1997)), to the contention that jury nullification is the thin edge of the wedge towards legal anarchy (see, for instance, *U. S. v. Dougherty, supra* note 2).

[9] For example, in the United States there were over 180 cases between 2000 and 2022 that directly touched on the issue of the *nullification instruction* in one way or another.

[10] See, for examples of such debates, Scheflin, Alan W., *Jury Nullification: The Right to Say No*, 45 Southern California Law Review 168 (1972); *Note: Jury Nullification: The Forgotten Right*, New Eng. L. Rev. 105 (1971); Simson, Gary J., *Jury Nullification in the American System: A Skeptical View*, 54 Texas Law Review 488, 490 (1976).

this another way, *de facto* powers are based on practical control and influence only, while *de jure* powers are based on legitimate recognition by laws, constitutions, or legal systems. An example: the government has the *de jure* (and, admittedly, *de facto*) power to appropriate some of your income (in the form of taxation). An armed gunman also has the power to appropriate some of your income, but this is, of course, merely a *de facto* power – such appropriation has no jural legitimacy.

Engaging in such a conceptual analysis into the intrinsic legal status and nature of jury nullification, according to this approach, can reveal the answer to the *nullification instruction* question. If juries have the right to nullify, such reasoning goes, then the courts have a responsibility to inform jurors of their power to nullify. This is because jurors, for the most part, only become aware of their responsibilities, duties, and rights *qua* jurors via instructions from the bench. While there may be little to no onus on the part of a trial judge to inform jurors of extremely obvious rights and responsibilities, such an onus exists where the rights in question are not obvious, such as, for example, the right (if it is a right) to disagree with, and disregard, the trial judge's instructions regarding the law (in other words, to nullify). Since such a right is not obvious, the failure to mention its existence to the jury would be seen, according to this position, as a *constructive denial* of the right.[11] The trial judge may not be actively preventing the jury from nullifying, but by refusing to inform the jury of its power to nullify, she is nevertheless materially interfering with the jury's ability to exercise that right. After all, it is difficult to exercise a right if one

---

[11] See, for example, Epps, D. and Ortman, W., *The Informed Jury*, 75 Vand. L. Rev. 823, 885 (2022): "Even so, there are plausible grounds to find a right to informed juries in the Constitution… In particular, keeping the jury ignorant is hard to square with the Court's cases on the scope of the Sixth Amendment jury-trial right;" Johnson, Julie, *The Jury Nullification Debate*, 5 U.S. A.F. Acad. J. Legal Stud. 139, 140 (1994-1995) (emphasis added): "American juries do have the inherent right to decide issues of both fact and law based on the historical development of our jury system. In order to completely recognize this right, juries must be instructed by the judge that they have such a right;" Scheflin, Alan W., *Jury Nullification: The Right to Say No, id.* at 187: "If the "man in the jury box" is to fulfill his role as the representative of the "conscience of the community," participating effectively in the making of public policy, then he must possess the power and the right to check the "misapplication" of any particular value distribution. Beyond this, he must be informed that he has such a power and the constitutional right to exercise it."

is unaware of its existence or possibility. Thus, proponents of the *nullification-is-a-right* view conclude, the jury ought to be informed that it is free to judge the law as well as the facts of the case.[12]

On the other hand, according to this *rights/power* perspective, if jury nullification is nothing more than a *de facto* power with no legitimate legal standing, then the courts have no such responsibility to inform jurors of their power to nullify. Jury nullification, according to this view, is a direct and clear violation of the juror's oath to take the law as given by the court; it is nothing more than a mere consequence of the right to a trial by jury – an *emergent property* of the combined principles of double jeopardy and jury independence, as it were. It has, therefore, no *de jure* status, and exists only as a *de facto* artifact of the jury system.[13] Yes, the jury has the *raw power* to

---

[12] This argument relies upon an understanding of 'right' as a positive concept – one that is predicated on the existence of a corresponding duty. Under this view, a duty-bearer has the obligation to provide or allow for both the material and epistemic conditions necessary to exercise that right.

[13] See, for example, *State v. Showell*, No. A-1981-12T1, at *11 (App. Div. Aug. 12, 2014): "It is well-settled that a jury does not have the "right" to nullification; rather, nullification is a "power" the jury possesses, which is undesirable;" *U.S. v. Thomas, supra* note 8, at 615: "[T]he power of juries to "nullify" or exercise a power of lenity is just that — a power; it is by no means a right or something that a judge should encourage or permit if it is within his authority to prevent;" *U.S. v. Lynch*, 181 F.3d 330, 338 (2d Cir. 1999): referencing "a century-old line of cases holding that jury nullification is a power and not a right;" *U.S. v. Kerley*, 838 F.2d 932, 938 (7th Cir. 1988): "[The jury] has the *power* to acquit on bad grounds, because the government is not allowed to appeal from an acquittal by a jury. But jury nullification is just a power, not also a right;" *Wofford v. Woods*, 969 F.3d 685, 709 (6th Cir. 2020): "The settled conclusion of American courts has been that nullification is a power but not a right;" *Craigmire v. State*, C.C.A. No. 03C01-9710-CR-00440, at *1 (Tenn. Crim. App. July 20, 1999): "Just as the jury's de facto power of nullification is not a "right" of the jury, the power confers no constitutional rights upon defendants;" *State v. Paredes-Solano*, 223 Ariz. 284, 293 (Ariz. Ct. App. 2009): [J]ury nullification is not the legal "right" of either the defendant or the jury; the jury merely has a power to acquit on bad grounds, because the government is not allowed to appeal from an acquittal by a jury;" *People v. Rodriguez*, 508 P.3d 276, 286 (Colo. App. 2022) (citations omitted): "A criminal defendant does not have a right to jury nullification. Nor does a juror have the right to nullify… Instead, what every juror has, notwithstanding his, her, or their sworn duty to follow the law, is the de facto power to nullify — a power made possible only by the rule that jury deliberations are secret."

nullify, proponents of this view acknowledge, but this power to so act is not by design and in no way translates into a *de jure* right:

> It nonetheless remains true that the power to acquit despite the law and the facts is not a right of juries but something which results from a number of things including the right of a criminal defendant to have a jury trial, the rule prohibiting postverdict inquiry into the thought processes of jurors, and the rules against appellate review of verdicts of acquittal... Certain things follow logically from the fact that the jury necessarily has this power of lenity... Other things do not follow logically from a recognition of this power... We do not believe that the constitution mandates an instruction in a criminal case which would encourage the jury to acquit for impermissible reasons — that is, an instruction which informed the jury of its raw power of lenity [i.e., jury nullification].[14]

Reasoning along similar lines, one could further assert that the jury also has the raw power to disregard the law by accepting bribes; this certainty does not translate into the legal right to accept bribes. According to this view, then, not only does the jury *not* have the right to nullify, the jury actually has – given both its oath and the instructions from the court – a duty to not-nullify. Thus, there is, and can be, no duty on the part of the court to give a *nullification instruction*.

A great deal of scholarship and debate has heretofore been devoted to the issue of whether nullification is a right (in the *de jure* sense) or merely a power (in the *de facto* sense). We can call this the *rights/power* view. Under this view we need only to investigate into the intrinsic legal nature of jury nullification to get our answer as regards the *nullification instruction* question: if jury nullification is a right, we give the instruction; if it is not a

---

[14] *State v. Perkins*, 353 N.W.2d 557, 561 (Minn. 1984). See, also: *Merced v. McGrath*, 426 F.3d 1076, 1079 (9th Cir. 2005): "Importantly, while jurors have the power to nullify a verdict, they have no right to do so. If jurors had a right to nullify, then a court would have a correlative duty to safeguard their ability to exercise this right. But courts manifestly do not have a [positive] duty to ensure a jury's free exercise of this power."

right, we do not give the instruction. The *rights/power* view, in fact, rests on the conjunction of 3 principles:

1. Jury nullification is either a *de jure* right that juries have, or it is simply a *de facto* power that they possess. These options are exhaustive.
2. If jury nullification is a *de jure* right, then the court is under an obligation to give the *nullification instruction.*
3. If jury nullification is merely a *de facto* power, then no such obligation exists.

This dichotomy between nullification as a right and nullification as a mere power is, I contend, misguided. The *rights/power* debate asks the wrong question, and, hence, gives an irrelevant answer. I do not take issue with either points ii) or iii), but I do believe that point i) is incorrect. Jury nullification is, in fact, neither a legally recognized *de jure* right nor merely a *de facto* power. This distinction between rights and mere powers is not, in other words, exhaustive; jury nullification has an altogether different legal status. To put this another way, jury nullification does have *de jure* status – it more than a mere *de facto* power – but this does not necessarily imply that it is a *de jure* right.

3.3 A Hohfeldian Analysis of the Issue

Up until this point I have been using terms 'rights' and 'powers' as if their meaning in the legal context was clear. However, such terms are notoriously ambiguous and imprecise. Thus, if any analysis into the legal status of jury nullification is to succeed in yielding an answer to the *nullification instruction* question, a more precise understanding of these terms and their related concepts is necessary. For such precision we can turn to the work of W.N. Hohfeld.[15] Hohfeld argued that legal debate was

[15] Hohfeld's analysis of legal terminology is widely accepted and employed by the U.S. courts at both the state and federal levels. See, for instance, Heller, Michael, *The Boundaries of Private Property*, 108 Yale Law Journal 1163, 1191-92 (1999): "The Hohfeldian view moved quickly from legal theory into the 1936 Restatement of Property and from there into mainstream scholarship and judicial decision-making." For a representative sample of cases that employ the Hohfeldian schema, see, generally, *Yu v. Paperchase Partnership*, 114 N.M. 635 (N.M. 1992); *Mabry v. Superior*

often clouded by the fact that many legal terms are ambiguous and equivocal, stating:

> One of the greatest hindrances to the clear understanding, the incisive statement, and the true solution of legal problems frequently arises from the express or tacit assumption that all legal relations may be reduced to "rights" and "duties" and that these latter categories are therefore adequate for the purpose of analyzing even the most complex legal interests.... Even if the difficulty related merely to inadequacy and ambiguity of terminology, its seriousness would nevertheless be worthy of definite recognition and persistent effort toward improvement; *for in any closely reasoned problem, whether legal or non-legal, chameleon-hued words are a peril both to clear thought and to lucid expression.*[16]

As it is used in legal discourse, the term "right," Hohfeld argued, has at least four distinct meanings: *claim right* (or, simply, "right"); *privilege; power;* and *immunity*. Hohfeld's goal was to disambiguate these various terms. In their jural context, stated Hohfeld, these terms are to be properly understood as describing legal relations between different parties. Though Hohfeld's analysis was meant to apply to the private law, it can be made to apply to the criminal law schema with little conceptual maneuvering.[17] Hohfeld thought that the key to understanding these terms was not to offer substantive definitions, but rather to situate them formally in the context of their *jural correlatives* and *jural opposites*. He offered the following model of analysis:

Court, 185 Cal.App.4th 208 (Cal. Ct. App. 2010); *Burns v. PA Department of Correction*, 544 F.3d 279, 281 n.1 (3d Cir. 2008); *Merriam v. Kunzig*, 476 F.2d 1233 (3d Cir. 1973); *Golden State Transit Corp. v. Los Angeles*, 493 U.S. 103 (1989); *United States v. Richardson*, 418 U.S. 166 (1974); *United States v. Molt*, 589 F.2d 1247 (3d Cir. 1978); *Flast v. Cohen*, 392 U.S. 83 (1968).

[16] Hohfeld, Wesley N., *Fundamental Legal Conceptions as Applied in Judicial Reasoning*, 23 Yale Law Journal 16, 18 (1913) (emphasis added).

[17] Indeed, the courts themselves have upon occasion applied the Hohfeldian model of rights to the criminal law sphere. See, for instance, *Khan v. United States*, 928 F.3d 1264, 1277 (11th Cir. 2019): "A lawyer's duty to provide effective representation is the correlate of a defendant's right to counsel under the Sixth Amendment. *Cf.* Wesley Newcomb Hohfeld."

Jural Opposites	claim rights	privilege (no duty)	power	immunity (no liability)
	no-rights	duty	disability (no power)	liability
Jural Correlatives	claim rights	privilege (no duty)	power	immunity (no liability)
	duty	no-right	liability	disability (no power) [18]

Figure 1: *The Hohfeldian Jural Scheme*

The idea of jural opposites is self-evident. The opposite of having a right to *x* is, of course, having no right to *x*, and so on. Correlatives, on the other hand, are meant to describe two ends of the same relationship – one between two parties: holders and bearers. Rights, powers, immunities, and privileges are things that parties hold. Duties, liabilities, disabilities, and no-rights are things that parties bear. Thus, if A holds the power to *x*, then there exists some B such that B bears a liability to be *x*'ed. If A bears a duty to B regarding *y*, then B has a claim right against A regarding *y*, and so on. An example using this Hohfeldian analysis: if A has a right against B that the latter stay off the former's land, then B is under a correlative duty towards A to stay off that land.

3.4 Jury Nullification as a De Jure Right

Applying this Hohfeldian analysis to jury nullification, it soon becomes evident and obvious that the *rights/power* view of nullification fails to accurately account for the phenomenon or thereby yield an answer to the *nullification instruction* question. Let us begin by inquiring as to what it would mean for the jury to have the right (in the Hohfeldian sense) to nullify. To begin with, recall that rights imply duties. The court is really the only party in any position to interfere with, or allow for the promotion of, jury nullification during trial. Thus, if jury nullification *is* a right, clearly the court would be the corresponding duty bearer. Continuing along this line of reasoning, if the jury has a right (a "claim right" to speak in the strict Hohfeldian sense), held against the court to nullify, then this would imply that the court has a correlative duty to, at the very least, not interfere (either actively or passively) with the exercise of the jury's ability to nullify. But,

[18] *Supra* note 16, at 18.

of course, this analysis merely exchanges one question for another; whether the court bears such a duty is, after all, precisely the question we are seeking to answer.

So, does the court bear such a duty towards the jury? We might reason along the following lines. Although guilty verdicts are always, at least in principle, open to review,[19] there are no such review mechanisms in place for not guilty verdicts (save for when those verdicts are shown to be the result of some prohibited form of malfeasance – bribery, for example).[20] Case law and legislation is conclusive that the court cannot cajole, pressure, or otherwise try to influence the jury into returning a particular verdict.[21] Moreover, and more importantly, the court is not at liberty to reject or deny a jury's verdict of not guilty resulting from jury nullification.[22] One view then is that this unreviewable power to nullify establishes the legal right to nullify. Clay Conrad argues for this view, stating: "The distinction between jury "rights" and jury "powers" is nonsensical and should be discarded. A legal power that can be exercised with legal impunity is a legal right... Where no injunction or penalty is possible, there is no real difference between a legal power and a legal right."[23] This view that the jury's *de facto* power to nullify is therefore equivalent to a *de jure* right to nullify was also asserted by Pennsylvania Chief Justice Sharswood in 1879: "[I]t has been strongly contended that though the jury have the power they have not the

---

[19] In some jurisdictions, for example, the trial judge may refuse to accept a guilty verdict if she concludes that it is unsupportable on the evidence. More often, though, the trial judge will enter a 'directed verdict' of not guilty if there is insufficient evidence to support a guilty verdict. In such cases, the jury is not even consulted.
[20] Not guilty verdicts can always be successfully appealed, of course, but only on issues of law. The important point here is that a not guilty verdict cannot be impeached *per se*. There must be some impropriety or legal error that is causally implicated in the not guilty verdict. Guilty verdicts, on the other hand, are reviewable *per se*. An appeals tribunal is, in principle, free to conclude that such a verdict was, due to the insufficiency of evidence, at trial, simply wrong. See, for example, *Sapir v. United States*, 216 F.2d 722 (10th Cir. 1954).
[21] See **CHAPTER 1, § 1.5.5 The Verdict**.
[22] *U.S. v. Siegelman*, 640 F.3d 1159, 1185 n. 36 (11th Cir. 2011) (emphasis added): "For example, we permit logically inconsistent jury verdicts as to different counts, and even as to different co-defendants. *We permit jury nullification*. We do not inquire whether a verdict is the result of compromise, mistake or even carelessness."
[23] Conrad, Clay S., *Jury Nullification: Evolution of a Doctrine*, 301-02 (Carolina Academic Press, 1998).

right to give a verdict contrary to the instruction of the court upon the law... The distinction between power and right, whatever may be its value in ethics, in law is very shadowy and insubstantial. *He who has legal power to do anything has the legal right.*"[24] The court in *People v. Croswell*[25] affirmed a similar point, stating:

> The law must...have intended, in granting this power to a jury, to grant them a *lawful and rightful power*, or it would have provided a remedy against the undue exercise of it. The true criterion of a legal power is its capacity to produce a definitive effect, liable to neither censure nor review. And the verdict of not guilty, in a criminal case, is, in every respect, absolutely final. The jury are not liable to punishment, nor the verdict to control.[26]

This view that the jury's unreviewable power to nullify thereby translates into a legal right was given explicit voice by the court in *State v. Croteau*:[27]

> [W]hen political power is conferred on a tribunal without restriction or control, it may be lawfully exerted; that the power of a jury in criminal cases to determine the whole matter in issue committed to their charge, is such a power, and may therefore be lawfully and rightfully exercised; in short, that such a power is equivalent to, or rather is itself, a legal right.[28]

The court, according to this *nullification-is-a-right* view, has a duty to accept (and not try to prevent) a jury verdict of not guilty (although with the above *proviso* regarding prohibited forms of malfeasance), even when the court believes that the evidence would not merit or support such a verdict. Again, decades of case law and legislative history do support this.[29] This duty does not exist as regards a jury verdict of guilty, however, for, as mentioned above, the court can, and sometimes does, intervene to prevent a jury from potentially returning such a verdict when it deems the evidence

---

[24] *Kane v. Commonwealth*, 89 Pa. 522, 525 (1879) (emphasis added).
[25] 3 Johns. Cas. 337 (N.Y. 1804).
[26] *Id.* at 368 (emphasis added).
[27] 23 Vt. 14 (1849).
[28] *Id.* at 47.
[29] See, for example, *U.S. v. Siegelman*, *supra* note 22, at 1185 n. 36.

insufficient to warrant conviction. Moreover, since jury nullification always results in a verdict of not guilty, and jury nullification *isn't* a prohibited form of malfeasance, it does seem to follow that the court is under a duty to accept (and not try to prevent) a jury verdict of not guilty resulting from jury nullification. Given this duty, we might further conclude that, therefore, the jury has a correlative right to have its nullification verdict accepted (and not interfered with in any way). And since (as was suggested above) failing to inform the jury of its right to nullify might count as a form of constructive interference or denial in the exercise of that right, we might therefore even further conclude that the court has a duty to inform, and the jury a correlative right to be informed of, its nullification abilities.[30]

As appealing as this line of reasoning initially appears, it is, as I alluded to above, ultimately, flawed. It is really nothing other than a slightly more sophisticated way of claiming that an unreviewable *de facto* power therefore confers a *de jure* right – an inference which is, frankly, a *non sequitur*. A *de facto* power – even an unreviewable one – does not therefore necessarily translate to a *de jure* right. The law can, and does, confer unreviewable *de facto* powers for any number of reasons. We should be reluctant, however, to assume that in each and every case the use of such powers would be appropriate and legitimate; we should be reluctant, in other words, to conclude that unreviewable *de facto* powers necessarily and always translate into *de jure* rights. Judges, for example, have the unreviewable *de facto* power ("the raw power,"[31] we might say) to acquit or convict a defendant based solely on, for example, purely racist motives (so long as such motives are not disclosed, at least).[32] It hardly seems correct, though,

---

[30] Note that one could argue the court also has a *liability* vis-à-vis the jury's verdict of not guilty, and perhaps even a *disability*. However, as Hohfeld points out (*supra* note 16, at 46), jural relations need not be mutually exclusive. The important point here is that it is a matter of law that the court is under a duty not to interfere with a jury verdict of not guilty.

[31] To paraphrase *State v. Perkins, supra* note 14.

[32] See, for example, *Kratz v. Newsom*, 251 So. 2d 539, 540 (Fla. Dist. Ct. App. 1971) (emphasis added): "Properly used, 'judicial discretion' implies a judgment which is, for practical purposes, unreviewable… *It involves a sense of situation which may be wrong, and may seem wrong to an appellate judge, but… it [is] more just to allow the matter to stand.*" See, also, Butler, Paul, *Racially Based Jury Nullification: Black Power in the Criminal Justice System*, 677, 688 105 Yale Law Journal (1995) (quoting the *Washington Times Editorial*, "Kente Cloth in the Dock," *WASH. TIMES*, D2 June 13, 1992) (emphasis added)

to claim that since judges have the *de facto* power to reach verdicts in such a manner that they therefore have the *de jure* right to reach verdicts in such a manner.[33] Or consider a hypothetical *perfect-crime* example – a crime that, in principle, cannot be sanctioned or redressed. If such a crime were possible to commit, then certainly we would all have the unreviewable *de facto* power to commit said crime. While in principle, no sanctions or legal redress are possible for so-called *perfect crimes*, it would nevertheless be absurd to conclude from this that we therefore have the *de jure* right to disregard the relevant laws in such cases.[34] The same can be said of jury nullification.

To be clear, I am not disputing that the court does, in fact, have a duty not to interfere with (or prevent in any way) the jury's freedom to return a not guilty verdict. That much is clear, and is a well-established part of criminal jury procedure. Furthermore, this necessarily implies that the court also has a duty not to interfere with (or prevent in any way) the jury from exercising its nullification powers. However, this does not imply that the *jury* therefore has a correlative right against the court that it not interfere with (or prevent in any way) the jury's exercise of this power. In other words, the court's legal duty to not interfere with a jury engaged in nullification

---

"...[W]hile most of us common folk are puzzled by this kind of judicial behavior, lawyers are widely inured to the fact that *judges are free to act like fools with impunity* - even when it is an abuse of discretion, an abuse of power, a waste of time and an injustice to someone who has come before the court seeking justice."

[33] To be perfectly clear, if a judge uses *overtly* racist language and reasoning in her ruling, the verdict will not withstand appeal; but to the degree that such reasoning is *covert*, the judge does indeed have an unreviewable power to behave in such an odious manner. I think this analogy works insofar as the jury's nullifying reasoning is also - due to the principle of jury secrecy - similarly covert. Regardless of the source of the unreviewability, however, we ought to resist this fallacious slide from *power* to *right*.

[34] Whether any co-called *perfect crimes* are actually possible is, of course, irrelevant; there are no principled reasons to suppose that they are not possible. But, for a real-world case, consider the following example: soon after the 2019 legalization of hemp in Ohio through Senate Bill 57, a directive was issued to Prosecutors statewide, advising them to abstain from pursuing cases involving low-level marijuana possession. At the time law enforcement agencies in Ohio lacked the necessary equipment to effectively differentiate between hemp and marijuana. This inadvertently created a loophole in the evidentiary process for prosecuting marijuana possession cases. Consequently, for a brief period of time, low-level marijuana possession in the State of Ohio was a criminal offense with no practicable sanctions attached; it was certainly still a crime, however.

does not imply that the jury therefore has a correlative legal right to engage in nullification. Why? Recall that jural correlatives describe relations between two parties. Thus, the court's duty not to interfere with (or prevent in any way) the jury's freedom to return a not guilty verdict certainly does imply that *someone* has a right against the court that it not interfere with (or prevent in any way) the jury's freedom to return a not guilty verdict (including the freedom to nullify). But this someone is not the jury. Instead, the reason why the court cannot interfere with the jury's verdict is out of respect for the *defendant's* right to a fair trial. A fair trial is understood to entail, in part, an uncoerced and impartial jury, one that favors neither the defense nor the prosecution. The limits placed on the court regarding its influence on the jury's deliberative procedures and ultimate verdict are limits placed so as to respect the *defendant's* right to a fair and impartial jury. Thus, the jury's unfettered power to nullify is a consequence of the court's obligations towards a *defendant*.[35] If the defendant has a right against the court that it provide her with a fair trial (which includes, in part, an impartial and uncoerced jury), then the court must have a correlative duty towards the defendant to provide her with a fair trial. Since the antecedent is true, so too must the consequent be. Clearly this duty upon the court to provide the defendant with an impartial and uncoerced jury – which includes, in part, a jury with the freedom to nullify – is thus demanded by the *defendant's* right to a fair trial, and not the *jury's* right to nullify. In other words, we can explain the existence of the court's duty to not interfere with a nullifying verdict without postulating the existence of a correlative right for the *jury* to return nullifying verdicts. The correlative relationship in this case is between the court and the *defendant* – not the court and the *jury*. And the right in question is not the right to jury nullification, but rather the right to a fair trial.[36] There is no other way to understand the existence of this duty upon the court. Where does it come from if not out of respect for the *defendant's* right to a fair trial? Given this, it is difficult to see how one could

---

[35] The fact that in certain circumstances the court can interfere with a jury verdict of guilt in no way infringes upon this right to a fair trial. Defendants have this right so as to ensure that no one's liberty is unduly affected at trial. Preventing a jury from returning a guilty verdict in no way negatively impacts upon a defendant's liberty.

[36] See, for example, *State v. Paredes-Solano, supra* note 13, at 293: "[J]ury nullification is not the legal "right" of either the defendant or the jury;" *People v. Rodriguez, supra* note 13, at 286: "A criminal defendant does not have a right to jury nullification."

successfully argue that the jury has the *legal* right to nullify, and hence ought to be given the *nullification instruction*.

3.5 Jury Nullification as a Mere De Facto Power

Let us examine the contrary view then, that jury nullification is merely a *de facto* power, and thus, the *nullification instruction* is, at a minimum, unwarranted. This view is commonly defended by appeal to one of three closely related arguments: i) the *division-of-labor* argument; ii) the *jurors-oath* argument, and iii) the *fair-trial* argument. Let's start with the *division-of-labor* argument.

3.5.1 The Division-of-Labor Argument

Jury nullification is, according to this perspective, nothing more than a *de facto* power that merely supervenes upon the principles of jury independence and a defendant's right to a fair trial, but is nevertheless contrary to all principles of legality.[37] So, what motivates this view? Recall that in a criminal case the jury is informed that they are to take the law according to the judge's instructions.[38] Thus, we might reason, it is clear that juries have no legal right to nullify – the judge's instructions to the jury on the adjudicative division of labor make this self-evident. See, for instance, *People v. Mesik*[39] where the court said, in part, that "*the jury must*

---

[37] See, for instance, *Wofford v. Woods*, *supra* note 13, at 709-10 (citations omitted) (emphasis added): "The settled conclusion of American courts has been that nullification is a power but not a right. That is to say, jurors *can* vote to acquit in defiance of the law, and courts in general cannot stop them – but courts will not encourage this, provide jury instructions acknowledging it, or allow lawyers to argue overtly for it. Therefore, when courts have crafted doctrines to protect against jurors' being removed for their views on the case, they are *not* doing so to protect jury nullification. Rather, they are acting to protect the right of the accused to "trial by an impartial jury," from which jury the judge cannot remove jurors for their views on the case, as well as to protect related concerns such as jury secrecy. *Jury nullification is a byproduct of those rights, but it is not coterminous with them.*"

[38] See **CHAPTER 1, § 1.5.3: Jury Instructions**.

[39] 775 N.W.2d 857, 863 (Mich. Ct. App. 2009).

take the law as given by the court."[40] Such a view was also strongly advanced by the U.S. Supreme Court in *Sparf and Hansen v. United States*:[41]

> We must hold firmly to the doctrine that *in the courts of the United States it is the duty of juries in criminal cases to take the law from the court and apply that law to the facts as they find them to be from the evidence.* Upon the court rests the responsibility of declaring the law; upon the jury, the responsibility of applying the law so declared to the facts as they, upon their conscience, believe them to be. Under any other system, the courts, although established in order to declare the law, would for every practical purpose be eliminated from our system of government as instrumentalities devised for the protection equally of society and of individuals in their essential rights. When that occurs our government will cease to be a government of laws, and become a government of men. Liberty regulated by law is the underlying principle of our institutions.[42]

Thus, not only do juries *not* possess the right to nullify, according to this view, they actually bear a positive duty *not* to nullify. There are many more examples of this view.[43] The claim then, is that this adjudicative division of

---

[40] *Id.* (emphasis added).

[41] 156 U.S. 51 (1895).

[42] *Id.* at 102-103 (emphasis added).

[43] See, for instance, *People v. Lem You*, 97 Cal. 224, 228 (Cal. 1893): "Of course, a jury, in rendering a general verdict in a criminal case, necessarily has the naked *power* to decide all the questions arising on the general issue of not guilty; but it only has the right to find the facts, and apply to them the law as given by the court," *State v. Kebbie* SUPREME COURT DOCKET NO. 2018-064, 2 (Vt. Nov. 21, 2018): "We conclude that there was no error in the instruction… [T]he court instructed the jury that it must follow the law as given by the court and to decide the case based on the evidence provided. This is an entirely accurate statement of the law," *In re Stankewitz*, 40 Cal.3d 391, 399 (Cal. 1985) (citations omitted): "In our system of justice it is the trial court that determines the law to be applied to the facts of the case, and the jury is bound . . . to receive as law what is laid down as such by the court. Of course, it is a fundamental and historic precept of our judicial system that jurors are restricted solely to the determination of factual questions and are bound by the law as given them by the court. They are not allowed either to determine what the law is or what the law should be," *U.S. v. Sepulveda*, *supra* note 5, at 1190: "The applicable rule is that, although jurors possess the raw power to set an accused free for any reason or for no reason, their duty is to apply the law as given to them by the court," *New v. State* 19 Ala. App. 140, 141 96 So. 720: "Under our system, evolved for the purpose of an orderly and fair

labor establishes a *de jure* duty on the jury not to nullify. Since the courts are clear and unambiguous that the jury must take the law as given, it follows that the jury has a duty to take the law as given – a duty which obviously extinguishes any claim of a right to nullify. Thus, the reasoning continues, it would be a direct contradiction to the legally established adjudicative division of labor and therefore an error of law to give the *nullification instruction*. It would be absurd, according to this reasoning, to suggest that the court has a duty to encourage the jury to violate its duty. In the words of the court in *United States v. Boardman*:[44] "Today jurors may have the power to ignore the law, but their duty is to apply the law as interpreted by the court, *and they should be so instructed*."[45]

As compelling as this line of reasoning initially appears to be, it is, I contend, based on a misguided reading of the adjudicative division of labor instruction. Certainly, it is clear that juries are to be informed that they must take the law according to the judge's instructions; the law is unambiguous on this point. But the law is equally unambiguous on another point: while juries are to be *informed* that they must take the law according to the judge's instructions, it is decidedly *not* the case that a jury must thereby *comply* with the judge's instructions regarding this division of labor. If this is not clear, it becomes so when we look to whom the law is addressed. If the law was simply that juries must take the law as given, then we can assume that such a law would be addressed to the jury. But it is not. All relevant case law on point is specifically addressed to the behavior of the trial judge and counsel. That is, it is immaterial to an appellate tribunal whether the jury did in fact nullify – did in fact disregard the adjudicative division of labor instruction. It is only the failure to *give* the adjudicative division of labor instruction (or give it incorrectly) or to do anything which might encourage the jury to believe otherwise which appellate courts have heretofore concerned themselves with.[46] And this is specifically limited to the judge's or trial

administration of justice, the court is the judge of the law, and the jury must take the law as given them by the court. Any other rule might tend to misapprehension and confusion."

44 1970 419 F.2d 110 (1st Cir. 1970).

45 *Id.* at 116 (emphasis added).

46 See, for instance, *United States v. Young*, 403 F. Supp. 3d 1131, 1148 (D.N.M. 2019) (citations omitted): "The instructions as a whole need not be flawless, but we must be

counsels' actions. It is in their behavior that the potential error in law lies, not in the behavior of the jury, so far as jury nullification is concerned, at least.[47] If the adjudicative division of labor instruction is given (and given properly, as judged by an appellate court), then, even if the court has strong reason to suspect that the jury nullified, no error in law has occurred.[48] All reversible legal errors to do with the adjudicative division of labor instruction focus on the behavior of the judge, and not the jury's behavior/response to this instruction, and case law affirms this.[49] The *division-of-labor* argument therefore fails to establish a positive duty on the jury to refrain from nullifying. As a final consideration there is, for these reasons, something akin to intellectual dishonesty whenever the courts assert that, contrary to its unfettered ability to acquit, the jury is *ever* under a *duty* to, or *must* convict a defendant, a point echoed by the court in *Sutton v. State*:[50]

> Duty implies an obligatory task, mode of conduct, or service to be performed by those persons bound by the duty. It also implies that non-compliance will engender a penalty from a superseding entity with the power to command and to coerce obedience. But a jury always possesses the de facto power to acquit the defendant, regardless of the strength of the evidence against him... How, then, may a jury possessed of the ultimate power of acquittal and its discretionary use, reconcile that power with a trial court's instruction mandating a duty to convict? The answer is that it may not, *at least,*

satisfied that, upon hearing the instructions, the jury understood the issues to be resolved and its duty to resolve them."

[47] See, for instance, *People v. Kriho*, 996 P.2d 158, 175 (Colo. App. 1999): suggesting that "instructions to the jury in the underlying case were not "court orders," and therefore could not support a finding of contempt."

[48] See, for example, *U.S. v. Siegelman, supra* note 22, at 1185 n. 36.

[49] See, for instance, *United States v. Manzano, supra* note 5, at 626 (citations omitted): "In this case, we are left with the firm conviction that the district court based its jury nullification ruling [allowing the defense to give a *nullification instruction*] on an erroneous view of the law. Our case law is clear: it is not the proper role of courts to encourage nullification."

[50] 262 Ga. 181 (Ga. 1992) (dissenting opinion).

while still retaining any integrity, intellectual honesty, or logical consistency.[51]

3.5.2 The Juror's-Oath Argument

The *juror's-oath* argument fares little better. Proponents of this view argue that since jurors take an oath to judge the case strictly on the facts, and to leave all considerations of law to the trial judge, this oath thereby creates a corresponding legal duty on the jurors to disavow any nullificatory conduct. This oath is an essential part of the trial process, after all, and while the exact wording varies from jurisdiction to jurisdiction, all variations of this oath contain the same essential elements: a promise to carry out one's duties truly (i.e., to refrain from returning a false verdict), and a promise to reach that verdict solely on the basis of the evidence adduced at trial. In other words, one might argue, jurors swear an oath to (among other things) refrain from nullifying. There is some advocacy for this view. The Court in *Thomas*,[52] for instance, held that "[n]ullification is, by definition, a violation of a juror's oath to apply the law as instructed by the court."[53] The Court of Appeals for the Sixth Circuit was also persuaded by this line of reasoning, finding no error in the trial court's response to a jury inquiry on nullification that included the admonition to the jury: "You would violate your oath and the law if you willfully brought in a verdict contrary to the law given you in this case."[54]

---

[51] *Id.* at 183 (citations omitted) (emphasis added).

[52] *U.S. v. Thomas*, *supra* note 8.

[53] *Id.* at 614.

[54] *U. S. v. Krzyske*, 836 F.2d 1013 (6th Cir.). See, also *United States v. Funches*, 135 F.3d 1405, 1408 (11th Cir. 1998): "But, while the federal courts acknowledge the jury's de facto power to refuse to apply the law as instructed by the court, exercise of such power is in dereliction of the jury's sworn duty." But, for the contrary view, see *United States v. Lynch*, 903 F.3d 1061, 1088-89 (9th Cir. 2018) (citations omitted): "[An] instruction stating "[y]ou would violate your oath and the law" by engaging in nullification was not only improper but an error of constitutional dimension, for it carried with it the implicit threat of punishment… Telling jurors that nullification is a violation of their oath, standing alone, implies the potential for punishment because violating one's oath could be deemed either perjury or contempt, both of which are punishable by fine and imprisonment. [Such an instruction violates a defendant's] Sixth Amendment right to trial by jury."

However, actual cases where the explicit violation of the jurors' oath have been the principle focus of litigation or prosecution are extremely rare in modern jurisprudence, so it is hardly a settled question in law as to what sorts of duties the jurors' oath is expected to place upon a juror, *vis-à-vis* jury nullification. But we can speculate. Does the swearing of this oath create a corresponding legal duty upon the jury to refrain from jury nullification? It does not, I maintain. A legal duty, recall, implies the existence of a corresponding legal right. However, we have already established that the court has no legal right to prevent a jury determined to nullify. Nullifying jurors are not subject to any legal sanction, their verdicts are not subject to impeachment, and the court is not at liberty to discourage them from returning a not guilty verdict. To behave in any other way would involve the courts in a reversible error. There is simply no legal remedy available to a court confronted with a nullifying jury.[55] In other words, we might say that the court has no right against the jury, as regards nullification, that it uphold its oath.[56] Thus, the jury has no legal duty towards the court that it uphold its oath in nullification cases.[57] Perhaps,

---

[55] See, Blackstone, W., *Commentaries on the Laws of England, Book the Third,* *3 (1768): "It is a general and indisputable rule, that where there is a legal right, there is also a legal remedy by suit, or action at law, whenever that right is invaded." This is a principle that the U.S. Supreme Court has affirmed on a number of different occasions, in a number of different contexts. See, for example, *Alden v. Maine,* 527 U.S. 706 (1999); *United States v. Stevenson,* 215 U.S. 190 (1909); *Fenwick v. Chapman,* 34 U.S. 461 (1835); *Dupont de Nemours v. Vance,* 60 U.S. 162 (1856). The logical correlative of this statement is, of course, *where there is no redress, there is no right.*

[56] Some courts have gone so far as to state that to imply otherwise would be contrary to the very notion of a fair trial. See, for instance, *United States v. Kleinman,* 880 F.3d 1020, 1032 (9th Cir. 2017) (citations omitted): "Although a court has the duty to forestall or prevent [nullification], including by firm instruction or admonition, a court should *not* state or imply that (1) jurors could be punished for jury nullification, or that (2) an acquittal resulting from jury nullification is invalid. More specifically, the court's statement that the jury "would violate [its] oath and the law if [it] willfully brought a verdict contrary to the law given to [it] in this case," could be construed to imply that nullification could be punished, particularly since the instruction came in the midst of a criminal trial."

[57] There is the broader issue of whether the jury has a *moral* obligation to uphold its oath. Oaths are a type of promise, after all, and promises are the kinds of things that, morally speaking, we ought, for the most part, to keep. However, it is obviously beyond the scope of this work to discuss the morality of promise keeping and whether, and under what conditions, one might be justified in not keeping a promise. To that end, though, see Conrad, *Jury Nullification: The Evolution of a Doctrine, supra* note 23, at

one might argue, this duty is not to the court, but to the defendant. However, the jurors' oath is an oath sworn to the court – to the State, in fact; the jury swears no oath to the defendant – a private citizen. If the jury does bear a legal duty towards the defendant, it does not spring from the jurors' oath.

3.5.3 The Fair-Trial Argument

This last consideration forms the basis of the third argument supporting the view that the jury has a duty to not nullify: the *fair-trial* argument. Since, according to this argument, the defendant has the right to a fair trial, which includes, among other things, the right to be tried by an impartial jury *according to the law*, this right is infringed upon whenever a jury nullifies; after all, the jury, when nullifying, is superimposing its judgement over, and contrary to, the demands of the law. Thus, the jury has a duty, not to the State, but to the defendant, not to nullify, lest her right to a fair trial be infringed upon. This view was starkly articulated in *State v. Lum*,[58] where the Court unambiguously stated: "Jury nullification is the antithesis to a right to a fair trial by an impartial jury."[59] This perspective has found voice in many other courts.[60] However, this argument also cannot successfully withstand scrutiny. Granted, defendants have the right to a fair trial,

---

257, where Conrad suggests that they very conditions that would motivate jurors to consider nullifying are the very conditions that would vitiate whatever moral duty may or may not exist to not nullify: "When a juror takes his oath, he must base his pledge on certain assumptions, including a presumption that the law will be fair, and fairly applied. It seems reasonable to claim that a citizen, conscripted into serving his government, should be entitled to make the presumption that his government will not require him to participate in an injustice… If the premises upon which a juror agrees to swear his oath are proven to be false, then the juror should be morally… absolved of any responsibility under the oath."

[58] I.D. No. 1408022157 A&B (Del. Super. Ct. June 29, 2016).

[59] *Id.* at *8.

[60] See, for instance, *United States v. Edwards*, 266 F. Supp. 3d 1290, 1302 (D.N.M. 2017): "[A]llowing juries to decide the law in a case, and to decide against the law as the court gave it to them, is inconsistent with the constitutional right for a fair trial;" *McDonough Power Equipment, Inc. v. Greenwood*, 464 U.S. 548, 554 (1984) (citations omitted): "One touchstone of a fair trial is an impartial trier of fact — a jury capable and willing to decide the case solely on the evidence before it;" *People v. Douglas*, 178 Misc. 2d 918, 930 (N.Y. Sup. Ct. 1998) (citations omitted): "In all criminal prosecutions, the accused shall enjoy the right to trial by an impartial jury. By extension, this right includes the right to a jury that is willing to apply the law as instructed by the court."

including the right to be judged according to the law, but, importantly, this right is held against the *court*, not the *jury*. The court is the duty bearer of that right, in other words, and is the one who must see to it that the defendant receives a fair trial. As long as the trial was conducted with legal integrity, a defendant's right to a fair trial will have been successfully met as regards the law – and again, irrespective of whether the jury nullified.

While it might appear that the defendant's right to be judged according to the law is being negatively impacted whenever the jury nullifies, which would then indirectly create a corresponding duty on the court to prevent the jury from behaving in this manner, this is also simply not the case. The right to a trial by jury, the right to be tried according to the law, the right to the presumption of innocence, are all granted a defendant in a criminal trial so as to protect her liberty from any unjust encroachment by the State. In the words of Swift C.J.: "It is in criminal cases that juries are considered to be the guardians of the rights of the people against the tyranny and oppression of the government."[61] The obvious implication here is that jury nullification simply has no *negative* impact whatsoever on a defendant's liberty, as all instances of jury nullification result in a not guilty verdict, which is, obviously, liberty *enhancing* for the defendant. Finally, nullifying juries are not necessarily unfair, partial, or biased juries; they simply judge the appropriate outcome using considerations of justice rather than the strict letter of the law, and what justice demands is, on the whole, neutral between the defendant and the State. A nullifying jury, in other words, in no way negatively affects, nor adversely impacts, a defendant's right to a fair trial.

Given the rhetorical failures of the *division-of-labor* argument, the *jurors-oath* argument, and the *fair-trial* argument, it is difficult to see how one could successfully argue that the jury has the *legal* duty to refrain from nullifying, and, for that reason alone, ought not be given the *nullification instruction*.

3.6 Jury Nullification as a De Jure Privilege

Using Hohfeld's model, we can now see how the *rights/power* view is unable to successfully parse this issue and yield a satisfactory answer to the

[61] *Bartholomew v. Clark*, 1 Conn. 472, 481 (1816).

nullification instruction debate. The jury does not have the legal right to nullify, but neither does it have the legal duty to not nullify.[62] Jury nullification is neither a right nor a mere power – it is, instead, a *privilege*. It has, in other words, a place in the Hohfeldian framework and, hence, an intrinsic, *de jure*, legal status.[63] As we saw in the previous chapter, the jury is free to return a verdict of not guilty based on considerations of what justice, not the law, demands. In other words, the jury is free to nullify without fear of legal redress. As we have already established, the jury is, therefore, under no legal duty to refrain from nullifying. According to Hohfeld, "A's privilege of *not* doing [*x*] is the very negation of a duty of *doing* [*x*]. Here again the duty contrasted is of a content or tenor exactly opposite to that of the privilege."[64] Since the jury has no legal duty to refrain from nullifying, we can therefore conclude that, given the correlative nature of these concepts, the jury has the *privilege* to nullify.[65] Again, this description accords with the received view on how much control can and

---

[62] Put another way, while the jury is under no legal duty to refrain from nullifying, this in no way, I argue, necessarily entails that the jury has a legal right to nullify.

[63] To say that nullification has an intrinsic legal status is simply to say that the power to nullify is something that must be given legal recognition of some sort. In other words, the exercise of the nullification power is, in some sense, legitimate; interference with the exercise of this power is, therefore, all things being equal, illegitimate. Thus, jury nullification has legal status because it is something the courts must give recognition to (no matter how begrudgingly), and this status is intrinsic because it arises from the very nature of the jury's role in the criminal justice system. We can contrast this with the gunman's *de facto* power to successfully rob me. The latter need not be (and most certainly is not) something that the law must recognize and respect as legitimate. This power has no *de jure* status (except in the prohibited sense), intrinsic or otherwise. This distinction is something I believe Hohfeld was trying to capture in his analysis of rights-talk.

[64] *Supra* note 16, at 46. This last point about the content or tenor of the duty being exactly opposite to that of the privilege is of particular importance. It is one of the reasons why the duty/privilege pairing is the proper way to describe nullification. None of the other three jural opposite pairings can preserve this grammatical continuity and still make sense. Pierre Schlag suggests another way to understand this relationship: 'the privilege to *x* is equivalent to the absence of a duty to ~x.' Schlag, Pierre, *How to Do Things with Hohfeld*, 78, Law & Contemp. Probs. 185, 234 (2015).

[65] Put formally: [~(a duty to *x*) ≡ a privilege to *not x*], where, in this case, *x* equals returning a non-nullifying verdict, and *not x* translates into a returning a *not* non-nullifying verdict – or: jury nullification. Thus, the jury has a *legal privilege* to nullify because, to reference Hohfeld again, a privilege is simply one's freedom from the right or claim of another.

cannot be exerted on the jury regarding its deliberative procedures and subsequent verdict; the court has *no right* to prevent the jury from nullifying, hence, the jury has the *privilege* to nullify.[66]

This last paragraph is important, and, admittedly, the line of reasoning is complicated, if not altogether byzantine. Here is a more formalized account of the preceding argument:

Let (x) stand for: "return a non-nullifying verdict."

	i)	~[The jury has a duty to (x)].	(argued for above)
	ii)	[The jury has a privilege to ~(x)]	
		≡ ~[The jury has a duty to (x)].	(Hohfeld)[67]
thus,	iii)	The jury has a privilege to ~(x)	

To reiterate, because the jury has *no duty* to not nullify, it therefore has the *privilege* to nullify.

Let us pause briefly and review where we are and what brought us to this point. The arguments in favor of jury nullification's status as a *de jure* right are, I contend, unmotivated, misguided, and conceptually confused, as are the arguments in favor of its status a mere *de facto* power. Jury nullification, is, I argue, best understood as having the status of a *legal privilege*. This is an important conclusion because it shows that the *rights/power* view is looking for the wrong answer when enquiring into the intrinsic legal status of nullification. Recall that the purpose of such an inquiry was to resolve the initial controversy over whether juries ought to be informed that they have the ability to nullify. The *rights/power* view holds that the key to answering this question is to look into the nature of jury nullification itself. If it has the status of a legal right, according to this view, then juries ought to be given the *nullification instruction*. If jury nullification does not have the status of a legal right, this argument continues, then it is a mere *de facto* power (one that, in fact, directly conflicts with the jury's *legal* duty to render a true and accurate verdict based solely on the facts), and juries ought not

---

[66] Thus, we can see how the description of nullification as a *privilege* also has the virtue of fitting into the Hohfeldian scheme of jural *correlatives*.

[67] *Supra* note 16, at 46.

to be so informed. What I have shown to this point is that jury nullification is neither a right in the *de jure* sense, nor merely a power in the *de facto* sense. The *rights/power* view is predicated upon a false dichotomy and must therefore be rejected as specious reasoning. Instead, jury nullification is a *de jure privilege* – it has a legitimate legal status. This analysis and understanding of jury nullification was articulated by Bazelon, C.J. in his dissenting opinion in *Dougherty*:

> My own view rests on the premise that nullification can and should serve an important function in the criminal process. I do not see it as a doctrine that exists only because we lack the power to punish jurors who refuse to enforce the law or to re-prosecute a defendant whose acquittal cannot be justified in the strict terms of law.[68]

3.7 The Paucity of Privilege

We must now see what, if anything, the *privilege* of jury nullification implies *vis-à-vis* the *nullification instruction*. Privileges are, essentially, a type of freedom or liberty. They do not, however, entitle their bearers to much of anything beyond the absence of a duty. Privileges do not, in other words, give one a positive entitlement to anything, or imply positive duties on others. Hohfeld spells out the distinction this way: "A right is one's affirmative claim against another, and a privilege is one's freedom from the right or claim of another."[69] If privileges do not entail a positive entitlement to some *x*, then the failure to be provided with that *x* is not, in and of itself, a denial of that privilege, constructive or otherwise. We can see how this applies to the *nullification instruction* debate: Clearly, if nullification is a *de jure* right that juries possess, then the courts must not interfere with a nullifying jury; I am willing to grant the advocates of the *rights/power* view that much. This means, among other things, that the court would indeed have a duty of some sort to inform the jury of its ability to nullify, for, as discussed above, the failure to do so would amount to a constructive denial of that right. Conversely, is jury nullification is viewed as a mere *de facto* power, then many, if not all, of the conceptual/analytic arguments offered in support of the *nullification instruction* would be, at best, unmotivated and

---

[68] *Supra* note 2, at 1141-42.
[69] *Supra* note 16, at 55.

lacking in rhetorical purchase, and at worst, antithetical to sound law and legal reasoning.

However, if jury nullification is framed as a *privilege*, then the most we can say about the court's correlative relation is that it has *no-right* to prevent the jury from nullifying. But refusing to inform the jury about jury nullification and actually preventing the exercise of such are two very different things when we are talking about privileges as opposed to rights. Refusing to inform may, in some circumstances, be inconsistent with a duty, and thus a constructive violation of a correlative right; refusing to inform, however, is not inconsistent with a *no-right*, and thus not a violation (constructive or otherwise) of a correlative privilege. Therein lies one of the crucial distinctions between jury nullification as a right and jury nullification as a *privilege*: framing jury nullification as a *privilege* does not impose upon the court any positive obligation or duty whatsoever to give the *nullification instruction*. Privileges simply grant the *de jure* power to their holders to perform certain acts or be exempt from certain duties free from legal redress, but they do not thereby create corresponding duties for others. The court may have *no right* to prevent, or otherwise interfere with, a nullifying verdict, but this in no way imposes any obligation or duty upon the court to aid or assist in such through giving the *nullification instruction*.

This conclusion is not a victory for the *de-facto power* view of jury nullification, however. It is true that those who argue for this view are primarily concerned with denying that jurors ought to be informed of their ability to nullify. We might therefore suspect that they would be just as happy to concede the claim that nullification is a *privilege* (as this does not imply that jurors ought to be so informed). However, the critical feature of the *de-facto* power view of jury nullification is that it imputes to nullification no legal status whatsoever. It is something that falls out of the legal system, as it were. Giving the *nullification instruction*, under this view, is therefore completely unjustified, and contrary to the best principles of legality. However, as we saw, such a strong claim becomes ideationally unwarranted once jury nullification is acknowledged to be a *privilege*. Privileges describe legal relations – legal relations which must be respected and acknowledged by the courts – they have *de jure* status, in other words, and as such, are obviously not contrary to the principles of legality, *pace* the *de-facto* power view of jury nullification. Pierre Schlag describes it thusly:

> [A]lthough it is clear that Hohfeld's jural relations are atomistic, discrete, and fixed at the formal level, their legal and economic effects once deployed are anything but. *It is thus wrong analytically to think of privilege-no right regimes as nonlegal.* Not only is a legal [privilege] itself a legal regime... but it also functions as a kind of extension of other legal entitlements and disablements that enables these to be brought into play.[70]

This is the point I have been illustrating. The binary framework for understanding jury nullification offered by advocates of the *rights/power view* is simply ill-equipped to properly address the *nullification instruction* question – it fails inasmuch as it implies that jury nullification is either a *de jure* right, or a *de facto* power. It is neither – it is, I have argued, a *de jure privilege*. The courts bear a *no-right* against the jury *vis-à-vis* jury nullification; hence, under this Hohfeldian analysis, we can conclude that the jury holds a *privilege* against the court *vis-à-vis* jury nullification. As a *privilege*, jury nullification therefore has legal legitimacy: it has, in other words (and regardless of its origin or justification), implications and limiting consequences on court behavior which must be acknowledged and respected. Failure to do so can invalidate an entire trial process. Jury nullification is, structurally, a part of the law. That is what it means to identify something as a *privilege*: it exists as a legal entity within our jural regime.

So, what does viewing jury nullification as a *privilege* get us? It shows us simply that jury nullification is not a mere *de facto* power, but, despite its *de jure* status, it nonetheless remains somewhat less than a *claim-right*. Nothing less, nothing more. Conceptualizing jury nullification as a *privilege* is, I contend, the correct and only way to view it. However, it turns out that this gets us no closer to resolving the *nullification instruction* debate. Privileges, it turns out, impose *nothing* in the way of positive obligations upon their correlative *no-rights* bearers, and certainly nothing so strong as a duty to

---

[70] Schlag, *supra* note 64, at 216 (emphasis added).

inform or instruct a privilege holder of said privilege.[71] In other words, identifying jury nullification as a *privilege* nevertheless leaves the *nullification instruction* debate fundamentally unaddressed and unresolved. Which brings me to my final and concluding point. Enquiring into the intrinsic legal nature of jury nullification can go a long way towards disambiguating exactly what it is we are talking about, but such an enquiry simply does not and cannot settle the question about whether jurors ought to be informed of their power to nullify.

The *rights/power* view gets at least two fundamental things wrong. For one, it relies on the false dichotomy between *de jure* rights and *de facto* powers – not everything with *de jure* status is thereby a right, nor is everything less than a right somehow and necessarily *de facto*; secondly, and most critically, it is predicated on the view that conceptual legal analysis alone can answer the *nullification instruction* question. I am not denigrating conceptual legal analysis in the least, mind you; engaging in such helps us better understand the issues we set out to explore and can map out the debates, questions, and issues that still remain unaddressed and/or unresolved. Such analysis allowed us to see, for instance, that jury nullification is best understood to be a *de jure privilege* – something that the jury has no legal duty to refrain from engaging in. However, as we have also seen, solving this conceptual question tells us nothing whatsoever about whether the *nullification instruction* ought to be given; it remains unaddressed and unresolved. This shouldn't necessarily surprise us; as Arthur Corbin advises:

> In all our discussions of legal analysis, in all our attempts at defining terms or at coining them, we should never cease to bear in mind and give warning that mere legal analysis does not by itself enable us to tell what the law is in a single case. The ability to recognize and to define rights and duties, powers and privileges, and the other

[71] One's legal privileges are no doubt legion; it hardly seems reasonable to imagine that this corresponds to a correlative duty on the courts, or anyone for that matter, to inform you of them all.

> relations, does not tell us whether or not they exist in a given case or what facts operate to create them.[72]

While the *rights/power* view does offer a solution to the *nullification instruction* debate, it is a wrong solution arrived at through specious methods, and we do best to reject it as a cursory and unsophisticated understanding of the issue. To answer the *nullification instruction* question, therefore, we must abandon our strictly analytical approach to the topic and turn to a more pragmatic strategy; we must, in other words, look to the *practical* effects or consequences of giving such an instruction – the *policy* considerations, as it were. If giving the *nullification instruction* somehow furthers the goals of the justice system and/or *promotes* the ends of the criminal jury trial system, then it would seem that there might be good reason to inform jurors of their *privilege* to nullify. On the other hand, if informing jurors of their *privilege* to nullify somehow *subverts* the goals or ends of the justice system, then we would seemingly have good reason to refrain from doing so. Accordingly, these consequence-based *policy* arguments will be the focus of the next two chapters.

---

[72] Corbin, Arthur L., *Jural Relations and Their Classification*, 30 Yale Law Journal 226, 237-38 (1921).

Chapter 4
Arguments Offered in Support of the Nullification Instruction

The specific focus of this chapter will be those consequence-based arguments offered in support of the *nullification instruction*, along with an analysis of potential objections to such arguments. As we saw in the previous chapter, there is nothing intrinsic to the legal status of jury nullification itself that reveals whether a *nullification instruction* ought to be given. Thus, if there is any reason for or against giving a *nullification instruction*, it must lie with the consequences of doing so – in legal parlance, we must search for compelling *policy* considerations.

There are three main effects-based arguments commonly put forth by proponents of the *nullification instruction*: the *freedom from government oppression* argument; the *community/democratic values* argument; and the *mercy/justice* argument. While all three of these arguments are somewhat inter-related in scope and substance, I think it is important to distinguish them conceptually from one another, as often, in practice, the justificatory principles they employ can get somewhat conflated and confused.

4.1 The Freedom from Government Oppression Argument

The *freedom from government oppression* argument begins with the assumption that even the most just and democratic government can occasionally, perhaps even inadvertently, oppress its citizens through the law, either in substance or in application. The jury, with its nullification *privilege,* this argument continues, acts as an important and essential guardian of citizen rights by ensuring that the citizenry cannot and will not be victims of oppressive legislation or oppressive enforcement of otherwise acceptable legislation. Consider the Court's pronouncement on the topic in *Duncan v. Louisiana*:[1]

[1] *Duncan v. Louisiana,* 391 U.S. 145, 156 (1968).

> Providing the accused with the right to be tried by a jury of his peers gave him an inestimable safeguard against the corrupt or overzealous prosecutor and against the compliant, biased, or eccentric judge. If the defendant preferred the common-sense judgment of a jury to the more tutored but perhaps less sympathetic reaction of a single judge, he was to have it. Beyond this, the jury trial provisions in the Federal and State Constitutions reflect a fundamental decision about the exercise of official power – a reluctance to trust plenary powers over the life and liberty of the citizen to one judge or to a group of judges. *Fear of unchecked power, so typical of our State and Federal Governments in other respects, found expression in the criminal law in this insistence upon community participation in the determination of guilt or innocence.*[2]

In *State v. Wilkinson*[3], the court asserted a similar view, stating that the ability of the jury to nullify was a safeguard against tyranny in the law, and stood as one of the criminal law's "great landmarks"[4] for all who view "liberty and law as almost synonymous."[5] This view was also endorsed by Roscoe Pound, who described jury nullification as "the greatest corrective of law [against oppressive government action] in its actual administration."[6] Indeed, the perspective that the jury is meant to play this occasionally nullificatory role in the face of oppressive state action enjoys near universal endorsement by both scholars and the courts.[7] This fear of

---

[2] *Id.* at 1451 (emphasis added).

[3] 2 Vt. 480 (1829).

[4] *Id.* at 531-2.

[5] *Id.*

[6] *Law in Books and Law in Action*, 44 Am. L. Rev. 12, 18 (1910).

[7] See, for instance, *U. S. v. Dougherty*, 473 F.2d 1113, 1131-2 (1972): "Human frailty being what it is, a prosecutor disposed by unworthy motives could likely establish some basis in fact for bringing charges against anyone he wants to book, but the jury system operates in fact so that the jury will not convict when they empathize with the defendant;" *Williams v. Florida*, 399 U.S. 78, 100, 90 S.Ct. 1893, 1906, 26 L.Ed.2d 446 (1970): [T]he essential feature of a jury obviously lies in the interposition between the accused and his accuser of the commonsense judgment of a group of laymen, and in the community participation and shared responsibility that results from that group's determination of guilt or innocence;" *United States v. Lynch*, 903 F.3d 1061, 1088 (9th Cir. 2018) (emphasis added): "A court may permissibly seek to discourage jurors from returning a verdict contrary to law or fact, but ever since *Bushel's Case* , what a court may not do is coerce jurors into obeying its instructions on the law by suggesting that

oppressive government action, and the need to safeguard against it, moreover, is not something we can easily dismiss as purely abstract or academic. In his dissent in *Neder v. United States*,[8] for instance, Scalia J. emphasized this last point:

> Perhaps the Court is so enamoured of judges in general, and federal judges in particular, that it forgets that they (we) are officers of the Government, and hence proper objects of that healthy suspicion of the power of government which possessed the Framers and is embodied in the Constitution. Who knows? — 20 years of appointments of federal judges by oppressive administrations might produce judges willing to enforce oppressive criminal laws, and to interpret criminal laws oppressively — at least in the view of the citizens in some vicinages where criminal prosecutions must be brought. And so the people reserved the function of determining criminal guilt *to themselves*, sitting as jurors.[9]

Jury nullification, under this view, is not the least bit contrary or antithetical to the role of the jury; it is an essential function of, and foundational justification for, the entirety of the criminal jury system: "[T]rial by jury has always been cherished, as the great security of the subject against the oppression of government; *but it never could have been a solid refuge and security, unless the jury had the right to judge of the intent and the law.*"[10]

The reasoning supporting the *freedom from government oppression* argument is fairly straightforward: if a jury is to protect the citizens of the State from

---

those who disobey could face fine or imprisonment. Threats of punishment subvert the jury's longstanding role as a safeguard against government oppression;"; *Apprendi v. New Jersey*, 530 U.S. 466, 477 (2000) (citations omitted): "As we have, unanimously, explained, the historical foundation for our recognition of these principles extends down centuries into the common law. To guard against a spirit of oppression and tyranny on the part of rulers, and as the great bulwark of [our] civil and political liberties, trial by jury has been understood to require that the truth of every accusation, whether preferred in the shape of indictment, information, or appeal, should afterwards be confirmed by the unanimous suffrage of twelve of [the defendant's] equals and neighbors."

[8] 527 U.S. 1 (1999).

[9] *Id.* at 32.

[10] *People v. Croswell*, 3 Johns. Cas. 337, 355-56 (N.Y. Sup. Ct. 1804) (emphasis added).

government oppression, it must be in a position to refuse to enforce those laws that are oppressive or are enforced in an oppressive manner. In other words, the very function of the jury – to act as a safeguard against government oppression[11] – demands, in part, that it have the *privilege* to nullify.[12] Since the *nullification instruction* puts the jury in the position to exercise its nullification *privilege* and thereby function as a check on state oppression, the instruction ought to be given, such reasoning continues. To do otherwise would be to subvert or undermine the role of the jury as a bulwark against government tyranny and oppression.[13] In *U.S. v. Polizzi,*[14] for instance, the Court considered the related issue of whether a jury should be informed of relevant mandatory minimum sentencing laws. Acknowledging that doing so "arguably would open the jury to the possibility of mercy [nullification],"[15] the Court nevertheless asserted: "Providing jurors sentencing information would enable the jury to more effectively *fulfill its historical Sixth Amendment role as the conscience of the community and guardian against government oppression*."[16] It is difficult to parse what the Court could mean by this in a way that does not imply that juries are empowered by design to occasionally resist the actions of the State – are structured, in other words, to play a nullificatory role when confronted with government oppression. If so, then, the *freedom from government oppression* argument concludes, the *nullification instruction,* as the direct, immediate, and efficient means of empowering the jury to play this role, ought to be given.

---

[11] See, for instance, *Baldwin v. New York,* 399 U.S. 66, 72 (1970): "But the primary purpose of the jury is to prevent the possibility of oppression by the Government."
[12] See, for example, *People v. Croswell, supra* note 10; *U.S. v. Green,* 346 F. Supp. 2d 259, 309 (D. Mass. 2004) (citations omitted) (emphasis added): "[T]he Supreme Court has recognized the jury's historic function, in criminal trials, as a check against arbitrary or oppressive exercises of power by the Executive Branch, *and there can be little doubt that jury nullification sometimes occurs, typically in response to a sense that a law is unjust or that applying it "correctly" in a particular case would be unjust*."
[13] From a purely practical standpoint, a jury can hardly be expected to play a particular role within the legal system if it is unaware that such a role exists, and that it is the appropriate – and expected – candidate to fill that role. This is a similar, but different, point to the *constructive denial* argument from **CHAPTER 3**.
[14] 549 F. Supp. 2d 308 (E.D.N.Y. 2008).
[15] *Id.* at 445.
[16] *Id.* at 433 (emphasis added).

4.2 The Community/Democratic Values Argument

The *community/democratic values* argument proceeds along similar lines as the *government oppression* argument. One of the virtues of a just democratic legal state, according to this argument, is that the content and administration of the law reflect the will and values of the people it governs. However, even the most just and democratic government can occasionally, perhaps even inadvertently, substantially depart from community standards/values, either in substance or application of the law. This could be for a variety of reasons, not the least of which is that social values often tend to change too quickly for legislation to accurately reflect or keep up with. According to the *community/democratic values* argument, then, the jury acts as a corrective to ensure that the standards or values of the community are brought to bear on the content and administration of the law; it functions as a form of immediate and direct democracy, as it were.[17] The jury, this reasoning continues, is an embodiment of those democratic ideals that underpin our entire system of criminal justice;[18] it is, according to Scalia, J., "the spinal column of American democracy."[19] The jury, according to this view, is therefore a necessary and essential mechanism for preserving democratic ideals in the application of the law:

> [T]he jury is an institution of central importance in our system of government... Its primacy is guaranteed by the United States Constitution, and *the American jury system is our most vital day-to-day expression of direct democracy*. There is no other routine aspect of our civic existence today where citizens themselves are the government. Moreover, beyond involving citizens directly in one of the most

---

[17] See, for instance, *U.S. v. Doherty*, 675 F. Supp. 726, 739 n.20 (D. Mass. 1987) (emphasis added): "To the extent that we are concerned about the highest quality of justice in our courts, however, the rules under which we operate ought reflect a concern for *the jury system — that vital expression of direct democracy which charges the entire judicial structure with its moral force.*"

[18] See, for instance, *Green v. United States*, 356 U.S. 165, 215-16 (1958): "The jury injects a democratic element into the law. This element is vital to the effective administration of criminal justice, not only in safeguarding the rights of the accused, but in encouraging popular acceptance of the laws and the necessary general acquiescence in their application."

[19] *Supra* note 8, at 30.

> fundamental processes of government, *the jury system injects community values into judicial decisions* and allows equitable resolution of hard cases without setting a legal precedent.[20]

Once again, this is a perspective that enjoys near universal endorsement by both the courts and legal scholars.[21] We see this vividly in *U.S. v. Gilliam,*[22] where the court stated:

> Our constitution guarantees the accused the right of a trial by a jury of his peers, primarily in order to ensure that the accused is judged by prevailing community mores...[O]ne of the most important functions any jury can perform... is to maintain a link between contemporary community values and the penal system. The jury is the oracle of the citizenry in weighing the culpability of the accused, and should it find him guilty it condemns him with the full legal and moral authority of the society. The public listens with rapt attention to the jury's pronouncement of guilt or innocence, for in that singular

---

[20] *U.S. v. Green, supra* note 12, at 316 (citations omitted) (emphasis added).

[21] See, for instance, *U. S. v. Dougherty, supra* note 7, at 1142 (emphasis added): "The drafters of legal rules cannot anticipate and take account of every case where a defendant's conduct is "unlawful" but not blameworthy, any more than they can draw a bold line to mark the boundary between an accident and negligence. *It is the jury — as spokesman for the community's sense of values — that must explore that subtle and elusive boundary;" United States v. Adams,* 126 F.2d 774, 775-76 (2d Cir. 1942): "The institution of trial by jury — especially in criminal cases — has its hold upon public favor chiefly for two reasons. The individual can forfeit his liberty — to say nothing of his life — only at the hands of those who, unlike any official, are in no wise accountable, directly or indirectly, for what they do, and who at once separate and melt anonymously in the community from which they came. Moreover, since if they acquit their verdict is final, no one is likely to suffer of whose conduct they do not morally disapprove; and this introduces a slack into the enforcement of law, tempering its rigor by the mollifying influence of current ethical conventions. A trial by any jury, however small, preserves both these fundamental elements and a trial by a judge preserves neither, at least to anything like the same degree;" Holmes, O.W., *Law in Science and Science in Law,* 12 Harv. L. Rev. 443, 459: "[O]ne reason why I believe in our practice of leaving questions of negligence to [the jury]... [is that jurors]... will introduce into their verdict a certain amount – a very large amount, so far as I have observed – of popular prejudice, and thus keep the administration of the law in accord with the wishes and feelings of the community."

[22] 994 F.2d 97 (2d Cir. 1993).

> moment the convictions and conscience of the entire community are expressed.[23]

Or consider this description of the role of the jury: "[Jurors] represent the conscience and mores of the community in which the crimes were committed. That jurors represent the conscience of the community is the historic fact which inspired and gives continued life to the constitutional guaranty of a speedy and public trial by impartial jury… The conscience of the community may affect their verdicts. It needs saying that this is no aberration. This is the constitutional scheme."[24]

The connection between the jury's role as a "stunning experiment in direct democracy"[25] and its *privilege* to nullify is once again fairly straightforward. The very function of the jury – to ensure that community values are given voice in the administration and content of the law – demands, in part, that it have the *privilege* to nullify: "By ensuring that the state's power will not be brought to bear without passing through the conscience of local laypeople, the government and the law achieve greater democratic legitimacy… For originalists, *jury nullification is an enshrined part of the Constitution.*"[26] The jury, with its *privilege* to nullify, according to this account, is therefore "a ground level exercise of democratic values."[27] Without this *privilege,* the argument continues, the jury would be unable to fulfill its central function and important role. Clay Conrad clearly articulates how jury nullification serves as the locus of this essential democratic tie between community values and the administration of the law, stating:

> Legislators and other elected officials are responsible for writing, revising, and modifying laws until the criminal code matches community consensus. The surest way to measure community values is to see what the people do when they are called on to judge their neighbors according to the legislature's statutes. A pattern of

---

[23] *Id.* at 101 (citations omitted) (emphasis added).

[24] *Beckwith v. State,* 386 So. 2d 836, 341 (Fla. Dist. Ct. App. 1980).

[25] *U.S. v. West,* 552 F. Supp. 2d 74, 75 (D. Mass. 2008).

[26] Jolly, Richard L., *Jury Nullification as a Spectrum,* Pepperdine Law Review 49 (2022): 341, 345 (emphasis added).

[27] *State v. Saintcalle,* 178 Wash. 2d 34, 50 (Wash. 2013).

hung juries, nullification acquittals, or ameliorated convictions is a sure sign to the legislature that the law needs to be changed.[28]

For Conrad then, jury nullification is, at least in some instances, direct and immediate democracy in action, with a nullificatory verdict being analogous to a 'yes' vote in a referendum to overturn the law in question.

According to the *community/democratic values* argument, if a jury is to ensure that the content and application of the criminal law best reflects community values and gives democratic voice to the will of the community, it must obviously be in a position to refuse to endorse those laws that are inconsistent with, or contradictory to, the democratic will of the community – it must be in a position, in other words, to exercise its nullificatory *privilege*. Of course, the jury can only exercise is nullificatory *privilege* in the defense of community mores and democratic values if it is aware that such a *privilege* exists.[29] Since the *nullification instruction* puts the jury in the necessary epistemic position to exercise its nullification *privilege,* and hence, fulfill this important role, the instruction ought to be given, such reasoning continues. To do otherwise would be to subvert or undermine the role of the jury as a guardian of community standards and democratic values.[30] For Conrad, denying the *nullification instruction* therefore might be akin to holding a referendum, but not promulgating the time or place of the polling stations. We are, according to this argument, committed to the *nullification*

---

[28] Conrad, Clay S., *Jury Nullification: Evolution of a Doctrine,* 161 (Carolina Academic Press, 1998).

[29] See note 13.

[30] Interestingly, even cases condemning the *nullification instruction* itself still venerate the jury system – and with it, jury nullification – as a valuable means of imbuing the strict application of the law with community standards and democratic values. See, for instance, *Washington v. Watkins,* 655 F.2d 1346, 1374 n.54 (5th Cir. 1981): "A jury, acting as a "community conscience" in disregarding the strict requirements of the law when it finds that those requirements cannot justly be applied in a particular case, undoubtedly possesses this power each time it determines a defendant's guilt or innocence; that power, of course, is not limited to capital cases, but extends to determinations of guilt or innocence in all criminal cases. The courts that have considered the question, however, have almost uniformly held that a criminal defendant is not entitled to an instruction that points up the existence of that practical power to his jury." There seems to be a cognitive disconnect, however, between the Court's expectation that the jury will 'act as a community conscience' when justice demands it while simultaneously denying them the practical means to so behave.

instruction to the degree that we are committed to giving practical democratic voice to the will of the community through the administration of the criminal law:

> Ultimately, the power of the jury to prevent government overreach is too important to lose, and jury nullification has always been an integral way for juries to invoke the voice of the community in the criminal justice system. Jury nullification both protects individuals unfairly targeted by the system and draws attention to laws that violate community standards. Elected legislators, who have vowed to represent the voice of the people, should be motivated to uphold this system... Whether this is done by requiring judicial instructions, allowing mitigating evidence related to nullification, or implementing an innovative system of nullification pleas, the agentic legislatures should take it upon themselves to codify the right to jury nullification.[31]

4.3 The Mercy/Justice Argument

Finally, the *mercy/justice* argument: this perspective on the issue is predicated on the view that the pragmatic and conceptual necessity for generalized legal rules within an effective and efficacious legal regime might occasionally result in particularized forms of injustice.[32] A nullifying jury, however, is in a position to add an element of mercy or justice to those situations where a strict adherence to the law might otherwise be cruel or unjust: "Permitting the jury to act as the voice and conscience of the community is required because *the very reason for the jury system is to temper*

[31] Royer, Caisa E., *The Disobedient Jury: Why Lawmakers Should Codify Jury Nullification*, 102 Cornell L. Rev. 1401, 1430 (2017).

[32] Consider, for example, the mandatory minimum sentencing laws extant in some jurisdictions which compel judges to enforce predetermined minimum punishments for specific offenses, regardless of context. Such laws preclude a judge from taking account of things like a defendant's history or level of involvement in the crime when sentencing. While these statutes were originally established to promote the overall goal of uniformity in sentencing – a generally just and fair approach – in application they often lead to situations where a defendant with no prior convictions might receive a quite severe sentence disproportionate to the actual offense committed, regardless of any and all mitigating factors, and in direct conflict with the best principles of justice.

the harshness of the law with the commonsense judgment of the community."[33] The "very core of the jury system,"[34] according to this perspective, is founded on this "free and unfettered exercise of individual judgment and expression of conscience."[35] One of the central justifications for the jury system, its *raison d'être*, as it were, is to therefore ameliorate the law's harshness when considerations of mercy or justice demand it – to nullify, in other words.

Like the *community/democratic values* and *government oppression* arguments, there is again widespread agreement that one of the many benefits of trial by jury is that the jury's nullificatory *privilege* allows the criminal law in its application to be just and merciful in situations where a literal application of the law might preclude this.[36] In *Dougherty*,[37] for example, the Bazelon, C.J. stated that: "[n]ullification is a mechanism that... *permits the jury to bring to bear on the criminal process a sense of fairness and particularized justice*."[38] This is exactly the reasoning used by Scheflin and Van Dyke when they described jury nullification in the following manner:

> The jury power at issue here is not a power to "nullify" statutes or precedents in order to create or substitute a new version of the law. Instead, it is a power to "complete" or "perfect" the law by permitting the jury to exercise that one last touch of mercy where it may not be appropriate and just to apply the literal law to the actual

---

[33] *State v. Scott*, 314 N.C. 309, 311-12 (N.C. 1985) (citation omitted) (emphasis added).
[34] *United States v. Johnson*, 432 F.2d 626, 633 (D.C. Cir. 1970).
[35] *Id.*
[36] See, for instance, Liu, Yingxi, *Does the Modern Jury Represent a Successful Exercise in Democracy?*, vol. 5, issue 13 Academic Journal of Humanities & Social Sciences 4, 7 (2021) (emphasis added): "Moreover, the positive significance of jury in democracy lies in its role in the wider judicial and political order, which not only *promotes fairness, justice and legitimacy* at the judicial level, but also protects the interests of citizens and supervises the government at the political level;" *Furman v. Georgia*, 408 U.S. 238, 313 (1972) (emphasis added): "[T]he policy of vesting sentencing authority primarily in juries [was] a decision largely motivated by the desire to *mitigate the harshness of the law* and to bring community judgment to bear on the sentence *as well as guilt or innocence*;" *Jurek v. State*, 522 S.W.2d 934, 940 (Tex. Crim. App. 1975) (emphasis added): "To eliminate all discretion on the part of the jury... would eliminate *the element of mercy, one of the fundamental traditions of our system of criminal jurisprudence*."
[37] *Supra* note 7.
[38] *Id.* at 1142 (emphasis added).

> facts… [Jury nullification is an] integral part of the law itself, serving the unique and vital function of smoothing the friction between law and justice, and between people and their laws.[39]

The *mercy/justice* argument, then, proceeds along the following lines: it is desirable for the criminal law to be just and merciful; a strict application of the law will sometimes conflict with justice and mercy; the jury is designed to act as a corrective to this;[40] the jury can only act as a corrective to this if it is able to nullify; the *nullification instruction* enables the jury to nullify;[41] therefore, the *nullification instruction* ought to be given, in the name of promoting justice and mercy into the application of the criminal law and allowing the jury to fulfill its essential function.[42] To quote Scheflin and Van Dyke once again:

> But the jurors should also be told that their function is to represent the community in this trial and that their ultimate responsibility is to determine the facts that occurred and to evaluate whether applying the law to these facts will produce, in the eyes of the community, a just and equitable verdict. This type of honest instruction would reinforce our nation's commitment to a government where the people are sovereign, and it would serve to bring the people and their laws together in closer harmony.[43]

The *mercy/justice* argument relies on an assertion of the intrinsic value of jury nullification for its rhetorical impact – on an unconditional justification

---

[39] Scheflin, Alan W. and Van Dyke, Jon M., *Merciful Juries: The Resilience of Jury Nullification*. 48 Wash. & Lee L. Rev. 165, 167-68 (1991).

[40] See, for instance, *State v. LaMere*, 298 Mont. 358, 372 (Mont. 2000): "Our jury system, no less than our system of representative government, is based upon a democratic ideal: that justice is best served by a broadly representative group of individuals 'drawn from the various walks of life;'" *United States v. Folse*, No. CR 15-2485 JB, at *9 (D.N.M. Nov. 9, 2015): "The criminal jury's role at the Founders' time was primarily that of a factfinder, but also included as a secondary role acting as the community's conscience to determine whether the law, or the application of law to the facts, was conscionable."

[41] See note 13.

[42] Of course, this argument assumes that when the law and justice (or mercy) are in conflict, the jury will at least occasionally choose to promote justice (or mercy) as an end, and refuse to endorse a strict application of the law – in other words, will nullify.

[43] Scheflin and Van Dyke, *Merciful Juries*, *supra* note 39, at 183.

for "the right of a jury, as a buffer between the accused and the state, to reach a verdict despite what may seem clear law."[44] Jury nullification, according to this argument, is "*one of the fundamental traditions of our system of criminal jurisprudence*,"[45] and hence does not need a further policy-based justification. Like the other two arguments, the *mercy/justice* argument relies on the pragmatic reality that a jury can hardly be expected to exercise an unknown privilege in a formal legal setting.[46] Thus, according to the *mercy/justice* argument, the *nullification instruction* is demanded as a practical means to realize the jury's principled ends.

At heart, the *freedom from government oppression*, the *community/democratic values*, and the *mercy/justice* arguments rest on three simple premises:

1. The jury has a laudable function[47] to fulfill in the criminal justice system.
2. In order to fulfill this laudable function, the jury must be in a position to nullify.[48]
3. In order to best be in a position to nullify, the jury must receive a *nullification instruction*.[49]

therefore,

4. The jury must receive a *nullification instruction*.

I think premise i) is pretty much unassailable historically speaking.[50] However, as we shall see later in this chapter, there is some controversy regarding both premise ii) and iii).

---

[44] *U.S. v. Krzyske*, 836 F.2d 1013, 1021 (6th Cir. 1988).

[45] *Jurek v. State*, *supra* note 36, at 940 (emphasis added).

[46] See note 13.

[47] To act as a safeguard against government oppression or to give voice to community standards and democratic values.

[48] Resisting oppressive or undemocratic state action entails, for jurors, a refusal to be complicit in such oppression through their verdict – it entails, in other words, jury nullification.

[49] See note 13.

[50] See, for instance, *United States v. Gaudin*, 515 U.S. 506, 510-11 (1995) (citations omitted): "This right was designed to guard against a spirit of oppression and tyranny

I am not going to spend any more time explicating these three arguments, as they are all quite straightforward, and it seems clear that the jury, with its nullification *privilege,* can indeed accomplish the laudable goals attributed to it, at least in some instances. One thing worth noting, however, is that these arguments are all somewhat inter-related. For instance, what counts as merciful or just often depends on a particular community's standards. The same can be said regarding government oppression or democratic will. What one community's standards might identify as oppressive legislation might be considered wise and prudent according to the standards of a different community. Finally, as noted earlier, many of the extant examples of these arguments tend to conflate and confuse these various principles and virtues with one another. It is the scholar's task to try to lend conceptual clarity to these issues.

4.4 Is the Instruction Necessary?

While these do appear to be powerful arguments in favor of giving the *nullification instruction,* we can question to what degree, if any, the *nullification instruction* is actually required in order to achieve those ends. Certainly, the *nullification instruction* is *sufficient* for accomplishing such goals – that much seems clear – but, we might ask, is it *necessary* for accomplishing such goals? Perhaps all of the desired consequences of jury nullification can be realized without the jury being informed of its *privilege* to nullify. In fact, this is exactly the approach adopted by some opponents of the *nullification instruction*. We will next turn our attention to two such objections: the *damn-good-reason* objection, which questions the veracity and wisdom of premise iii): "in order to best be in a position to nullify, the jury must receive a *nullification instruction;*" and *contextualism,* which challenges the truth of premise ii): "in order to fulfill its laudable function, the jury must be in a position to nullify."

---

on the part of rulers, and was from very early times insisted on by our ancestors in the parent country, as the great bulwark of their civil and political liberties;" *Spaziano v. Florida,* 468 U.S. 447, 462 (1984): "We do not denigrate the significance of the jury's role as a link between the community and the penal system and as a bulwark between the accused and the State."

4.4.1 The Damn-Good-Reason Objection

This view – that the *nullification instruction* is unnecessary to achieve the benefits of jury nullification – is given particular voice in the *damn-good-reason* objection to the *nullification instruction*. This objection is discussed by Mortimer and Sanford Kadish in their book, *Discretion to Disobey*.[51] Kadish and Kadish acknowledge the jury's unreviewable power to nullify, and even go so far as to claim that such a power is a legitimate part of the jury system,[52] and in some cases ought to be praised:

> The jury's fundamental function is not only to guard against official departures from the rules of law, but on proper occasions themselves to depart from unjust rules or unjust applications.[53]

But, they continue, not all instances of jury nullification are praiseworthy. Kadish and Kadish emphasize that there is a principled distinction between a jury nullifying *at-will* and jury nullifying for a *damn-good-reason*.[54] So, what constitutes a *damn-good-reason* to nullify? While Kadish and Kadish admit that the line between nullifying *at-will* and for a *damn-good-reason* is by no means a clear one, they state that in order for a reason to be *damn-good* it must be consistent with the overall goals and values of the legal system. Conversely, *at-will* nullification would be, in a sense, inconsistent with, or contrary to, the overall goals and values of the legal system. And what might these goals be? According to Kadish and Kadish:

> [t]he rules of law have presumably been formatted to achieve justice. The jury liberty [to nullify] is extended because in some unknown and hence unstatable circumstances [the law] may [be unjust], and the determination of these circumstances is left at large to the jury.[55]

---

[51] Kadish, Sanford H. and Kadish, Mortimer R., *Discretion to Disobey: A Study of Lawful Departures from Legal Rules* (Stanford University Press, 1973).
[52] *Id.* at 67.
[53] *Id.* at 53-4.
[54] *Id.* at 62.
[55] *Id.* at 63. Note that Kadish and Kadish never say that a juror has a *right* to nullify given a *damn-good-reason*. Only that given such a reason, nullification must be seen as a legitimate exercise of the juror's role in the justice system.

In other words, a juror in a criminal trial may ignore the judge's otherwise obligatory instructions regarding the law, according to Kadish and Kadish, if and only if doing so is absolutely necessary for preserving the overall goals of the criminal justice system. For Kadish and Kadish, *damn-good-reason* nullification is, in this sense, a *legitimate* form of jury nullification – it is, on the whole, a positive influence *vis-à-vis* justice – whereas *at-will* nullification is an *illegitimate* form of jury nullification insofar as it promotes outcomes contrary to justice. We want a legal system, argue Kadish and Kadish, that preserves *damn-good-reason* nullification, while simultaneously screening out instances of *at-will* nullification.

By not giving the instruction, they continue, the justice system can ensure that jury nullification will only occur in those instances where jurors have a *damn-good-reason* for doing so. Instructing the jury that they must obey the law, imposes, in their words, an "extra surcharge"[56] on instances of nullification. This limits jury nullification to those instances of (perceived) great injustice where the jury is prepared, on the basis of conscience or a commitment to the principle of justice (at least as the jurors understand it), to override or ignore completely the judge's explicit instructions regarding the law.[57] We can count on jurors to nullify, according to Kadish and

[56] *Id.* at 65.

[57] There is one question we might ask of Kadish and Kadish's account of jury nullification: from whose perspective is a reason determined to be '*damn-good*?' Is the determination of what best serves the interest of justice and preserves the overall goals of the criminal justice system a subjective or objective one? Kadish and Kadish are willing to bite the bullet on this; they assert that juries who nullify in order to promote their own particularized (and some might argue, mistaken) view of justice nevertheless behave in a legitimate (but not necessarily commendable or desirable) manner. They discuss the example of an acquittal by a white southern jury of white defendants accused (and clearly guilty) of murdering blacks and civil rights workers. Is this, they ask, a legitimate example of jury nullification? "The answer, we think, has to be yes. One is entitled to say that the jury is egregiously wrong in its interpretation of the ends of its role, both institutional and background; that its ventured justification rests on premises that contravene the basic ethos of the Constitution and the legal system founded on it; even that it has violated the law insofar as one may regard policies and ends of this kind as part of the law, as we do. But… one cannot say that this jury has acted lawlessly, in the sense of usurping an authority it did not have, any more than one could say of a judge that he acted lawlessly when in good conscience he grossly misread the law." *id.* at 68-69. Although the jury, they continue, may occasionally "act in crass and damaging ignorance… the law has chosen to take that chance in the case of the jury." *id.* at 69.

Kadish, when there is a *damn-good-reason* to do so, even in the absence of any *nullification instruction*. Correlatively, they continue, we can also count on jurors to nullify in ways that occasionally conflict with the ends and goals of justice (*at-will* nullification) when the *nullification instruction* is given.[58] This then, is the claim that Kadish and Kadish are making: if jurors feel that they have a *damn-good-reason* to nullify, they will do so and nothing the trial judge does or does not say will affect this. The *nullification instruction*, in other words, is inefficacious as regards *damn-good-reason* jury nullification. In all other cases (that is, cases where, from the jury's perspective, a commitment to the overall goals of the legal system does not demand that it nullify), the judge's instructions will not conflict with the jury's conscience or commitment to justice. Thus, they conclude, there is no reason to instruct the jury on its nullification *privilege*.

There is some historical support for their reasoning. *Bushel's Case*,[59] the acquittals of those charged with breaking the *Fugitive Slave Act* in the nineteenth century,[60] and instances of jury nullification involving the prohibition laws of the early twentieth century,[61] all took place against the background of court procedures that made it clear that the jury was to take the law as given by the judge and decide only the facts. Yet in these examples the jury nevertheless asserted its *privilege* to nullify despite the absence of any instruction informing them of its existence. As one pair of scholars observed: "the Prohibition era provided the most intense example of jury revolt in recent history"[62] even in the absence of explicit *nullification instructions*. Correlatively, Kadish and Kadish express concern that if the instruction is given, this may encourage the jurors to return not guilty verdicts in those cases where a guilty verdict really wouldn't conflict with their understanding of what justice demands – instances of *at-will* nullification. Perhaps, we might say, Kadish and Kadish are concerned that

---

[58] See *id.* at 59-66, for a complete discussion of this view.

[59] *Bushel's Case*, (1670) 124 E.R. 1006.

[60] See, Scheflin, Alan W., *Jury Nullification: The Right to Say No*, 45, Southern California Law Review 168, 177 (1972).

[61] See, for instance, Conrad, *supra* note 28, at 109 for a further discussion of this history.

[62] Kalven, Harry and Zeisel, Hans, *The American Jury*, 291 (Little Brown Co., 1966).

giving the instruction encourages nullification in those cases where the jury has only a *pretty-good-reason* for doing so.

Kadish and Kadish here are worried that by giving the *nullification instruction* jurors will thereby be encouraged to *actively* enquire as to the justice of applying the facts as believed to the law as given. If jurors are actively searching for injustice, Kadish and Kadish explain, they may believe they find it where none actually exists. On the other hand, by not giving the instruction the court can ensure that the jury will nullify only in those cases where a guilty verdict would be so contrary and egregious to the jurors' sense of justice that they are forced to confront the issue. In other words, if the jurors receive no *nullification instruction,* and are instructed only to apply the law as given to the facts as believed, then the issue of whether the law is just simply will not enter into their decision-making calculus – except in those extremely rare cases where a strict application of the law would obviously and clearly result in a direct and fundamental assault on the jurors' sense of justice.

While Kadish and Kadish do not specifically state this, their worry about the increased cases of nullification appears to stem from a belief that jurors informed of their nullification *privilege* will acquit in cases where, for example, they have undue sympathy for the defendant. The received view is, of course, that considerations of sympathy, if they have any place in the legal system at all, are relevant only at the sentencing stage of the trial. They are not relevant to determinations of guilt. Because such considerations are taken account of at a different stage of the trial process (at the sentencing stage), there is no reason nor necessity for the jury to take account of them at the adjudicative stage. Such behavior on the part of the jury is, according to the received view, therefore unnecessary, unwarranted, and undesirable. Letting considerations of sympathy for the defendant influence determinations of responsibility and criminal culpability is, on this view, inconsistent with a core function of the criminal justice system. Rather, the jury is letting some external, extra-legal consideration – sympathy for the defendant, for example – influence its verdict. Thus, the issue for Kadish and Kadish can most accurately be put in the terms of how best to encourage (or at least allow for) legitimate *damn-good-reason* jury nullification while at the same time minimizing illegitimate *at-will* jury nullification. Their answer is to refrain from informing the jury of its nullification *privilege* altogether. To put this another way, when the *nullification instruction* is given, argue Kadish and Kadish, we don't necessarily achieve more instances of *damn-good-reason* jury nullification, but we do increase the likelihood of *at-will* jury nullification. This, state Kadish and Kadish, would invite the twin dangers of increasing the amount of arbitrary verdicts as well as "removing the criminal law still further from the control of the court and legislature."[63] One can see their logic: if it is true that the number of legitimate cases of jury nullification will not substantially increase regardless of whether the instruction is given, and it is also true that the number of overall cases of jury nullification will rise if the instruction is given, then those additional cases of jury nullification that result from the instruction must be, in some sense, illegitimate.

But do jurors actually behave the way that Kadish and Kadish assert? That is, can we expect jurors to behave in an irresponsible manner and return not guilty verdicts in circumstances that can neither be justified by the law nor by an appeal to some generally accepted sense of justice? The courts appear, at various times, to believe so. Judicial support for Kadish and Kadish's view can be found in the majority opinion of the *Dougherty* case,[64] where Leventhal, J., writing for the majority, ruled that the defendant's right to a fair trial had not been subverted by the trial judge's refusal to allow the jury to be informed of the doctrine of jury nullification. Moreover, Leventhal thought the very idea of the *nullification instruction* was inconsistent with sound jurisprudence. The nature of human reasoning, he argued, points to the danger of articulating the discretion to depart from a rule: "the breach will be more often and casually invoked,"[65] he reasoned. There is no place in the sound administration of justice, he continued, for such a casual and capricious approach to the consistent application of the law:

> There is reason to believe that the simultaneous achievement of modest jury equity and avoidance of intolerable caprice depends on

[63] Kadish and Kadish, *Discretion to Disobey, supra* note 51, at 65.
[64] *U. S. v. Dougherty, supra* note 7.
[65] *Id.* at 1135.

> formal instructions that do not expressly delineate a jury charter to carve out its own rules of law... The danger of the excess rigidity that may now occasionally exist is not as great as the danger of removing the boundaries of constraint provided by the announced rules.[66]

Besides, Leventhal continues, there is no reason to articulate to the jury their *privilege* to nullify. "The jury knows well enough that its prerogative is not limited to the choices articulated in the formal instructions of the court."[67] In other words, the instruction is unnecessary because jurors are already aware that they can nullify. And how do jurors come to have such knowledge if not through its explicit articulation in court? Apparently through "informal communication from the total culture — literature (novel, drama, film, and television); current comment (newspapers, magazines and television); conversation; and, of course, history and tradition."[68] Leventhal responds to the worry that by not explicitly informing the jury the court is thereby being duplicitous, stating that: "[t]he limitation to informal input is, rather a governor to avoid excess: the prerogative [to nullify] is reserved for the exceptional case, and the judge's instruction is retained as a generally effective constraint."[69] Thus, states Leventhal, the court is not attempting to deceive the jury when it refrains from giving the *nullification instruction*. Rather, the court is ensuring that the jury exercises this *privilege* in a responsible manner. Quoting Kadish and Kadish, Leventhal continues: "We recognize a constraint as obligatory upon us when we require not merely reason to defend our rule departures, but *damn good reason*."[70] Leventhal acknowledges that jurors who do not receive the *nullification instruction* may feel compelled to the point of rigidity to convict despite being convinced that to do so would be unjust. However, he suggests that in such cases a juror may convict with a clear conscience by reasoning that it is not "he who fashions the rule that

[66] *Id.* at 1134-35 (emphasis added).

[67] *Id.* at 1135.

[68] *Id.*

[69] *Id.*

[70] *Id.* (citation omitted).

condemns," and that "he was merely following the reasoning of the court."[71]

It is important to note that Leventhal does not condemn outright all instances of nullification, and even goes so far as to claim that "the pages of history shine on instances of the jury's prerogative to disregard uncontradicted evidence and instructions of the judge."[72] However, he states, "[w]hat makes for health as an occasional medicine would be disastrous as a daily diet."[73] The point that Leventhal is trying to make is the same one that Kadish and Kadish argue for: that by not giving the *nullification instruction,* the threshold is set sufficiently high to ensure that juries will only nullify in those cases where a conviction would be, while strictly speaking legally warranted, nevertheless an egregious miscarriage of justice, a violation of community values, and/or unconscionably cruel (at least from the perspective of the jurors). Leventhal sums up his argument this way:

> [I]t is pragmatically useful to structure instructions in such wise that the jury must feel strongly about the values involved in the case, so strongly that it must identify the case as establishing a call of high conscience, and must independently initiate and undertake an act in contravention of the established instructions. This requirement of independent jury conception confines the happenings of the lawless jury to the occasional instance that does not violate, and viewed as an exception may even enhance, the overall normative effect of the rule of law. *An explicit instruction to the jury conveys an implied approval that runs the risk of degrading the legal structure requisite for true freedom, for an ordered liberty that protects against anarchy as well as tyranny.*[74]

As initially appealing as the *damn-good-reason* objection to the *nullification instruction* might appear, however, it ultimately fails to be convincing. Bazelon C.J., writing in dissent in the *Dougherty* case, took specific issue with the majority's reliance on the *damn-good-reason* objection, stating that

[71] *Id.* at 1136.
[72] *Id.* at 1130.
[73] *Id.* at 1136.
[74] *Id.* at 1136-7 (emphasis added).

"I see no justification for, and considerable harm in, this deliberate lack of candor."[75] He offered two arguments in support of his rejection of the majority opinion.

To begin with, Bazelon invites us to inquire as to why it is that the more knowledgeable jurors become the less likely we should be confident that they will behave in a conscientious and responsible manner. That is, after all, one of the key assertions of the *damn-good-reason* objection – that fully informed jurors cannot be trusted to act responsibly, or at least not as responsibly as jurors not so informed. The majority opinion, Bazelon states, holds that "the spontaneous and unsolicited act of nullification is thought less likely, on the whole, to reflect bias and a perverse sense of values than the act of nullification carried out by a jury carefully instructed on its power and responsibility."[76] Is not the opposite more likely, he opines. Ought not we to expect that a properly informed jury will behave in a consistent and responsible manner? There is no reason to assume, continues Bazelon, that jurors who are given the *nullification instruction* will make rampantly abusive use of this *privilege*. "Trust in the jury is, after all, one of the cornerstones of our criminal jurisprudence, and if that trust is without foundation, we must re-examine a great deal more than just the nullification doctrine."[77]

Bazelon is attacking the central premises of the *damn-good-reason* objection: that not only will the jury nullify more often if the *nullification instruction* is given, but that it will nullify more often *and in less desirable ways* (i.e., acquittals motivated by racism, undue sympathy for the defendant, and so forth) if the instruction is given. This is an interesting objection inasmuch as it turns the *damn-good-reason* objection on its head. Bazelon is suggesting that it is a *non-sequitur* to reason from more instances of jury nullification to more instances of illegitimate jury nullification. Where is the evidence for such an assumption, he demands. As Bazelon points out, commonsense dictates that jurors would be very reluctant to free someone back into their community who was, for instance, clearly guilty of a violent criminal act. Considerations such as these, he continues, act as internal checks and

[75] *Id.* at 1139.
[76] *Id.* at 1141.
[77] *Id.* at 1142.

balances against a jury's possibly over-enthusiastic embrace of their nullification *privilege*:

> As for the problem of unjust acquittal, it is important to recognize the strong internal check that constrains the jury's willingness to acquit. Where defendants seem dangerous, juries are unlikely to exercise their nullification power, whether or not an explicit instruction is offered. Of course, that check will not prevent the acquittal of a defendant who may be blameworthy and dangerous except in the jaundiced eyes of a jury motivated by a perverse and sectarian sense of values. But whether a nullification instruction would make such acquittals more common is problematical, if not entirely inconceivable. In any case, the real problem in this situation is not the nullification doctrine, but the values and prejudice that prompt the acquittal.[78]

Bazelon concludes that the key premise to the *damn-good-reason* objection – that the *nullification instruction* would thereby result in an increase in illegitimate acquittals – remains unproven, unmotivated, and, importantly, contrary to common-sense.[79]

Moreover, though Bazelon makes no mention of this,[80] there is some empirical evidence to suggest that he is correct in his claim that jurors familiar with the doctrine of nullification *do not* behave the rather capricious way that Justice Leventhal and the Kadishs suggest. A 1974 Yale Law Journal survey of the literature surrounding this issue addressed both Judge Leventhal's and Chief Justice Bazelon's decisions in the *Dougherty* case and concluded:

> Social psychological research indicates that the internal checks referred to by Chief Judge Bazelon are very real and that, even where he knows of his power of nullification, a juror has a strong

---

[78] *Id.* at 1143.

[79] Of course, one is free to ask whether giving the instruction would increase the likelihood of illegitimate or unjust *convictions*. However, this is a topic I will turn to towards the end of the next chapter.

[80] Most like because this information was published two years *after* the *Dougherty* case.

> psychological need to see the case settled according to his sense of equity. This need should act as a restraint on the juror's feelings of sympathy for the defendant. In light of a judge's probable influence as an authority figure on the way jurors perceive their own roles, an instruction which informed the jury of its power of nullification but at the same time conveyed the legal system's expectation that it follow the general law in reaching its verdict would likely retain the necessary tension in the jury's role.[81]

Scheflin and Van Dyke sum up this view in the following manner:

> We feel that logic, common sense, and the available evidence support the conclusion that a carefully drafted instruction informing the jury of its nullification power would not produce unjust acquittals or increase the likelihood of departures from the law except in rare situations justifying departures. The burden now falls on nullification opponents to demonstrate that their fears [regarding giving the *nullification instruction*] are justified.[82]

Bazelon also provides a second, and even stronger argument against Leventhal's objection to the *nullification instruction*. Leventhal, he argues, is engaged in reasoning that is internally inconsistent: he is simultaneously condemning and praising the idea of an informed jury. Bazelon's objection is clear, concise, and to the point, and his reasoning is lucid and persuasive; rather than paraphrase what he says, therefore, I will let his words speak for themselves:

> [I]f it were true that nullification which arises out of ignorance is in some sense more worthy than nullification which arises out of knowledge, the Court would have to go much further. For under the Court's assumption, the harm does not arise because a jury is *told* of its power to disregard the law, but because it *knows* of its power.

---

[81] *Note: Toward Principles of Jury Equity,* 83 Yale Law Journal 1023, 1051-52 (1974), as quoted in Scheflin, Alan W. and Van Dyke, Jon M. *Jury Nullification: The Contours of a Controversy,* 43 Law & Contemp. Probs. 51, 104 (1980).

[82] Scheflin, Alan W. and Van Dyke, Jon M. *Jury Nullification: The Contours of a Controversy, id.* at 105.

> Logically construed, the Court's opinion would seem to require the disqualification at *voir dire* of any prospective juror who admitted to knowledge of the doctrine. By excluding jurors with knowledge of the doctrine the Court could ensure that its invocation would be spontaneous. And yet, far from requiring the exclusion of jurors who are aware of the power, the Court takes comfort in the fact that informal communication to the jury "generally conveys adequately enough the idea of prerogative, of freedom in an occasional case to depart from what the judge says." One cannot, it seems to me, have the argument both ways. If, as the Court appears to concede, awareness is preferable to ignorance, then I simply do not understand the justification for relying on a haphazard process of informal communication whose effectiveness is likely to depend, to a large extent, on whether or not any of the jurors are so well-educated and astute that they are able to receive the message. *If the jury should know of its power to disregard the law, then the power should be explicitly described by instruction of the court or argument of counsel.*[83]

If knowledge of jury nullification is to be praised as a means for jurors to best fulfill their laudable role within the criminal justice system in those rare cases where the strict application of the law to the facts would result in a material injustice, it seems odd, if not entirely inconsistent, challenges Bazelon, to simultaneously condemn the means for acquiring that knowledge.

To summarize: I think it is fair to say that the *damn-good-reason* objection fails to adequately indict the advisability of giving the *nullification instruction*. While it is perhaps true, as Kadish and Kadish, as well as the Court in *Dougherty* assert, that some, if not all of the benefits of nullification could be realized in the absence of the instruction, there is little reason to believe that the negative consequences of giving the instruction proposed by this objection would actually manifest themselves. Indeed, Bazelon argues persuasively that the opposite is true. Mind you, this is not to say that there are no negative consequences whatsoever to giving the instruction – only that those negative consequences as proposed by the

[83] *Id.* at 1141 (emphasis added).

damn-good-reason objection (so-called *at-will* nullification or unwarranted acquittals) remain unproven. Thus, while the *damn-good-reason* objection may raise the question of the *necessity* of the *nullification instruction* for achieving the desired ends that the proponents of the instruction attribute to it, this objection does little to impeach the *sufficiency* of the instruction for achieving such ends. Thus, we might ask, if giving the instruction is an efficient means to a worthy end, should it not be given?

4.4.2 Contextualism

Norman Finkel, professor of psychology, suggests a negative answer to the above question. Whereas the *damn-good-reason* objection states that the instruction is unnecessary because juries will nullify without it, Finkel claims instead that the instruction is unnecessary (and therefore, inefficacious) because juries do not, in fact, actually nullify all that often. Finkel acknowledges that all of the proposed benefits attributed to nullification do, in fact, manifest within the jury system. However, he continues, these positive consequences arise, not from juries *nullifying* when some deeply held principle(s) conflicts with and trumps strict fealty to the letter of the law. Rather, the positive and advantageous effects of the jury system exist, argues Finkel, because juries genuinely believe, in cases where a guilty verdict would clash with such deeply held principles, and despite what may seem to outside observers as near-irrefutable proof to the contrary, that the defendant is, in fact, legitimately not legally guilty. This is a view he refers to as *contextualism*. The upshot is that Finkel rejects premise ii) of the above arguments: "In order to fulfill its laudable functions, the jury must be in a position to nullify." Juries accomplish these ends through almost exclusively non-nullificatory means, he asserts; thus, there is no need for a *nullification instruction*.

Finkel, in *Common Sense Justice: Jurors' Notions of the Law*,[84] examined jury behavior in a wide range of issues (including euthanasia, insanity cases, capital punishment, self-defense, and crimes of passion) making use of social-psychological experiments involving mock juries. His goal in undertaking this research was to understand the jury decision making

[84] *Harvard University Press*, 1995.

process, particularly in cases involving rather notorious and unexpected verdicts. His theory of *contextualism,* he claims, explains jury behavior which, from an external perspective, otherwise appears irrational or unmotivated. Finkel asserts that at heart juries rely on their commonsense notions of morality and justice to render verdicts, and for the most part do not really take the law into account when deliberating. He begins his analysis of jury behavior by noting that the ambiguity of both the legal standards that need to be applied, and the factual questions that need to be resolved at trial give jurors substantial discretion to bring in their own underlying values of justice to the verdict:

> In today's parlance, jurors facing conflicting evidence are said to grope for the "story line" that is most plausible; but since there are plenty of stories to go around, they are able within limits to select to the story which points to the most satisfying verdict. This is all the more the case since jurors often must look for *mens rea,* criminal intent, in addition to figuring out who did what. In short, jurors can have their cake and eat it too – heeding [their understanding of the] judicial instructions about sticking to the law and the evidence, while simultaneously responding to their instincts.[85]

For Finkel, therefore, the jury's behavior is best described as involving a search, not for *legal* culpability, but for *moral* culpability, with its associated concept of blameworthiness.[86] To illustrate this idea, Finkel gave mock jurors a range of insanity defense cases involving, at one end of the spectrum, such organic disorders as epilepsy, and, at the other end, disorders classified as more psychological in nature, such as stress and anxiety disorders. Jurors were then given one of six alternative legal instructions defining insanity, including the *Wild Beast* test, the *M'Naghten* rule, and instructions from the Federal Insanity Defense Reform Act.[87]

---

[85] Levine, James, *Review Essay/Jury Wisdom,* 8 Crim. Just. Ethics 49 (1997).

[86] *Id.*

[87] The *Wild Beast* test states that a person is legally insane if he was "totally deprived of his understanding and memory, and doth not know what he is doing, no more . . . than a brute, or a wild beast." *Rex v. Arnold,* 16 How. St. Tr. 695, 764–65 (1724). The *M'Naghten* test states that: "the test of insanity… is whether the defendant knew the nature and quality of his actions at the crucial time. In the alternative, the test requires that the defendant be able to distinguish right from wrong." *State v. Hudson,* 152 Ariz.

According to Finkel, while there was a wide variety of verdicts based on the nature of the cases, differences in what insanity test the jurors were told to use made almost no difference at all in the verdicts returned. His conclusion: the jurors used their commonsense notion of justice and responsibility in trying to sort the 'bad from the mad.' They distinguished between those who actually possessed self-control and who thereby deserved to be held accountable for their actions, and those who were truly unable to control themselves and thereby deserved leniency. Legal distinctions between these two categories that did not comport with the jurors' sense of justice and responsibility were simply not applied, Finkel states. Finkel ran similar tests with mock juries involving self-defense claims. Despite the fact that the law requires an objective test to determine whether a forceful response to a perceived threat was reasonable, the mock jurors tended to bring the moral integrity of both the victim and the defendant claiming self-defense into account when judging whether the force was reasonable. That is, particularly virtuous defendants accused of assaulting particularly disreputable victims were far more likely to be given the benefit of the doubt that their actions were, in fact, legally justified.

Contextualism, for Finkel, can therefore best be described as this tendency for jurors to look to the moral context in which an alleged crime occurred when deciding issues of culpability. The jurors' views of alleged criminal conduct, claims Finkel, encompasses many more elements than a strict reading of the law would allow; jurors are concerned with reaching verdicts that correspond with their idea of justice and thus tend to put the case in a larger perspective. The jury, using this *commonsense* notion of justice, continues Finkel, thereby takes into account many factors that the law considers irrelevant to the issue of guilt or innocence:

> Across a number of venues, the paths of law and commonsense justice diverge, sometimes rather sharply. One reason for the

---

121, 125 (Ariz. 1986). Finally, the Federal Insanity Defense Reform Act of 1984,18 U.S.C. § 4241 states that a defendant must prove, by "clear and convincing evidence," that "at the time of the commission of the acts constituting the offense, the defendant, as a result of a severe mental disease or defect, was unable to appreciate the nature and quality or the wrongfulness of his acts."

> divergence is *context*. At times, citizens seem to frame cases in a way that differs from the law's, thereby seeing a different "picture" of what the case is about and of the relevant factors to be included or excluded. An easy generalization, albeit an overgeneralization, is this: the commonsense context is typically *wider* than the law's... The commonsense context, like a motion picture, conveys actions before, during, and even after the moment of the act.[88]

Considering the importance Finkel places on the concept of commonsense justice in jury deliberations, it is fair to inquire as to what exactly he believes this term refers to. In fact, he uses the term in two different, but related, ways.[89] On the one hand, Finkel takes 'commonsense justice' to be grounded in the word 'common,' as in the judgment of the common people – the community taken as a whole, as it were. This, claims Finkel, is one of the great strengths of the jury: it is the conscience of the community, engaging in sound practical judgement, that acquits or convicts:

> Juries thus infuse a decidedly populist element into the judicial process. They are a font of commonsense in both senses implied by the term: they are "down-to-earth" and they are representative of the social ethos. The moral knowledge that guides us in everyday life is the stuff out of which sound verdicts are made.[90]

Just like the proponents of jury nullification discussed above, Finkel views this populist element in the jury system to be a very positive thing. It tempers the sometimes-abstract application of the law with justice, compassion, community mores, and it situates claims of responsibility with their concomitant implications for punishment within the wider context in which such actions occurred. While the law treats the hitman for hire as equally deserving of punishment as the parent who tracks down and kills their child's rapist, many of us might feel that there are (or ought to be) legally relevant distinctions between the two cases. For Finkel, one of the great advantages of the jury system is that it allows the criminal law, in its

---

[88] *Supra* note 84, at 319.

[89] See Levine, *supra* note 85, at 51-52 for a detailed discussion of this point.

[90] *Supra* note 84, at 52.

administration, to reflect the community's commonsense notion of justice in exactly these sorts of cases.

More to the point, however, Finkel uses 'commonsense justice' to refer the idea that issues of criminal culpability should be based on the specific moral dimensions of concrete situations rather than on attempts to apply somewhat abstract principles of right and wrong to unique and specific cases:

> [T]he broad-based taxonomies of the law are simply too clumsy to make the minute distinctions which must be the basis for ascertaining appropriate commensurate deserts. In contrast, the fine-grained and nuanced decision-making of jurors is tailor-made to assay degrees of moral infirmity.[91]

Jurors, according to Finkel, size up the nuanced fact constellations of subjective motives and objective facts emerging from the trial process in order to figure out just how bad a defendant's conduct really was and therefore the extent to which punishment is warranted. The jurors' scope of what is and is not legally relevant *vis-à-vis* culpability is, therefore, both wider and more subtle than the law's. Jury verdicts, for Finkel, are ultimately moral judgments. It is therefore not jury nullification that jurors rely on and employ when returning seemingly merciful verdicts, according to Finkel. Rather, jurors use their commonsense notion of justice and moral culpability – *contextualism* – when reaching such verdicts. From the jurors' perspective, states Finkel, justice demands a fine-grained examination of the particulars of each case, and the moral status of the parties involved in the case is one of the relevant particulars to be examined. As evidence that jurors view justice as demanding fine-grained moral evaluations, Finkel points to the issue of capital punishment. Whereas polls indicate that the majority of Americans are in favor of the death penalty,[92] juries impose this punishment rather infrequently, reserving this most severe of punishments for the worst offenders and the most heinous of crimes. Even in situations and contexts where a strict and literal application of the law may not allow

---

[91] *Id.* at 51.

[92] Pew Research Center, Report: *Most Americans Favor the Death Penalty Despite Concerns About Its Administration* (June 2021).

it, juries want the punishment to fit the moral, as well as legal, contours of the crime, concludes Finkel.

At this point, we might well begin to wonder whether *contextualism* is simply a different way of talking about jury nullification. Are these not just two ways of describing the same phenomenon? According to Finkel, his experiments with mock juries reveal that outright jury nullification – in the sense of jurors acquitting those they truly believe to be legally guilty – is an extremely rare occurrence. What jurors are doing when reaching otherwise legally problematic verdicts, asserts Finkel, is *construing* the law as they see fit.[93] Again and again, Finkel states, the mock jurors explained their verdicts by reference to what they took to be legally germane aspects of the cases they adjudicated. Jurors who wished to acquit, in other words, did not ignore the judge's instructions regarding the law. Rather, says Finkel, they took a merciful view of the facts, and interpreted the judge's instructions in a charitable fashion. That is, when jurors believed that justice demanded an acquittal, they resolved ambiguities in the law and uncertainties in the evidence in the direction of leniency. Nevertheless, states Finkel, the jurors who acted in such a manner took themselves to be behaving in a way *consistent with*, and not *contrary to*, their oath and the judge's instructions regarding the law:

> CSJ [commonsense justice] typically reaches for more ingredients than the Law… Even when both the Law and CSJ agree about the ingredients, CSJ's approach to weights and measures is decidedly unformulaic: instead of using simple and invariant rules, CSJ's method is richly interactive and highly contextual… Even if the Law and CSJ agree about the ingredients, and agree about their respective weights, jurors are likely to flavor, combine, and cook them in more subjective and psychological ways, throwing in past experiences, intuitions, sentiments, biases, heuristics, construals, and prototypes.[94]

---

[93] *Supra* note 84, at 51.

[94] *Id.* at 33.

In his critical notice of Finkel's book,[95] James Levine expands upon this view. He points to the example of the Michigan jurors who on three separate occasions acquitted Dr. Jack Kevorkian of murder. In explaining their verdict after the fact, some jurors argued that Kevorkian connected the patients to his 'suicide machine' with the intention of alleviating their pain rather than causing their death. The necessary criminal intent to support a murder conviction was therefore lacking.[96]

> To outsiders this may sound illogical and even preposterous, but the jurors to a person claimed to be acting within the law. It is impossible to disprove [that they did not genuinely believe this].[97]

Finkel's research has led Levine to conclude it will "have a dampening effect on the seething debates about jury nullification raging in both popular and legal circles… [J]ury nullification is a tempest in a teapot."[98] Perhaps this is overstating the case somewhat! Nevertheless, if Finkel is right about how juries actually reach their verdicts – and given his impressive compilation of empirical evidence there is no reason to believe that he is not – it is easy to see how one might reach the conclusion that much of the debate regarding jury nullification is therefore somewhat otiose. Nullification is, after all, intentional behavior: the jury reaches a certain conclusion regarding a set of factual questions, and is aware that, strictly speaking, the law demands a guilty verdict given such a factual conclusion, and yet decides to acquit. A *contextualizing* jury, on the other hand, believes that it is operating within the bounds of the law when it is acting in way that appears, from the outside, as overly merciful, if not outright nullificatory – the jury genuinely believes that the defendant's conduct was, in fact, legally permissible; the extra-legal nature of its deliberative process was, therefore, unintentional. Finkel and Levine's point: the jury's behavior in these *contextualized* verdicts simply does not count as nullification; there is no intent to reject the law.

---

[95] Levine, *supra* note 85, at 49-56.

[96] *Id.* at 52.

[97] *Id.*

[98] *Id.* at 52-3.

So, what does this distinction imply for the debate about the *nullification instruction*? Again, if Finkel's research is to be believed then one might well argue that the *nullification instruction* is unnecessary and irrelevant: juries don't nullify (or do so with such infrequency as to be, for all intents and purposes, negligible), so why inform them of the *privilege*? Proponents of the *nullification instruction* argue that it promotes justice and community values into the application of the criminal law. But since in the overwhelming number of cases where these values actually come into conflict with the strict application of the law, jurors promote them in a way that can almost be described as intellectually unreflective, there does not seem to be any need to give the instruction, according to Finkel. While a nullifying and *contextualizing* jury behave in extensionally equivalent manners, it is this unconscious aspect of the jury's behavior in the latter case that is, from Finkel's perspective, most relevant. For Finkel, since a *contextualizing* jury is, strictly speaking, already going beyond its defined legal purview and tempering the literal application of the law with an extended (and extra-legal) sense of justice and mercy, but is doing so unconsciously, there is simply no point to explicitly informing them that such behavior is allowed.[99] How would such an instruction be efficacious? Proponents of the *nullification instruction* will still get what they want – justice, mercy, the promotion of community values, a watchdog on government oppression – without the instruction being given, while any of the real or imagined dangers of giving the instruction will thereby be avoided.[100] Since the only reason to give the instruction is to promote jury nullification, and since the only reason to promote jury nullification is to promote those values, the instruction is simply unwarranted given that these values already are being promoted and given voice within the jury system through the jury's *contextualized* sense of commonsense justice. Finkel offers his descriptive analysis of the jury's commonsense reasoning as a justification, therefore, for rejecting the *nullification instruction*.

While the preceding line of reasoning does initially have the ring of cogency to it, under closer scrutiny it becomes clear that it actually fails to

---

[99] There is, after all, a certain psychoemotional contradiction in asking or encouraging jurors to intentionally adopt unconscious behavior and/or motivations.

[100] See Finkel, *supra* note 84, at 19 for his discussion of some of the potential dangers of a *nullification instruction*.

address the issue of jury nullification whatsoever. To begin with, to claim that jury nullification does not actually occur very often is beside the point. The fact of the matter is, jury nullification can and sometimes does occur, and this possibility is entrenched into the very structure of the criminal jury system. Thus, the real question is, and always has been: given that juries have the *privilege* to nullify, ought they to be informed of this fact? And this question simply cannot be answered by replying that juries don't actually make use of this *privilege* all that often.

Let us assume, for the sake of argument, that Finkel's data and the conclusions he draws from it are accurate. It follows, therefore, that the supposed benefits of jury nullification – justice, community values, etc. – will be instantiated in the *contextualized* commonsense justice embedded within the jury system, and a great deal more often than they would be if these values could only be given voice through an actively nullifying jury. But what does this prove? Simply that jury nullification is not *necessary* for these values to be given voice – that jury nullification is not the only way to temper the strict application of the law with mercy, justice, community values, etc. Of course, nullification is still a *sufficient* way for these values to be instantiated in the law through the jury system, even if Finkel is correct that such behavior is quite rare. Moreover, we have to assume that tempering the law with mercy and justice is, in fact, a good and desirable thing, all things being equal. Presumably we should want to maximize opportunities for this.

4.5 The Best of Both Worlds

Rather than condemn the *nullification instruction* outright on the grounds that it is unnecessary, I think a better, and less controversial route would be to first acknowledge that a criminal justice system that favors some generally accepted principles of justice over a strict application of explicitly promulgated laws when the two come into conflict is normatively superior and more desirable than one that does not. It seems reasonable to conclude that in our courts we want more justice, not less. If jury nullification and *contextualism* both accomplish the same ends, and those ends are desirable on the whole, then why not have both? While nullification may not be necessary for making the application of the criminal law more just (or more merciful, or less oppressive, etc.), it is certainly sufficient for doing so. Moreover, it is a very efficient way of doing so – at least according to the proponents of the *nullification instruction*. Thus, if we allowed for the *nullification instruction*, we would have two ways to promote justice in the application of the criminal law through the jury: one, *contextualism* – the result of purely unreflective behavior; the other, jury nullification – the result of purely intentional behavior. One could easily imagine a proponent of the *nullification instruction* arguing that this would thereby maximize the jury's ability to prevent miscarriages of justice. This would be, in a sense, the best of both worlds. While we can hope that the jury's commonsense, *contextualized* sense of justice would catch and prevent all or most miscarriages of justice, the *nullification instruction* would alert them to their *privilege* to do so for those (perhaps few) cases that might otherwise slip through.[101]

This response gets to the heart of what *contextualism* actually implies *vis-à-vis* the *nullification instruction* – very little. Let us assume once more that Finkel is correct about how juries reason. On the one hand, an opponent of the *nullification instruction* is not free to argue that the jury is behaving in an undesirable and unjustifiable manner when it reasons *contextually*, as this would be an indictment of the entire jury system itself. If the jury cannot help but behave in such a manner – if it does so in a morally instinctive and intellectually unreflective fashion – and such behavior has no place in the criminal justice system, then the jury itself has no place in the criminal justice system. Presumably, however, if one felt that the institution of trial by jury had no place in the criminal justice system, one would not have much of an opinion one way or the other regarding the *nullification instruction*. On the other hand, if one is of the opinion that a jury that reasons *contextually* is often behaving in a desirable and morally permissible manner, then this is tacit acknowledgment that the aims of such a jury – to prevent miscarriages of justice where the law does not, for instance – are worthy aims. And if one reaches that conclusion, then it would appear to be but a small step in reasoning to conclude that a

[101] While it may be possible for there to be too many checks and balances on government overreach, two does not seem, in this instance, to be unduly excessive or burdensome.

nullifying jury that accomplishes the same goals is also behaving in a desirable and morally permissible manner. It would therefore be somewhat *ad hoc* to endorse *contextualism* while simultaneously rejecting the *nullification instruction*, as both are committed to achieving the same ends.

4.6 Associated Negative Consequences?

Perhaps one way to avoid this charge of arbitrariness would be to point out that there are dangers associated with jury nullification and the *nullification instruction* that are simply not associated with *contextualism*.[102] This might at first glance appear to be a difficult argument to make, as it would seem that since the two types of behavior are extensionally equivalent then whatever dangers are associated with one would more than likely be associated with the other. There are differences between the two phenomena, however: one is intentional behavior and the other is unconscious behavior. Since jury nullification and *contextualism* are both, for the most part, not really the sort of behavior that can be actively prevented, then, if there are negative consequences associated with either of them, one might easily conclude that, at the very least, such behavior ought not to be actively promoted. And since jury nullification, as intentional behavior, is the only one of the two that can be actively promoted[103] (through the *nullification instruction*), this would thereby give an opponent of the *nullification instruction* good grounds for objecting to it. One could grant to the proponents of the instruction that the aims of nullification are worthy, but then point out that these aims can be met in other, potentially safer, and less capricious ways. One could then further argue that since jury nullification has some associated negative consequences, any move to promote jury nullification would thereby be a move to concomitantly promote those associated negative consequences. Given that the positive goals associated with jury nullification can be met in other ways, we might therefore conclude that the *nullification instruction* ought not to be given. However, and this is important, some reason or evidence must be given that jury nullification does, indeed, have associated

[102] Finkel, for instance, is particularly worried about instances of what he calls "vengeful nullification" if jurors were to be instructed on jury nullification. *supra* note 84, at 33.

[103] See note 99.

negative consequences or somehow invites unjust verdicts; otherwise, this line of reasoning is simply and entirely unmotivated.

As we saw with the *damn-good-reason* objection, and with Finkel's theory of *contextualism*, the crux of these objections to the *nullification instruction* is that it is not necessary for realizing the jury's good consequences, and that giving it has potentially bad consequences – instances of *at-will* nullification,[104] for instance, or perhaps *vengeful-nullification*.[105] Let us grant the first point, that the instruction is not necessary to generate the positive consequences its proponents attribute to jury nullification. As was mentioned above, this is hardly much of a complaint: it doesn't have to be necessary. So long as it is sufficient for generating such consequences, that is a point in its favor. The other point, that nullification has some bad consequences attached to it, is a promising approach, but both of the objections examined above do not go far enough with it. They both imply that there are negative consequences to the practice, but do so in rather vague, speculative, and unspecific manners, and little evidence is given to support such claims. In the next chapter, we will therefore focus on this issue: what are the negative consequences attributed to jury nullification and the *nullification instruction*, and what evidence is provided to support such claims?

Appendix: Butler's Model of Racially Based Jury Nullification

Paul Butler, in *Racially Based Jury Nullification: Black Power in the Criminal Justice System*,[106] defends a compelling yet controversial model of jury nullification as, in part, a *self-help remedy* for those communities victimized by a racist legal system. However, since Butler is not advocating for a *nullification instruction*, but rather extrajudicial forms of community-based *nullification education*, it seems most appropriate to discuss his view in this appendix. Accordingly, I intend to acknowledge Butler's importance to the current jury nullification debate by providing here a brief exegesis of his project. Given that I am engaged with confronting the jurisprudential

[104] See note 54.

[105] See note 102.

[106] Butler, Paul, *Racially Based Jury Nullification: Black Power in the Criminal Justice System*, 105 Yale Law Journal 677 (1995).

nature of jury nullification as it operates *within* the justice system, however, I will reserve any in-depth critical analysis of Butler's project here; his project is tangential to mine. Regardless, many of the issues raised by Butler's analysis and defense of jury nullification will come into play in the next chapter; to that end, it is both worthwhile and edifying to examine his model for racially based jury nullification.

Butler's primary concern is to demonstrate how the African-American community can affect positive change to an otherwise racist criminal justice system through the use of their nullificatory power within that system as jurors. While he admits that his goal is, in a sense, the subversion of the criminal justice system as it now stands, his project is ultimately constructive – advocating for, in part, restorative, community-based responses to antisocial conduct.[107] Importantly, and like all 'remedies,' Butler's prescription (racially based jury nullification) is designed to expire when the malady (racially harmful outcomes within the criminal justice system) is 'cured:' "In an ideal world, whether the victim is rich or poor or black or white would be irrelevant to adjudication of the defendant's culpability."[108]

Of course, it is not an ideal world, and as Butler argues, one place this imperfection shows up vividly is in how the criminal justice system responds to crime within the African-American community. Despite our normative ideals for the law, Butler argues that the race of a black defendant does, in fact, play a role in the outcome of a trial, and the consequences of such have been devastating to the African-American community.[109] The legal system betrays such defendants, and the African-American community at large, by failing to openly address this relationship between crime and race.[110] Antisocial behavior within the African-American community is, states Butler, often a consequence of, and reaction to, oppression. Instead of seeking to eliminate or reduce the social

---

[107] *Id.* at 608.

[108] *Id.* at 721.

[109] *Id.* at 719 "African-Americans make up 13% of the nation's regular drug users, but they account for 35% of narcotics arrests, 55% of drug convictions, and 74% of those receiving prison sentences."

[110] *Id.* at 686: "...the reality [is] that race matters, in general and in jury adjudications of guilt or innocence."

factors that function so as to promote such conduct, the law adopts a punitive, retributivist approach to criminal conduct among African-Americans: "The law uses punishment to treat social problems that are the result of racism and that should be addressed by other means such as medical care or the redistribution of wealth."[111] Given that the law, in its outcomes, treats race as a legally relevant factor, Butler argues that "the race of a black defendant is sometimes a legally and morally appropriate factor for jurors to consider in reaching a verdict of not guilty."[112]

It is very important to understand exactly what Butler is advocating for. His is not a knee-jerk reaction to the perceived failings of the justice system – he is not, for instance, suggesting that black jurors always or even often nullify the verdicts for every guilty African-American defendant. Rather, he carves out a very narrow model of *justified,* or *morally-permissible,* jury nullification for the African-American community to engage in through their capacity as jurors. This last qualification is important. Jury nullification already occurs within the African-American community, asserts Butler, but it does so in a sometimes capricious, *ad hoc,* and potentially harmful manner.[113] Butler's aim is, at least in part, to sketch a prolegomena for the *principled* use of jury nullification with the expressed end of resisting and/or ameliorating the harmful effects of the criminal justice system on the African-American community.[114] Black jurors must ask themselves, states Butler, "whether the operation of the criminal law in the United States advances the interests of black people. If it does not, the doctrine of jury nullification affords African-American jurors the opportunity to control the authority of the law over some African-

---

[111] *Id.* at 709.

[112] *Id.* at 679.

[113] *Id.* at 723: "Black jurors are already nullifying on the basis of race because they do not want to send another black man to prison… It appears that some black jurors now excuse some conduct – like murder – that they should not excuse."

[114] *Id.* "My proposal… provides a principled structure for the exercise of the black juror's vote."

American criminal defendants."[115] It is, for Butler, a simple cost/benefit analysis of justice.[116]

As an actual strategy or practice, Butler offers the following parameters for principled, morally justified implementation: For nonviolent, yet *malum in se*[117] offenses, such as theft or perjury, black jurors should be sensitive to the possibility of nullification, but not necessarily predisposed in favor of it. There is, presumably, some social value to punishing such behavior, though, of course, also some concomitant social costs. The particulars of the offense and associated circumstances should guide the jurors in such cases. For nonviolent 'victimless' crimes (Butler includes narcotics offenses under this description),[118] on the other hand, black jurors should be predisposed to favor nullification.[119] Again, though, the particulars of the offense and associated circumstances should guide the jurors in such cases. In every case, continues Butler, jurors need to be guided by their particularized sense of what is 'just,' specifically as this concept applies to the interests of the African-American community.[120] This is the "principled basis"[121] upon which his defense of racially based jury nullification is predicated.

Butler is well aware of the potential for controversy that his proposal engenders. Certainly, some will object to the very idea of using a defendant's race as a means of determining legal culpability. On the surface, such a proposal might seem antithetical to our fundamental

---

[115] *Id.* at 714.

[116] *Id.* at 698: "But what about when locking up a black man has no or little net effect on public safety, when, for example, the crime with which he was charged is victimless? Putting aside for a moment the legal implications, couldn't an analysis of the costs and benefits to the African-American community present an argument against incarceration? I argue "yes," in light of the substantial costs to the community of law enforcement."

[117] Latin: "Wrong or evil in itself."

[118] While Butler admits that nullification in the case of drug offenses "carries some societal risk," *supra* note 106, at 719, he nevertheless believes the risk to be less than with violent crimes and that the community costs of enforcing narcotics laws are often higher than the community costs of nullification in such instances. For his full discussion on this point, see *id.* at 719-20.

[119] *Id.* at 715.

[120] *Id.*: "I have more faith in the average black juror's idea of justice than I do in the idea that is embodied in the 'rule of law.'"

[121] *Id.* at 705.

notions of justice, truth, and equality under the law. Andrew Leipold, in his rebuttal to Butler's advocacy for jury nullification,[122] makes such a point: "[W]hether you go to jail or get set free should not depend on the color of your skin. Using race as the reason for acquitting or convicting is a bad idea, and no matter how strategic the reasoning and no matter how good our intentions, it is still wrong."[123] Objections such as Leipold's miss the point, however.[124] Butler seems willing to concede that, all things being equal, race *ought not* be a factor in determining criminal liability. But, as he argues, the actual outcomes of the criminal justice system paint an entirely different picture: the law treats race (perhaps intentionally, perhaps not) as relevant, and negatively so, as regards the criminal liability of African-American defendants. Moreover, the participation of African-American citizens on petit juries is often used to hide this negative race-consciousness and is instead used to demonstrate its very opposite – the illusion of so-called 'color-blindness' or race-neutrality in the criminal justice system.[125] Thus, not only is a black defendant's race a relevant factor, but the law also pretends that it is not, using the participation of black jurors to make its racist outcomes appear neutral. And it is precisely the law's duplicity in this regard that justifies the black juror's race-based nullificatory acts: "Is the black juror's race-conscious act moral? Absolutely. It would be farcical for her to be the sole color-blind actor in the criminal process, especially when it is her blackness that advertises the system's fairness."[126]

Not all race-based jury nullification is principled or just under this model, and Butler is quick to distinguish his concept of principled or just race-based jury nullification from those that are not: "I distinguish racially based nullification by African-Americans from recent right-wing proposals for jury nullification on the ground that the former is sometimes morally right

[122] Leipold, Andrew D., *Race-Based Jury Nullification: Rebuttal (Part A)*, 30 J. Marshall L. Rev. 923 (1997).
[123] *Id.* at 926.
[124] For one thing, Leipold seems to conflate Butler's claim that 'black jurors should sometimes consider returning not guilty verdicts for some guilty black defendants,' with the claim that 'all jurors should allow the race of the defendant to influence verdicts of guilty *or* not guilty.' These two statements are clearly not logically equivalent, nor do they imply similar consequences in application.
[125] Butler discusses this point in some detail: Butler, *supra* note 106, at 712-714.
[126] *Id.* at 714.

and the latter is not."[127] While he does not say so in so many words, his view appears to be that the calls for race-based jury nullification by, for instance, right-wing, white-supremacist groups lack moral legitimacy precisely because these latter groups do not suffer disproportionately at the hands of the criminal justice system. Thus, their nullificatory responses are not predicated on a reaction to systemic injustice, but instead, mere self-interest; as such, this delegitimizes their moral standing. Such jurors, states Butler, have simply "erred in their calculus of justice."[128] Butler's scope for the principled or just exercise of race-based jury nullification is therefore quite narrow. He offers four justifications for the moral permissibility of his model: i) violent antisocial behavior would still be punished, eliminating any fear that nullification will somehow lead to an increase in violent crime;[129] ii) fewer African-Americans would be jailed and imprisoned, ameliorating "one of the severe consequences of law enforcement in the African-American community."[130] As Butler explains: "Black people have a community that needs building, and children who need rescuing, and as long as a person will not hurt anyone, the community needs him there to help;"[131] iii) the current penal system has "antirehabilitative effects,"[132] and as such, jurors have a morally legitimate reason (if not a duty) to resist convicting defendants in the absence of a reasonable expectation of some useful treatment for offenders;[133] and, iv) his proposal is offered as a temporary solution to current injustice, "an intermediate step, a stopping point between the status quo and real justice."[134] As such, Butler is advocating for a temporary response to current systemic injustice; when the injustice ends, so too, presumably, will Butler's advocacy for race-based

[127] *Id.* at 705. See, also, 680, note 11: "I do not think that the use of jury nullification by these [white supremacist] groups has the same moral legitimacy as its use by African-Americans based on the racial bias of the criminal justice system."

[128] *Id.* at 705.

[129] *Id.* at 716: "Under my proposal, violent lawbreakers would go to prison."

[130] *Id.* at 715-716.

[131] *Id.*

[132] *Id.* at 718.

[133] *Id.*: "Unfortunately, however, rehabilitation is no longer an objective of criminal law in the United States... For that reason, unless a juror is provided with a specific, compelling reason to believe that a conviction would result in some useful treatment for an offender, she should not use her vote to achieve this end, because almost certainly it will not occur."

[134] *Id.* at 725.

jury nullification as its solution.[135] Butler has since developed and expanded on his work and has elsewhere[136] suggested a fifth moral justification for his proposal: traditional means and mechanisms for affecting positive change have proven ineffective in addressing systemic racism within the criminal justice system. Untraditional means are therefore required: "I do not want to hear that African-Americans should write to Congress. We tried that. It did not work. The house that African-Americans live in is on fire, and when your house is on fire, you do not write to Congress. You do not ask the people who set the fire to put it out; you leave the building. That is what my proposal for selective jury nullification encourages."[137]

The entirety of this past chapter was taken up by addressing the arguments offered in favor of an in-court *nullification instruction*, along with their conceptual and jurisprudential implications and deficits. Butler's article, however, neatly side-steps these issues entirely by focusing on community-centered extrajudicial education as the locus of epistemic activity: "Because *Sparf*, as well as the law of many states, prohibits jurors from being instructed about jury nullification in criminal cases, information about this privilege would have to be communicated to black jurors before they heard such cases."[138] In other words, Butler is concerned with negotiating the law as it is to get the best results for the African-American community rather than postulating long-term structural changes in trial procedures to achieve those ends.[139] As such, his solution is grounded in a more realist/pragmatic, as opposed to normative, approach; he is not concerned here with advocating for an in-trial *nullification instruction*. Butler may well be correct in this approach – the weight of nearly one hundred and fifty years of

---

[135] *Id.*: "Other policy questions are not as easily answered, including the issue of how long (years, decades, centuries?) black jurors would need to pursue racially based jury nullification. I think this concern is related to the issue of the appropriate time span of other race-conscious remedies, including affirmative action."

[136] Butler, Paul, *Race-Based Jury Nullification: Case-in-Chief*, 30 J. Marshall L. Rev. 911, 922 (1997).

[137] *Id.* at 922.

[138] Butler, *supra* note 106, at 723.

[139] He does not imply that these are in any way mutually exclusive, however, and indeed, the entire goal of his model is to affect such long-term structural changes. See note 135.

judicial precedent and case law leans heavily on the view that such in-trial *nullification instructions* run contrary to both the notion of a fair trial, and the sound and efficient operation of the criminal justice system. It seems unlikely that the courts will reverse their position on the subject anytime soon. If black jurors are to use their nullification *privilege*, therefore, they cannot rely on the legal system to educate them on their power. However, as Butler points out, "*Sparf* is one Supreme Court decision whose holding is rather easy to circumvent: If the defense attorneys cannot inform the people of their power, the people can inform themselves."[140] To that end, Butler offers a picture of a community-based educational initiative for promulgating information regarding jury nullification:

> Disseminating this information should not be difficult. African-American culture - through mediums such as church, music (particularly rap songs), black newspapers and magazines, literature, storytelling, film (including music videos), soapbox speeches, and convention gatherings - facilitates intraracial communication. At African-American cultural events, such as concerts or theatrical productions, the audience could be instructed on the proposal, either verbally or through the dissemination of written material; this type of political expression at a cultural event would hardly be unique - voter registration campaigns are often conducted at such events. The proposal could be the subject of rap songs, which are already popular vehicles for racial critiques, or of ministers' sermons.[141]

Butler goes on to suggest that more direct approaches, such as distributing jury nullification pamphlets outside of courthouses, might also be effective.[142]

Education and advocacy are, ultimately, the lynchpins to the success of Butler's project. His premise that jury nullification can be a powerful means to affect change within the legal system is generally undisputed and well-

[140] Butler, *supra* note 106, at 724.
[141] *Id.* at 723.
[142] *Id.* at 724.

confirmed through robust historical examples.[143] The effectiveness and efficacy of his community-based educational model, on the other hand, is speculative – particularly given the trend in recent years for the courts to use the *voir dire* process as, in part, a tool to weed out potentially nullifying jurors.[144] While obviously an in-trial *nullification instruction* would be the most direct and efficient way to educate jurors of their *privilege,* so long as the courts remain immune to the advisability of such, Butler's model offers an alternative path for those who see jury nullification as a legitimate tool to affect positive social change. For those wanting justice now, and not justice deferred, Butler offers a means to a constructive transformation of the law's impact on the African-American community – directly, through racially based jury nullification, and indirectly, through advocacy and education in the promotion thereof.

---

[143] See **CHAPTER 1** for a detailed discussion of this phenomenon.

[144] Butler does point out, however, that even one informed juror would be sufficient "to prevent the conviction of a defendant. The prosecution would then have to retry the case, and risk facing another African-American juror with emancipation tendencies." Butler, *supra* note 106, at 724.

Chapter 5
Arguments Offered in Opposition to the Nullification Instruction[1]

At this point it might be appropriate to review the overall project that I am engaged in and the question that I am trying to answer. Ought the jury to be informed of its nullification *privilege*? Chapter 3 explored why we cannot answer this question by engaging strictly in pure conceptual analysis into the legal status of jury nullification. Therefore, I suggested, the most profitable course of action would be to attempt to address this question by looking to the effects or consequences of giving the *nullification instruction*. In the previous chapter we looked at consequence or policy-based arguments in favor of giving the *nullification instruction*, as well as some corresponding objections and their concomitant shortcomings. In this chapter now we turn to an investigation of what the negative consequences of the instruction are purported to be. After looking at what these objections to the instruction are, I end the chapter by balancing the benefits versus the costs of giving the instruction and conclude that it is in the best interests of that fundamental value of any just legal system, a respect for personal liberty, that jurors ought *not* be informed of their *privilege* to nullify. The costs are potentially too great.

5.1 The Anarchy Objection

Some critics of the *nullification instruction* argue that it ought not to be given because: i) the instruction will lead to more instances of jury nullification;

[1] Some of the thoughts and ideas expressed in this chapter have been previously explored in Hreno, Travis, *Jury Nullification and the Bad-Faith Juror*, vol. 1, no. 1 LEAP: The Journal of Legal Ethics and Philosophy 53 (Spring 2013), and Hreno, Travis, *The Rule of Law and Jury Nullification*, vol. 34, no. 2 The Commonwealth Law Bulletin 297 (June 2008). However, it is important to note that the substantive content and conclusions drawn have undergone substantial revisions, developments, expansions, and updates to reflect current jurisprudence, as well as the specific focus and tenor of this project. The author acknowledges these earlier publications as a foundation for the present work.

and, ii) this is therefore an invitation to anarchy in the justice system – a total breakdown of an orderly legal system. We can call this the *anarchy* objection. Leventhal, J. gave voice to this particular objection when he stated, in *U. S. v. Dougherty*,[2] that "[t]his so-called right of jury nullification is put forward in the name of democracy, but its explicit avowal *risks the ultimate logic of anarchy*."[3] Leventhal went on to cite with approval *United States v. Moylan*[4] where Sobeloff, J., also commenting on jury nullification, made the following claim:

> To encourage individuals to make their own determinations as to which laws they will obey and which they will permit themselves as a matter of conscience to disobey is to invite chaos. No legal system could long survive if it gave every individual the option of disregarding with impunity any law which by his personal standard was judged morally untenable. Toleration of such conduct would not be democratic, as appellants claim, but inevitably anarchic.[5]

This view was repeated by the Kansas Supreme Court, which, in commenting on the advisability of giving the *nullification instruction* stated that "[d]isregard for the principles of established law creates anarchy and destroys the very protections which the law affords."[6]

It is important here to clarify exactly what is meant by 'anarchy' in this context. Proponents of the *anarchy* objection are, almost exclusively, using the term as equivalent to 'chaos' or 'disorder'. More specifically, the foundational claim of the *anarchy* objection is that the *nullification instruction* will lead to (or is even equivalent to) some form of *jural* anarchy: a widespread, inconsistent, disordered, and chaotic approach to applying and administrating the criminal law to the extent that the legal system could no longer be relied upon to function as a reliable "legal structure requisite for true freedom, for an ordered liberty that protects against anarchy as well as tyranny."[7] In a state of legal/jural anarchy, our

---

[2] 473 F.2d 1113, (D.C. Cir. 1972).
[3] *Id.* at 1133 (emphasis added).
[4] 417 F.2d 1002 (4th Cir. 1969).
[5] *Id.* at 1009.
[6] *State v. McClanahan*, 212 Kan. 208, 510 P.2d 153, 159 (1973).
[7] *Supra* note 2, at 1137.

fundamental and essential legal rights would be, in a very real sense, forfeit. Or, at least, that is the concern.

There are many more examples of this type of thinking, but all that is important to note here is that, especially amongst the judiciary opposed to jury nullification in general, and the *nullification instruction* in particular, this is a relatively common objection.[8] And, like many of the arguments for

---

[8] See, for instance, *People v. Dillon*, 34 Cal.3d 441, 488 n.39 (Cal. 1983): "Whatever the result of that exercise, it cannot seriously be urged that, when asked by the jurors, a trial judge must advise them: 'I have instructed you on the law applicable to this case. Follow it or ignore it, as you choose.' Such advice may achieve pragmatic justice in isolated instances, but we suggest the more likely result is anarchy;" *Arshack v. United States*, 321 A.2d 845, 851 (D.C. 1974): "No doubt juries sometimes act out of compassion and in disregard of the law. But we will not place upon such conduct by juries the stamp of judicial approval through an instruction from the court. To do so would actually encourage anarchy in the courtroom, and that might in the end harmfully infect organized society;" *United States v. Simpson*, 460 F.2d 515, 520 n.12 (9th Cir. 1972): where the court referred to jury nullification as "a kind of anarchy; that is, a system in which the ultimate test of socially permissible conduct is, to a significant degree, the random reaction of a group of twelve people selected at random. Acceptance of this as the principle governing individual conduct which collides with the rules adopted by governmental processes would, of course, amount to rejection of law as the controlling principle of society;" *State v. McClanahan, supra* note 6, at 216 where the court stated, in regard to jury nullification that "[d]isregard for the principles of established law creates anarchy and destroys the very protections which the law affords;" Crispo, Lawrence W.; Slansky, Jill M.; and Yriarte, Geanene M., *Jury Nullification: Law Versus Anarchy*, 31 Loy. L.A. L. Rev. 1, 60-61 (1997): "Jury nullification does and will continue to occur, but courts should never encourage it… If individuals were allowed to decide that certain laws apply to some and not to others, true anarchy would reign;" Royer, Caisa E., *The Disobedient Jury: Why Lawmakers Should Codify Jury Nullification*, 102 Cornell L. Rev. 1401, 1406 (2017): "Without any consequences, jury nullification may involve less integrity than other acts of conscientious lawbreaking wherein the lawbreakers willingly suffer penalties for their actions. Juries can, in theory, mercurially acquit defendants which would create a system of anarchy instead of a system of democracy;" Abramson, Jeffery, *Two Ideals of Jury Deliberations*, 1998 U. Chi. Legal F. 125, 147 (1998), stating that if courts allow jurors to "deliberate whether they happened to agree with the law, then there effectively would be no law at all, only an anarchy of conscience, an unpredictable series of ad hoc judgments by isolated groups of twelve;" Yorke, Susan, *Jury Nullification Instructions as Structural Error*, 95 Wash. L. Rev. 1441, 1148-1149 (2020): "Nullification thus simultaneously occupies dissonant roles in our jurisprudential universe. It is anarchy, subverting the most basic tenets of our adjudicative process. And it is itself a fundamental tenet of that process, instilling in the people the power to resist government tyranny and prevent injustice. Law values order; nullification is mayhem;" See, also, Scheflin, Alan W. and Van Dyke, Jon

or against the *nullification instruction*, the real focus of this objection actually turns on the desirability of jury nullification itself. That is, the *anarchy* objection only has purchase because its proponents feel that jury nullification is, on the whole, undesirable (due to its consequences – jural anarchy). The *nullification instruction*, therefore, is only undesirable indirectly, to the degree that it promotes instances of jury nullification, which then in turn would lead to, or promote, an anarchic justice system. The underlying point of the *anarchy* objection, then, is that jury nullification promotes jural anarchy – the breakdown of the very "protections afforded by the rule of law"[9] – and that therefore, the *nullification instruction* ought not be given, lest we risk such anarchy.

This, therefore, seems to be a logical place to begin our investigation of the *anarchy* objection: does (or would) the *nullification instruction* actually lead to such widespread substantive jural anarchy? Or, to put the question more accurately: does jury nullification itself lead to widespread substantive jural anarchy? If the answer to either of these questions is no, then there is no need to go any further and inquire as to whether jury nullification or the *nullification instruction* would be inconsistent with the existence of, and respect for, an orderly legal system consistent with the protection of basic human rights. And as we shall see, there is very good reason to believe that answer to these questions is, in fact, no. As Alan Scheflin and Jon Van Dyke point out, advocates of the *anarchy* objection exaggerate or "over-dramatize what jury nullification means."[10] When juries nullify, they are not making new law, nor are they redefining the meaning and application of extant laws. Nullification, they assert, does not give the jury the ability to take the law into its own hands. Rather, jury nullification "is a power of conscience which permits the jury to suspend the application of a particular law in a particular instance to a particular defendant in the interest of conscience and justice."[11] In other words, jury nullification gives the jury the discretion to decide whether to apply the law in a particular case. That, argue Scheflin

M., *Jury Nullification: The Contours of a Controversy*, 43 Law & Contemp. Probs. 51, 85-90 (1980).

[9] *State v. McClanahan*, *id.* at 216.

[10] Scheflin and Van Dyke, *Jury Nullification: The Contours of a Controversy*, *supra* note 8, at 87.

[11] *Id.*

and Van Dyke, is the correct way to view jury nullification – as an *ad hoc* discretionary ability. And there is no reason to assume, Scheflin and Van Dyke continue, that the exercise of such a discretionary ability on the part of the jury in individual instances will somehow lead to widespread legal/jural anarchy. After all, they continue, such *ad hoc* discretionary abilities abound in the administration of the criminal justice system without anarchy thereby resulting. Police officers investigating criminal matters have discretion whether to make an arrest, they point out. Prosecutors have discretion whether to bring criminal charges to court. Trial judges have discretion whether to allow a case to proceed to trial, or whether to allow the verdict to go to the jury. These discretionary abilities, according to Scheflin and Van Dyke, are analogous to the jury's. Since anarchy does not result when the police officer, the prosecutor, or the judge makes use of their discretion, there is little reason to conclude that anarchy will result when the jury makes use of its discretion, they conclude. Jurors, for the most part, prefer justice to anarchy, and it is difficult to imagine that they would use their discretionary abilities in a way that promotes the latter over the former.[12] The *anarchy* objection fails to be persuasive the degree that it equates knowledge of a discretionary ability with jural anarchy, despite the robust evidence against such a relation in any and every other facet of the criminal justice system.

However, *pace* Scheflin and Van Dyke, it might be pointed out that these discretionary powers are unlike the jury's in one important sense. When a police officer, prosecutor, or trial judge exercise their discretion in the manner mentioned above, the motivating factor is supposed to be the reasonable expectation of obtaining a conviction. That is, the police officer will not (ideally) make an arrest where the evidence will not support a criminal conviction, even if she believes the suspect to be guilty; the prosecutor will not (ideally) proceed to trial where the evidence will not support a criminal conviction – again, even if she believes the accused to be guilty; and the judge will not (ideally) let the case proceed to trial, nor let the jury render a verdict where she believes that the evidence will not reasonably support a criminal conviction. However, where there is a reasonable expectation of conviction, none of the aforementioned

---

[12] See **CHAPTER 4**, notes 81 and 82 for a detailed discussion of this point.

discretionary abilities are supposed to come into play. In that situation, the police officer who doesn't make the arrest, or the prosecutor who doesn't proceed to trial, for instance, have both made legal errors which can and, in the eyes of the law, should, be corrected.[13] The jury's discretionary power to nullify, on the other hand, *only* comes into play when there is (at the very least) a reasonable expectation of conviction. And unlike those aforementioned discretionary abilities, jury nullification has no available redress – in practice or in principle. Thus, perhaps Scheflin and Van Dyke's comparison of the jury's *ad hoc* discretionary powers to those of the police, prosecutors and judges is somewhat of a false analogy. Certainly, when police, prosecutors and judges exercise such discretion we do not expect anarchy, but this is only because, in exercising such discretion, they are (supposed to be) behaving in accordance with the law, not contrary to it. Moreover, we can easily (for the most part) distinguish those examples of discretion used properly by legal officials from those examples which are not. Redress, as I mentioned above, is often available (if only conceptually) for the latter. This is not the case when juries exercise their discretionary *privilege* to nullify; no such structural checks and balances exist or apply.

There is, however, a more telling reply to the *anarchy* objection. We begin by noting that jury nullification is a phenomenon that currently takes place without any jural anarchy thereby resulting. To put this plainly, we are not currently living in an anarchic legal environment that "harmfully infect(s) organized society,"[14] despite the continued existence of jury nullification within the legal system.[15] A charitable reading of the *anarchy* objection therefore suggests that the real concern is that *informed* jurors will nullify in ways radically different from *uninformed* jurors – that informed jurors will behave in ways substantively injurious to "our system of government… devised for the protection equally of society and of individuals in their essential rights."[16] When Leventhal stated, in *Dougherty*, for instance, that an "explicit [nullification] instruction to a jury conveys an implied approval

---

[13] At least in principle. In practice, such correction may be difficult to achieve.

[14] *Arshack v. United States, supra* note 8, at 851.

[15] According to one researcher, roughly 4% of all acquittals are the result of jury nullification. Black, Robert C., *FIJA: Monkeywrenching the Justice System*, 66 UMKC L. Rev. 11, 16 (1997).

[16] *Sparf and Hansen v. United States*, 156 U.S. 51, 102-03 (1895).

that runs the risk of degrading the legal structure requisite for true freedom, for an ordered liberty that protects against anarchy as well as tyranny,"[17] it is safe to assume that he was not referring to instances of juries nullifying, for instance, minor drug possession laws. He even acknowledges as much earlier in his judgement, begrudgingly admitting to the (very minor) value of jury nullification when "the liberty vindicated by the verdict relates to the defendant's... purchase during Prohibition of alcoholic beverages."[18] The *anarchy* objection, therefore, understood properly, proposes that, jurors, if informed of their discretionary ability to nullify, will feel free to judge, evaluate, and even reject such fundamental societal laws as the prohibitions against murder, theft, assault, etc., etc. These are, after all, exactly the kinds of laws whose random, chaotic, and non-uniform enforcement might very well entail widespread jural anarchy, with all the associated negative consequences.[19] For the sake of clarity, I will call this: *radical jury nullification*. Let's grant then, for the sake of argument, that such radical jury nullification would indeed result in a form of jural anarchy where the law could no longer function as a reliable protector of essential rights. I think that much is uncontroversial: if jurors were to make use of their nullificatory discretion in such a radical manner, jural anarchy would most certainly follow. But, of course, the same can be said of the other actors in the criminal justice system who are trusted with discretionary powers: if judges, prosecutors, or police officers were to use their discretionary powers in similarly radical ways, we would also expect significant breakdown in "the protection equally of society and of individuals in their essential rights."[20] And yet, this is not seen as a well-motivated reason to remove or conceal such discretion from these actors. No one argues for the position that judges, prosecutors, or police officers should have no discretionary powers whatsoever, or that such powers

[17] *Supra* note 2, at 1137.

[18] *Id.* at 1130.

[19] See, for instance, Hart, H.L.A., *The Concept of Law,* 191 (Oxford University Press, 1961): "Even the strongest must sleep at times and, when asleep, loses temporarily his superiority. This fact of approximate equality, more than any other, makes obvious the necessity for a system of mutual forbearance and compromise which is the base of both legal and moral obligation. Social life with its rules requiring such forbearance is irksome at times; but it is at any rate less nasty, less brutish, and less short than unrestrained aggression for beings thus approximately equal."

[20] *Supra* note 16.

ought to be hidden from them, lest they use such discretion *radically*, with widespread jural anarchy thereby the result. So why should this be a good reason to treat jurors and their discretionary powers this way? Doing so appears somewhat *ad hoc* and arbitrary.

Perhaps, one might argue, jurors, unlike the other actors in the criminal justice system, simply cannot be relied upon to use their discretion in a wise and conscientious manner. This would remove the element of arbitrariness from the *anarchy* objection, at least. But this line of reasoning is, of course, more of an attack on the entire integrity of the jury system itself than a direct objection to jury nullification. It is a response predicated on the view that the jury simply cannot be trusted to discharge its duties in a responsible and reliable manner. As Bazelon C.J. stated: "Trust in the jury is, after all, one of the cornerstones of our criminal jurisprudence, and if that trust is without foundation, we must re-examine a great deal more than just the nullification doctrine."[21]

The biggest problem with *anarchy* objection, however, is that it is simply unrealistic; it paints a highly inaccurate picture of human social psychology and motivation. For the *anarchy* objection to have any rhetorical purchase whatsoever, one would have to imagine that jurors, once informed of their nullification *privilege*, would routinely and cavalierly engage in *radical jury nullification* and free defendants back into their own communities despite believing such offenders to be violent, dangerous, or in some other way, actively anti-social. This claim beggars belief, and yet the entire persuasive power of the *anarchy* objection seems to rely on this substantively counter-factual conception of human behavior. See, for instance Bazelon C.J.'s statement affirming this very point: "As for the problem of unjust acquittal, it is important to recognize the strong internal check that constrains the jury's willingness to acquit. *Where defendants seem dangerous, juries are unlikely to exercise their nullification power, whether or not an explicit instruction is offered.*"[22] I think we can therefore safely dismiss *radical jury nullification* as a realistic concern, and with it, the *anarchy* objection.

---

[21] *Id.* at 1142.

[22] *Id.* at 1143 (emphasis added).

5.2 The Racist-Juror Objection

An oft mentioned and potentially troubling challenge to the *nullification instruction* involves instances of juries acquitting based on racial considerations. I call this the *racist-juror* objection. Alan Dershowitz made this very point, stating: "Jury nullification is a double-edged sword. It is sometimes used, in a nonracist manner, to counter the unfairness of particular laws... But jury nullification also has an ignoble and racist history."[23] One example of this 'ignoble and racist history' often used by opponents of jury nullification refers to the troubling pattern of racist juries acquitting white defendants accused of committing violent hate crimes against African-Americans:

> [A]lthough the early history of our country includes the occasional Zenger trial or acquittals in fugitive slave cases, more recent history presents numerous and notorious examples of jurors nullifying — cases that reveal the destructive potential of a practice Professor Randall Kennedy of the Harvard Law School has rightly termed a "sabotage of justice." Consider, for example, the two hung juries in the 1964 trials of Byron De La Beckwith in Mississippi for the murder of NAACP field secretary Medgar Evers, or the 1955 acquittal of J.W. Millam and Roy Bryant for the murder of fourteen-year-old Emmett Till... — shameful examples of how "nullification" has been used to sanction murder and lynching.[24]

Certainly, in such cases, this objection runs, if the jurors do vote to acquit contrary to what they believe the evidence establishes, and based purely on reasons that can only be described as racist, this is nevertheless still a form of jury nullification. And just as certainly, such action is morally deplorable – the type of thing that, even if we cannot completely prevent it from occurring, we should nevertheless take every step we can to minimize. When we allow race to become a factor in the determination of criminal liability at any point in the criminal law, according to this objection, justice

[23] *Editorial - Barry Employs a Redneck Trick: Jury Nullification Play Appeals to Racist Instincts*, Buffalo News C3 (June 9, 1990).

[24] *U.S. v. Thomas*, 116 F.3d 606, 616 (2d Cir. 1997).

is perverted.[25] Proponents of the *racist-juror* objection[26] argue that to give the *nullification instruction* is to thereby license the jury to behave in a potentially racist manner, or at the very least to tacitly suggest to the jury that racist motivations for reaching a verdict are, in some sense, legitimate. To encourage or suggest this, the objection runs, would be to pervert everything that the justice system stands for. Advocates of this view therefore conclude that we ought to, in the name of our commitment to justice, refrain from giving the *nullification instruction.*

A number of things can be said in response to the *racist-juror* objection. To begin with, in such a case where a racist jury is sitting in judgment of "one of its own," accused of racist criminal activity, it is hard to imagine that the absence of the *nullification instruction* will materially affect the outcome one way or another. The jury in this case will, we can safely assume, vote to acquit no matter what the evidence presented at trial. Paul Butler offers such a response: "One concern is that whites will nullify in cases of white-on-black crime. The best response to this concern is that often white people do nullify in those cases. The white jurors who acquitted the police officers who beat up Rodney King are a good example."[27] Butler's claim here is that racist juries will most likely return not guilty verdicts in such cases regardless of what the evidence establishes and regardless of whether they are explicitly told they have the *privilege* to nullify. As such, a *nullification instruction* therefore plays no role one way or the other in promoting racist

---

[25] But for a different view see Butler, Paul, *Racially Based Jury Nullification: Black Power in the Criminal Justice System,* 105 Yale Law Journal 677, 679 (1995), where Butler argues that black communities in America are better off when some nonviolent black lawbreakers remain in the community rather than being convicted. To that end he concludes that "the race of a black defendant is sometimes a legally and morally appropriate factor for jurors to consider in reaching a verdict… The decision as to what kind of conduct by African-Americans ought to be punished is better made by African-Americans themselves, based on the costs and benefits to their community, than by the traditional criminal justice process, which is controlled by white lawmakers and white law enforcers." See **CHAPTER 4: Appendix** for a detailed discussion of this perspective.

[26] See, for instance, Simson, Gary J., *Jury Nullification in the American System: A Skeptical View,* 54 Texas Law Review 488 (1976); Schmidt, Jr., Benno C., *Juries, Jurisdiction, and Race Discrimination: The Lost Promise of Strauder v. West Virginia,* 61 Texas Law Review 1401 (1983); Hoffman, Paul, *Double Jeopardy Wars: The Case for a Civil Rights 'Exception,'* 41 UCLA Law Review 649 (1994).

[27] Butler, *supra* note 25, at 722.

verdict outcomes, concludes Butler.[28] In those specific cases where a jury of bigots is allowed to sit in judgment of a racist defendant accused of some sort of racially motivated crime, I think it safe to assume, along with Butler, that a nullified verdict of not guilty is often almost a foregone conclusion. Hence, the problem of racially motivated and racist verdicts cannot be adequately addressed merely by the court's refusal to allow the jury to learn of its *privilege* to nullify.

Rather, the problem of racist verdicts points to a more fundamental problem: that of non-representative juries. Presumably the more racially diverse a jury is, and the more representative it is of the community at large, the less likely that particular racial prejudices will affect the verdict in such cases, especially considering that, in many jurisdictions, jury verdicts must be unanimous to be legally binding. Our concern here should not be that defendants will not receive a fair trial, nor victims justice, if the jury uses its nullification *privilege* – rather we should worry that defendants will not receive a fair trial, nor victims justice, where the legal system allows non-representative and racist juries to be empaneled. Juries that are biased against minority members of the community are, by definition, non-representative of the community as a whole. If we wish to address the issue of juries returning unwarranted race-based acquittals, we can start by ensuring that we empanel juries that are representative of the community as a whole and properly screened at *voir dire* for any such racial biases. There is no reason to suspect that such properly empaneled and representative juries will exercise their nullificatory *privilege* in the pursuit of racist ends. This, I believe, is the most direct and telling response to the *racist-juror* objection.[29]

---

[28] See, also, *U. S. v. Dougherty, supra* note 2, at 1143 (emphasis added): "As for the problem of unjust acquittal, it is important to recognize the strong internal check that constrains the jury's willingness to acquit. Where defendants seem dangerous, juries are unlikely to exercise their nullification power, whether or not an explicit instruction is offered. *Of course, that check will not prevent the acquittal of a defendant who may be blameworthy and dangerous except in the jaundiced eyes of a jury motivated by a perverse and sectarian sense of values. But whether a nullification instruction would make such acquittals more common is problematical, if not entirely inconceivable.*"

[29] Bazelon, J., in addressing the issue of racist acquittals makes a similar point: "In any case, the real problem in this situation is not the nullification doctrine, but the values

Clay Conrad makes a very similar, though more extensive claim, arguing that attempts to accuse the jury of racist acquittals are a form of "scapegoating the jury,"[30] and that so-called racist acquittals are far more often indicative of systemic failures on the part of other elements of the criminal justice system rather than a failure of the jury system in general and jury nullification in particular:

> Violently racist communities cannot help but seat violently racist jurors. It would be unrealistic to expect otherwise. That, however, is only part of the story. Violently racist communities cannot help but elect violently racist legislators, sheriffs, judges, and prosecutors. There is no reason [however], to expect the jury system to be any worse than any other actors in the system.[31]

Conrad spent considerable effort researching the transcripts from various state-level trials involving white defendants in the American South accused of murdering civil rights workers during the 1950s and 60s. He mentions one trial in particular where a number of spectacular legal and procedural errors were committed. These included the prosecutor's closing remarks to the jury (where he apologized to the jury for even taking the case to trial), as well as a *voir dire* process that failed to exclude one of the defendant's close friends from sitting on the jury.[32] His conclusion: in a great many of these cases there was a palpable unwillingness on the part of state officials at all levels to prosecute with any real enthusiasm. It is hardly surprising, concludes Conrad, that, given such anemic attempts to prosecute on the part of the state, the jurors would return verdicts of not guilty. This lack of prosecutorial enthusiasm did not go unnoticed by the Federal Government, however, who responded by re-trying many of the defendants, not for murder, but for depriving the victims of their civil rights. Unlike their state-level analogues, Conrad points out that these federal prosecutions very often did result in convictions, despite the fact that these cases were

---

and prejudice that prompt the acquittal." *United States v. Dougherty, supra* note 2, at 1143.

[30] Conrad, Clay S., *Jury Nullification: Evolution of a Doctrine*, 167 (Carolina Academic Press, 1998).

[31] *Id.* at 202.

[32] *Id.* at 183-5.

nonetheless often tried in front of all-white juries taken from the very same jury pools as the state-level cases. As Conrad concludes: "Of the jury pool, the investigators, the prosecutors, and the judge, the only factor that remained unchanged between the successful federal and the failed state prosecutions has been the jury pool, and yet it is juries that have taken the brunt of public condemnation."[33] It seems likely then, that if these differences in verdicts were the result of racism, the blame cannot be laid entirely at the feet of the jury using its nullificatory *privilege* for racist ends.

To summarize: the *racist-juror* objection states that racially motivated jury nullification is a perversion of justice and that to give the *nullification instruction* is to thereby encourage jurors to pervert justice. This ought not to be done, argue proponents of this objection, and hence, the *nullification instruction* ought not to be given. However, as I noted above there is very little reason to believe that a racist jury wouldn't nullify even if no such instruction were given. As Bazelon C.J. stated, when describing the problem of "the acquittal of a defendant who may be blameworthy and dangerous except in the jaundiced eyes of a jury motivated by a perverse and sectarian sense of values… [W]hether a nullification instruction would make such acquittals more common is problematical, if not entirely inconceivable."[34] Moreover, there is a great deal of reason to think that where the jury is representative of the community at large, and at least minimally vetted for racist attitudes, such racially motivated nullification will not occur. Finally, there is Conrad's point that where the officials of the justice system, the investigators, prosecutors, and the judges, do their jobs sincerely and free of prejudice, the jury will most likely respond in kind. While racism in the criminal justice system is a very significant problem, it does not appear that limiting the jury's knowledge of its nullification *privilege* is an efficacious way of dealing with it. Thus, the *racist-juror* objection to the *nullification instruction* is a non-starter.

5.3 The Rule-of-Law Objection

Another objection often raised against the *nullification instruction* is that the exercise of the jury's *privilege* to nullify is, in some sense, incompatible with,

---

[33] *Id.* at 186.

[34] *U. S. v. Dougherty*, *supra* note 2, at 1143.

or subverts, the rule of law. Thus, the jury ought not to be encouraged to behave in such a manner. For instance, the Court in *U.S. v. Thomas*[35] stated: "We categorically reject the idea that, in a society committed to the rule of law, jury nullification is desirable or that courts may permit it to occur when it is within their authority to prevent."[36] A similar view was expressed in *State v. McClanahan*,[37] where the Court stated that "the administration of justice cannot be left to community standards or community conscience but must depend upon the protections afforded by the rule of law."[38] The Court in *United States v. Moylan*[39] issued a particularly forceful condemnation of the idea of issuing a *nullification instruction*:

> However, this is not to say that the jury should be encouraged in their "lawlessness," and by clearly stating to the jury that they may disregard the law, telling them that they may decide according to their prejudices or consciences (for there is no check to insure that the judgment is based upon conscience rather than prejudice), we would indeed be negating the rule of law in favor of the rule of lawlessness. This should not be allowed.[40]

The gist of these objections is that a legal system that allows for jury nullification to occur is incompatible with the rule of law. Notice that this is not really an objection to the *nullification instruction* specifically, but rather to jury nullification in general. Therefore, this objection indirectly indicts the *nullification instruction*, and only to the degree that it promotes, or increases the incidence of, jury nullification.

In addressing this objection two questions need to be asked: i) does the practice of jury nullification actually subvert the rule of law; and, ii) is this such a bad thing? We need to ask the first question because, for the most part, advocates of this view tend merely to assert it on the grounds that its truth is self-evident; rarely is any sort of positive argument given for this

---

35 *Supra* note 24.
36 *Id.* at 615.
37 *Supra* note 6.
38 *Id.* at 216.
39 *Supra* note 4.
40 *Id.* at 1006.

view. The second question can perhaps be understood better if we phrased it as such: If a legal system that allows for jury nullification is, in fact, incompatible with the rule of law, why should we prefer the latter to the former? After all, just to say that jury nullification and the rule of law are incompatible with one another is not necessarily, on the face of it, a sufficient objection to either practice. More needs to be said as to why the loss of the rule of law would be such a bad thing, or if it is *prima facie* a bad thing, why it would be worse than the loss of a legal system that allows for jury nullification. I will return to this second question in a few pages.

5.3.1 The Minimalist Conception of the Rule of Law

Before any of these questions can be answered, however, we need to investigate exactly what is meant by the phrase 'the rule of law.' For the most part proponents of the *rule-of-law* objection tend not to explain what this term means, or when pressed tend to respond with the answer that the rule of law stands for the principle of 'rule by laws, not by men.' Sometimes the rule of law is claimed to be the principle that no person is above the law.[41] These are hardly helpful answers to our project at hand. More needs to be said about just what is entailed by these ideas. The problem here is two-fold. On the one hand, legal scholars have written a plethora of articles and books explicating this concept, each with their own take on what it entails. On the other hand, it does no good to simply choose at random a particular understanding of this concept if it does not correspond to how it is being used by proponents of the *rule-of-law* objection to nullification; one runs the risk of engaging in straw-person reasoning. To address this problem, I have adopted what I call a minimalist/formal account of the rule of law. Examining the work of three fairly theoretically disparate legal theorists, Joseph Raz, Lon Fuller, and John Rawls, I have taken those elements of the concept of the rule of law that they all share. If three philosophers from such distinct backgrounds and commitments can all agree on these elements as being essential and necessary to the concept of the rule of law, I reason, then this is as good a starting point as any for making sense of the term. Moreover, and more importantly, the account of

[41] See, for instance, *United States v. Zubaydah*, 142 S. Ct. 959, 991 (2022) "In this country, no one stands above the law; not even the President may deflect evidentiary inquiries just because they may prove inconvenient or embarrassing."

the rule of law that I offer here reflects how the term is used by those who employ it to object to jury nullification and the *nullification instruction*.

So just what are these basic elements that make up the minimalist/formal account of the rule of law? The first thing to understand is that the rule of law actually refers to a cluster of principles meant to guide and limit the impact of laws and the legal system on the lives of persons.[42] In its simplest expression, then, the rule of law is merely an articulation of the general requirement that the law be action guiding for its subjects. This is an area of fundamental agreement between academics and the courts.[43] Raz, for instance, claims that "[t]his is the basic intuition from which the doctrine of the rule of law derives: the law must be capable of guiding the behavior of its subjects."[44] This rather general principle, of course, can be interpreted in a number of ways. To best understand this requirement for efficacy in guiding behavior, I propose breaking it down into four specific sub-principles:

1. The law must be composed of rules.[45]
2. These rules must be stable. This includes the requirements that the law be general, clear, and not subject to unannounced change.[46]
3. These rules must be conformable. This includes the requirements that the law be prospective in nature, it cannot demand the impossible, and that the law be promulgated.[47]

---

[42] Thus, just as only governments and their agents can act unconstitutionally, only the justice system and its agents can be said to behave contrary to, or in conformity with, the rule of law.

[43] See, for instance, *Thornburgh v. American College of Obstetricians & Gynecologists*, 476 U.S. 747, 786-87 (1986) (emphasis added), where the Court stated: "The rule of *stare decisis* is essential if case-by-case judicial decision-making is to be reconciled with the principle of the rule of law, for when governing legal standards are open to revision in every case, deciding cases becomes a mere exercise of judicial will, *with arbitrary and unpredictable results*."

[44] Raz, Joseph, *The Authority of Law: Essays on Law and Morality*, 214 (Oxford University Press, 1979).

[45] Raz, *id.* at 215; Fuller, Lon, *The Morality of Law*, 46-49 (Yale University Press, 1969); Rawls, John, *A Theory of Justice*, 238 (Harvard University Press, 1971).

[46] Raz, *id.* at 215; Fuller, *id.* at 79-81.

[47] Raz, *id.*

4. There must be non-arbitrary enforcement of these rules. This includes the requirements that like cases be treated alike,[48] that all persons regardless of position or standing, are subject to the authority of the law,[49] and that there must be congruence between the law as promulgated and the law in its application.[50]

This, notice, is a rather modest conception of the rule of law; it is purely formal in nature with little to no substantive content. The advantage of this model, as I have stated, is that it captures the term both as it is used by proponents of the *rule-of-law* objection to jury nullification, as well as how it is generally understood by legal scholars and philosophers. As regards this last point, it bears repeating that while Raz, Fuller and Rawls all have differing conceptions of what the specifics of the rule of law are (and, indeed, even disagree on such fundamental issues as to whether the notion is a substantive one or a formal one), the principles that I have listed in my minimalist conception of the rule of law represent those areas where their respective theories more or less overlap and agree. Indeed, these principles are seen to be essential to the concept of the rule of law, to a greater or lesser degree, in the theories of a great many other theorists besides Raz, Fuller and Rawls.[51] It is also worth noting that all of the above principles are necessary elements of the rule of law. That is, a legal system that fails completely or substantially to conform to even one of the principles or sub-principles that make up the rule of law is a legal system that therefore fails to be consistent with the entirety of the rule of law. Moreover, these principles have the character of categorical imperatives; even occasional lapses are inconsistent with the rule of law. In other words, it is not good enough that a legal system's laws are *mostly* prospective, or that *most* trials are orderly and free from prejudice – they must always be so. However,

---

[48] Rawls, *supra* note 45, at 237-8.

[49] Raz, *supra* note 44, at 218.

[50] *Id.*

[51] See, for instance, Hayek, Friedrich, *The Political Ideal of the Rule of Law*, lecture III (N.B.E. Press, 1955); Kennedy, Duncan, *Legal Formality*, 2 J. Legal Stud. 31-2, 38-9 (June 1973); Dicey, A. V., *Introduction to the Study of the Law of the Constitution*, (Liberty Fund, 1982); Holmes, Stephen, *Passions and Constraint: On the Theory of Liberal Democracy*, (University of Chicago Press, 1995); Weber, Max, *Economy and Society*, ed. G. Roth and R. Wittich (University of California Press, 1978); Finnis, John, *Natural Law and Natural Rights* (Oxford University Press, 1979).

this last point may need clarification: the requirement is not that these sorts of failures cannot ever happen; rather, to be consistent with the rule of law a legal system must not intentionally allow for, approve of, license, or otherwise endorse, these types of failures.

Given this conception of the rule of law, we can now return to the question raised earlier: does jury nullification subvert the rule of law? This is, as noted, a question the courts have felt it is easy to answer. In *Willis*,[52] for instance, the court stated: "[j]ury nullification exalts the goal of particularized justice above the ideal rule of law. We are persuaded the rule of law should not be subverted. A central theme in our constitutional system is that no [person] is above the law and all are equally accountable to it. The people are sovereign, but they exercise their sovereignty through government rather than juries."[53] Of course, it is one thing to assert that jury nullification subverts the rule of law, and quite another to actually provide an explanation as to how it does so. Thus, we must first ask what exactly it means to subvert the rule of law. Clearly, if jury nullification does subvert the rule of law, it must, in some sense, conflict with one or more of the sub-principles that make up the rule of law. For now, let us see how jury nullification and the minimalist account of the rule of law might be said to conflict.

Briefly, I think it is clear that jury nullification does not conflict with the first three of these principles. To begin with, these three are all meant to address the law on books, not the law in action. In other words, the requirement that the law be composed of rules is meant to address how laws are to be established - they must be in the form of rules, not in the form of specific orders issued in an *ad hoc* way by a sovereign or ruling legislative body. Obviously, there is no conflict between the way a jury behaves at trial and the requirement that the law as *written* be comprised of rules. Nor can we read this requirement to hold that the both the law as written and as practiced be comprised of rules, as that requirement is voiced in the fourth principle, that there be congruence between the law as written and as applied. As for the second and third principles, these also both specify what

[52] 218 N.W.2d 921 (Iowa 1974).
[53] *Id.* at 924.

is necessary to properly establish a law, and, for the most part, are not directly addressed to how the actors in a legal system ought to behave. The fourth principle, however – the principle of non-arbitrary enforcement – does directly address how the actors in a legal system ought to behave. In this regard, it directly maps onto the issue of jury nullification, which is, after all, about the behavior of the jury in so nullifying, or, perhaps, the behavior of the bench in giving a *nullification instruction*.

I do think it obvious that there are substantial areas of *prima facie* conflict between this fourth principle and jury nullification. Take the requirement that like cases be treated alike. A nullifying jury - one that refuses to apply the law as given to the facts as believed - is no doubt behaving very differently than another jury hearing the same case and not nullifying. The cases are not being treated alike, despite the fact that both juries agree on what the facts of the case are as well as what the relevant law to apply to those facts would be. When two different tribunals reach the same conclusion regarding the facts and relevant laws of two relevantly similar cases, and yet return different verdicts (which would occur if one of the juries nullified), the principle that like cases be treated alike has obviously been compromised. To the degree that jury nullification allows such an outcome, it seems obviously incompatible with the rule of law. Jury nullification, it can be argued, is also in direct conflict with the requirement that all persons be subject to the authority of the law. Nullification is, essentially, the action of excluding a particular defendant in a particular case from the general authority and applicability of the law. Since this exclusion applies to only that particular defendant, and for only that particular charge, jury nullification appears to add an element of the *ad hoc* to the law's authority. Finally, a nullifying jury clearly seems to be in conflict with the principle that the law in its application must mirror the law as promulgated. If a particular law says that all those who do action *A* are subject to punishment *p*, and a defendant *D* appears before the court who, on the evidence, has, beyond a reasonable doubt, committed *A*, the requirement of congruence demands that *D* be liable to *p* for *A*. A nullifying jury, however, will by definition exclude *D* from *p*, thereby violating this mirroring principle. I am willing, therefore, and for the most part, to concede that jury nullification is in *prima facie* conflict with, at the very least, some of the fundamental elements of the rule of law. However, as I said earlier, merely acknowledging that jury nullification conflicts with the rule of law is not enough to show that there is therefore a problem with jury nullification; this simply is not, on the face of it, a sufficient objection to the practice. More needs to be said as to *why* the loss of the rule of law would be such a bad thing, or if its loss is *prima facie* a bad thing, why it would be worse than the loss of jury nullification.

5.3.2 The Value of the Rule of Law

It is to this question I shall now turn: what is implied by this apparent conflict between jury nullification and the rule of law? The answer, it might be surprising to find out, turns out to be: very little. To support this conclusion, I propose to return to the works of the three theorists discussed earlier: Raz, Fuller, and Rawls. The first question we need to ask is why we even value the rule of law in the first place? Given that there are, in fact, regimes that do not instantiate the rule of law, why should we prefer one that does? What, in other words, is the value of a legal system that effectively guides the action of its subjects – that instantiates the rule of law? We value the rule of law, according to these three legal scholars, precisely because it promotes liberty – personal freedom. Here I am using the term liberty as Isaiah Berlin uses it,[54] and as I understand Raz, Rawls, and Fuller to use it – as a term to be used interchangeably with the idea of personal freedom or autonomy. We do not wish our legal system to restrict liberty unduly (as Rawls puts it: "liberty can be restricted only for the sake of liberty itself."),[55] and conformity with the rule of law is a way of trying to achieve this. Consider Raz's defense of the rule of law:

> We value the ability to choose styles and forms of life, to fix long-term goals and effectively direct one's life towards them. One's ability to do so depends on the existence of stable, secure frameworks for one's life and actions. The law can help secure such fixed points…by a policy of self-restraint designed to make the law

---

[54] See, Berlin, Isaiah, *Four Essays on Liberty* (Oxford University Press, 1969).

[55] Rawls, *supra* note 45, at 244.

> itself a stable and safe basis for individual planning. This… is the concern of the rule of law.[56]

For Raz, then, the rule of law serves to preclude laws and procedures that unduly affect one's liberty through unpredictability of state action. In other words, where state response to behavior is unpredictable, the laws of the State fail to be any sort of practical guide to action. This unduly interferes with our liberty "to choose styles and forms of life, to fix long-term goals and effectively direct [our] life towards them,"[57] something we value intrinsically. Furthermore, considerations of liberty, argues Raz, demand that the law treat individuals as rational choosers, as capable of deducing the consequences of their actions and basing their choices to act in part upon such expected consequences.[58] The rule of law promotes such treatment by making vivid just what those expected consequences are.

Fuller also appeals to considerations of liberty to explain the value of the rule of law. The law, according to Fuller,

> furnishes a baseline for self-directed action… [and] is not… a matter of directing other persons how to accomplish tasks set by a superior, but is basically a matter of providing the citizenry with a sound and stable framework for their interactions with one another, the role of government being that of standing as a guardian of the system.[59]

Fuller is concerned that the law not interfere with liberty and personal freedom except to the extent that doing so is necessary to maintain a stable society with maximum liberty for all. For Fuller, therefore, a legal system that preserves the rule of law is a legal system that refrains from unduly and unnecessarily restricting liberty. Concomitantly, a legal system that fails to conform to the rule of law is a legal system that fails to provide a stable framework for decision-making. And without such a stable

---

[56] Raz, *supra* note 44, at 220.
[57] *Id.*
[58] *Id.* at 221. Note: Raz actually claims that it is, in fact, respect for *human dignity* that demands that the law be action-guiding. It is clear, however, from the context that Raz means much the same thing by "human dignity" as Rawls and Fuller mean by "liberty": personal freedom and autonomy.
[59] Fuller, *supra* note 45, at 210.

framework, argues Fuller, the limits of one's personal freedoms – one's liberty – are unknown and unknowable. Assuming that rational agents are somewhat risk averse, it is easy to see how such ignorance regarding the boundaries of acceptable action could have the effect of constraining ones liberties – if not formally, then at least on a practical level. Fuller also ties liberty to the rule of law by stating that regimes involved in gross violations of personal liberty could never be law-like. In such situations, argues Fuller, "the principal object of government seems to be, not that of giving the citizen rules by which to shape his conduct, but to frighten him into impotence."[60] Fuller is claiming here that regimes where personal liberties are severely constrained thereby violate the rule of law.

Finally, we can turn to Rawls's defense of the rule of law. Like Raz and Fuller, Rawls's conception of the rule of law is tied to considerations of liberty. At its most basic, Rawls takes liberty to mean nothing more than treating individuals as rational choosers with the intrinsic right to determine their life choices (subject, of course, to the *proviso* that one not unduly interfere with another's acceptable choices). Rawls claims that the rule of law is an aspect of his overall conception of justice as fairness: the rule of law is justice applied to a legal system with the expressed purpose of promoting liberty, the prime value in justice as fairness.[61] He states his position most explicitly when he claims: "The dangers to liberty are less where the law is impartially and regularly administered in accordance with the principle of legality [the rule of law]."[62]

In all three of these theorists, we find the normative claim that whatever form a legal system takes, it ought always to promote the individual liberty of its citizens. And the rule of law is valued because, it is argued, it functions so as to promote the individual liberty of citizens. How does it do this? Again, all three theorists agree: by providing protection against arbitrary state action. Indeed, for Fuller this is very foundation of the rule of law:

---

[60] *Id.* at 40.

[61] Rawls, *supra* note 45, at 235.

[62] *Id.* at 241.

> Surely the very essence of the Rule of Law is that in acting upon the citizen... a government will faithfully apply rules previously declared as those to be followed by the citizen and as being determinative of his rights and duties. *If the Rule of Law does not mean this, it means nothing*.[63]

His point seems to be that, while conformity to the rule of law may not guarantee that liberty is promoted, nevertheless, substantive departure from the rule of law will most certainly negatively impact on personal liberties. For Raz, we value the rule of law up until the point that it promotes, or allows for the pursuit of, individual liberties, but no further. Again, this is a perspective shared by the courts.[64]

To be as precise as possible then, the claim we have been looking at runs like this: we want our legal system to instantiate the rule of law because we want our legal system to promote or allow for the pursuit of personal liberty. I am going to assume that this is correct – that, all things being equal, we do want our legal system to promote liberty. I am also going to assume that we are justified in this – that we are correct in thinking that a legal system ought to promote liberty. I am also going to assume that the claim that the rule of law actually functions to promote or allow for the pursuit of liberty is correct. Finally, I am going to assume that a legal system that allows for jury nullification does, on the face of it, seemingly conflict with the rule of law. Does it follow from this that we ought to prefer a legal system that preserves the rule of law to one that allows for nullification? Though it might seem obvious that the answer is yes, I argue that a more nuanced examination of the phenomena in question will show that this question, by its very nature, is predicated on a category error.

---

[63] See Fuller, *supra* note 45, at 209-10 (emphasis added).

[64] See, for instance, *State ex Rel. Kincaid v. Parsons*, 191 W. Va. 608, 611 (W. Va. 1994): "Everyone must understand that his right to swing his arm ends at the other chap's nose." See, also, *Perlot v. Green*, 609 F. Supp. 3d 1106, 1111 (D. Idaho 2022): "An oft-quoted statement – attributed to various Supreme Court Justices and legal scholars – explains that the 'right to swing your arms ends just where the other man's nose begins.'"

5.3.3 The Conformity of Jury Nullification with the Rule of Law

If it were simply the case that the conflict between the rule of law and jury nullification was between, respectively, a legal system that promoted liberty and one that failed to promote liberty or even actively discouraged it, then the decision would be clear, and jury nullification should and would be rejected, for obvious reasons. But the conflict between jury nullification and the rule of law does not turn on the inclusion or exclusion of considerations of liberty. For one thing, recall that jury nullification can only result in an acquittal, never a conviction – it is simply not jury nullification otherwise.[65] Jury nullification is, in this respect, a purely liberty enhancing mechanism. So, while jury nullification certainly appears indicative of a departure from the requirement that there be congruence between the law as promulgated and the law as applied, this departure in no way negatively impacts a defendant's liberty – the person whose liberty is, after all, the one at stake. While there is no doubt that there is certainly a formal conflict here, it is, nevertheless, hardly one of great significance *vis-à-vis* considerations of liberty. While one may object to such a conflict on many different grounds, one is simply not free to claim that jury nullification is incompatible with the promotion and protection of liberty and autonomy; nullification has no direct negative impact on anyone's liberty. To put this explicitly: jury nullification flows in one direction only – always and only towards a verdict of not guilty. Such a verdict can therefore only directly *increase* a defendant's liberty, and in no way negatively impacts her freedom or autonomy. Whether it is just, appropriate, or wise for any particular defendant to receive her liberty is a different issue altogether: liberty is liberty, and jury nullification can only function so as to directly increase it for the defendant.[66] Given that the justificatory foundation of the rule of law is to promote or allow for the pursuit of liberty, and given that jury nullification is an exclusively liberty-

---

[65] See my detailed analysis of this point at CHAPTER 1, note 7.

[66] Whether jury nullification can, in some sense, *indirectly* decrease the liberties of a community faced with a dangerous offender released into their midst, is, I admit, a possible concern. But in reply, we can say: i) it is implausible to imagine that juries would routinely behave in such a manner; and, ii) we are here, for the most part, only concerned with the *direct* and identifiable relationship between the rule of law and jury nullification.

enhancing mechanism, the two are seemingly consistent with, and not contrary to, one another.

Jury nullification, I argue, therefore not only does *not* subvert the rule of law, it actually serves to promote the same fundamental ends and goals as the rule of law. To begin with, we value the rule of law instrumentally, recall, because it promotes liberty. How does it do this? In part, by guarding against arbitrary state action. In other words, when what we are free to do safely (that is, safe from state action) is vague and imprecise (as it would be if state action could be exercised arbitrarily and without check), then in the words of Rawls, the "boundaries of our liberty are uncertain. And to the extent that this is so, liberty is restricted by reasonable fear of its exercise."[67] Just like the rule of law, the jury system (with its *privilege* to disregard judicial instructions regarding the law) is also a powerful tool in the promotion and protection of liberty. Moreover, it is precisely the jury's ability to nullify that allows it to function in this manner. Such a view was certainly advocated by the U.S. Supreme Court in *Duncan v. Louisiana*.[68] This key passage from White J.'s majority opinion provides insight into the Court's reasoning: "A right to jury trial is granted to criminal defendants in order to prevent oppression by the Government… Fear of unchecked power… found expression in the criminal law in this insistence upon community participation in the determination of guilt or innocence."[69] The majority in *Dougherty* begrudgingly admitted a similar point, describing the jury with its *privilege* to nullify as a "necessary counter to case-hardened judges and arbitrary prosecutors."[70] The Court in *Williams v. Florida*[71] reasoned along the same lines, referring to the jury "as a safeguard against arbitrary law enforcement."[72]

Clearly the courts in all of these cases viewed the jury system to be a very important, if not essential, check and balance against arbitrary action by the State against its citizens – to be, in other words, an essential tool in the

[67] Rawls, *supra* note 45, at 239.
[68] 391 U.S. 145 (1968).
[69] *Id.* at 155-6.
[70] *U. S. v. Dougherty*, *supra* note 2, at 1136.
[71] 399 U.S. 78, (1970).
[72] *Id.* at 86 (citations omitted).

protection and promotion of individual liberty *vis-à-vis* arbitrary state action.[73] Any attempt to prosecute in an *ad hoc* and arbitrary manner by the State will, due to the jury's nullificatory *privilege*, fail if confronted by a jury that refuses to be complicit in such actions. Presumably, the more arbitrary, unprincipled, and oppressive the State's actions are, the less chance there is of jury approval, and hence, less chance of individuals becoming victims of such arbitrary state action. If so, then obviously the jury – with its *privilege* to nullify – functions as a valuable mechanism in the promotion and protection of individual liberties against arbitrary and oppressive state action. Concomitantly, if the jury were not able to disregard the State's position on how the law ought to be applied – if it was unable to nullify, in other words – then its ability to effectively promote and protect individual liberty would obviously be severely constrained, if not eliminated altogether, when confronted with arbitrary state application and enforcement of the law.

Put explicitly: the jury system (given its *privilege* to nullify) is essential to protect an accused against some forms of arbitrary state action; protection against arbitrary action by the State is essential if liberty is not to be unduly restricted; hence, the jury system (due in large part to its nullificatory *privilege*) is, at least in some instances, a powerful tool for the protection and promotion of personal liberties against arbitrary state action. Thus, while the jury system (with its intrinsic *privilege* to nullify) may appear to conflict with the rule of law, upon closer inspection, the significance of this conflict appears to be greatly exaggerated. In other words, while there is,

---

[73] See, also, *United States v. Young*, 403 F. Supp. 3d 1131, 1157 (D.N.M. 2019), where the Court asserted that "the Sixth Amendment jury trial right guarantees the 'historical foundation' of the jury as "guard[ing] against a spirit of oppression and tyranny on the part of rulers, and as the great bulwark of our civil and political liberties;" *United States v. Baker*, 342 F. Supp. 3d 1189, 1221-22 (D.N.M. 2018): "The Court has made clear its belief that the jury has the power to put off the law as the Court gives it and to convict according to the jury's conscience. This power has been a long-standing bulwark against the threat of judicial despotism and congressional tyranny;" also, *Duncan v. Louisiana*, *supra* note 68, at 151-52, quoting Blackstone: "Our law has therefore wisely placed this strong and two-fold barrier, of a presentment and a trial by jury, between the liberties of the people and the prerogative of the crown… [T]he truth of every accusation, whether preferred in the shape of indictment, information, or appeal, should afterwards be confirmed by the unanimous suffrage of twelve of his equals and neighbours, indifferently chosen and superior to all suspicion."

indeed, a *prima facie* conflict between the fourth principle of the minimalist/procedural account of the rule of law and jury nullification, this conflict in no way undermines the essential virtue of the rule of law – that it promotes and protects liberty through, in part, minimizing arbitrary state action. In fact, jury nullification plays the exact same role through the exact same mechanism – it too promotes and protects liberty through, in part, minimizing arbitrary state action. Thus, there really is very little to no substantive conflict between jury nullification and the rule of law, despite initial appearances to the contrary. As Raz states: "Some infringements [of the rule of law] are worse than others. Some violate the principles in a formal way only, which does not offend against the spirit of the doctrine."[74] Furthermore, he states, conformity to the rule of law is "only one of the many virtues that a legal system should possess."[75] I believe that this best captures my view on the subject; despite its formal conflict with the principle, jury nullification is entirely *consistent with* the substantive, liberty-promoting goals instantiated within the rule of law. Moreover, nothing of much significance can be deduced from this purely *formal* conflict – certainly nothing as significant as whether a jury *nullification instruction* would function so as to subvert essential liberties.

I am going to pause here for a moment and review what has been established so far in this chapter. The objections to nullification based on, respectively, anarchy, racism, and the rule of law, are, I argue, all less than successful. The fears of jural anarchy are exaggerated, unrealistic, and conceptually arbitrary. And while it is true that jurors may use their *privilege* to nullify in order to promote racist ends and thereby 'pervert' the justice system, it is not at all clear that the presence or absence of the *nullification instruction* would make much of a difference one way or another in how such jurors act. Moreover, where the legal system is administrated fairly and without bias, and juries are representative of the community at large, such racially motivated verdicts are not apt to occur. It is hard, therefore, to make persuasive the claim that the jury, particularly in its use of its nullification *privilege*, is to blame for such verdicts. Finally, even if we were to admit that a legal system which allows for jury

---

[74] Raz, *supra* note 44, at 221.

[75] *Id.* at 219.

nullification is, in some way, formally inconsistent with the rule of law, this, in and of itself, hardly stands as an objection. Once we look at why one might attach importance to the rule of law, we see that the jury system, with its *privilege* to nullify, also promotes the very same value and ends as the rule of law – namely, the protection and promotion of personal liberty, (understood in this case as protection from arbitrary state action). The only way, therefore, to prefer a legal system *formally* consistent with the rule of law to a legal system that allows for jury nullification would be if there were some argument that the former model promoted liberty more effectively or efficiently than the latter. No such argument appears to be available; to the contrary – the ability of the jury to refuse to convict where the Government is acting in a manner unjust, vindictive, or overly biased, is an incredibly strong and direct safeguard to personal liberty in the face of arbitrary state action.

5.4 The Bad-Faith-Juror Objection

Recall that in Chapter 4, I suggested what a successful argument against the *nullification instruction* might look like. To begin with, we could assert that the laudable goals of the instruction[76] can be met without actually giving the instruction.[77] The *nullification instruction,* we might conclude, is therefore unnecessary. We could then further argue that jury nullification has some associated negative consequences; thus, any move to promote jury nullification would be a move to concomitantly and unnecessarily promote those negative consequences. Hence, we might conclude, the *nullification instruction* is unwarranted. For this argument to have any rhetorical purchase, however, I explained how we must first have a genuine and justified reason to believe that there are, indeed, unwelcome negative consequences associated with the *nullification instruction.* Moreover, we would also need a good reason to believe that such consequences clearly outweigh the associated positive consequences of

[76] To: i) ensure that the standards of the community are brought to bear on the administration of the criminal law; and/or ii) ensure that the citizenry will not be victimized by unwarranted and oppressive state action; and/or iii) add an element of mercy/justice to situations where a strict adherence to the law might otherwise be cruel.

[77] Through *contextualism,* perhaps, or through *damn-good-reason* nullification.

giving the instruction. Heretofore, the objections to the instruction that we have been looking at have, as I demonstrated, failed to establish a genuine and justified foundation for either belief.

There is, however, one objection to the *nullification instruction* that I believe to be not only successful (that is, it is both relevant and persuasive), but is also able to meet the challenges posed by the arguments in favor of the instruction discussed in Chapter 4. I call it the *bad-faith-juror* objection. The *nullification instruction* has, I argue, the unforeseen, but unavoidable consequence of, not only encouraging jurors to nullify the law, but to also deliberate in *bad-faith* and in such a way so as to increase the likelihood of unwarranted and unjust *convictions*. The *nullification instruction* thereby negatively affects the integrity of a fair, just, and impartial trial, and, importantly, negatively and unjustly impacts the liberty of some defendants.[78] What do I mean by *bad-faith*? Jurors act in *bad-faith* when they use certain *de facto* (but, importantly, not *de jure*) discretionary abilities to convict a defendant who would otherwise, according to the law, be found not guilty.

Consider: a judge, in giving the *nullification instruction*, is saying to the jury something akin to: "I am going to give you an order regarding how the law in this case is to be interpreted and applied. However, you are free to disregard that order at your discretion." But given that instruction, what is to prevent the average juror from wondering whether all such orders and instructions from the bench are similarly discretionary in nature?[79] Once a juror is told that she can safely ignore a specific judicial instruction free from reprimand or redress, she might thereby also infer that *all* such orders given by the judge are similarly discretionary in nature. Moreover, such an inference would not be entirely unjustified – at least from a practical point

---

[78] It is important to note the distinction I am making here. I am not arguing that jury nullification *itself* compromises the integrity of a fair, just, and impartial trial, or has a negative impact on the liberty of some defendants. Rather, the position I am arguing for is that it is the *nullification instruction* that has these specific deleterious effects.

[79] There is a recursive nature to this problem. After all, the judge could inform the jurors that her instructions regarding the law are the only such instructions they are free to ignore, but again, once that door has been opened, what is to prevent a juror from wondering whether that first order too is also discretionary? It too, after all, is an instruction regarding the law.

of view. This might seem an odd thing to say, and I am certainly not suggesting that the jury has any sort of *de jure* power to ignore any and all judicial instructions. However, given the combined principles of deliberative secrecy and privacy regarding jury verdicts, jurors do, in fact, have a substantial and robust *de facto* power to ignore or reject many of the procedural constraints considered central to the notion of a fair trial, such as, among other things, the presumption of innocence (included in this presumption is the idea that a defendant's decision not to testify in his or her defense is not to be taken as *prima facie* evidence of guilt), fair rules of evidence (based on traditional notions of legal relevance: for instance, if potential evidence does not make any element of the crime more or less likely, such evidence is deemed irrelevant and, hence, inadmissible), and a burden on the prosecution to prove the defendant's guilt 'beyond a reasonable doubt.' All of these elements of a fair trial are given to the jury via instructions from the bench; if a juror is of the mind that she can safely ignore any or all of these other judicial instructions free from sanction, impeachment, or redress, then the very notion of a fair trial becomes corrupted. Of course, in principle some form of relief is always available to those convicted as a result of this type of *bad-faith* jury discretion, but since juries do not issue written decisions, nor are their deliberations monitored, it is not at all clear that such an avenue is effectively open in most cases. We simply do not know most of the time *why* a jury decides to convict and thus cannot impeach their reasons for doing so. The jury's discretionary power to ignore or reject most judicial instructions is, in practice, nearly unreviewable; for all intents and purposes, the jury has *bad-faith* discretion in a very practical, powerful, and *de facto*, sense.

I think it obvious that, were the jury to become cognizant of such widespread *de facto* discretion to convict in spite of the law and evidence, this would present significant challenges to the notion of a fair trial. For instance, it is not uncommon for evidence or testimony to be introduced in court that is subsequently ruled to be inadmissible. Often judges will simply instruct the jury to ignore such evidence or testimony and not let it play any part in their deliberations.[80] But, of course, this is a judicial order,

[80] We can debate whether such an order can be completely followed. After all, once the jury has heard something, they cannot very well un-hear it, and presumably it will

and, as argued above, the jury has a very real *de facto* power to ignore it. If this order is intentionally ignored (because the jurors feel they have the discretion to so act), and the evidence or testimony in question *is* taken into consideration, then the defendant will not have been convicted solely on the evidence relevant to the alleged crime, but, also, on extraneous, extra-legal factors. This would be a paradigmatic case of *bad-faith* reasoning or deliberating. Or consider the principle that the decision not to defend oneself on the stand is not to be taken as evidence of guilt. Judges give that particular order precisely because it is human nature to consider it suspicious when someone accused of iniquitous behavior does not try to defend themselves. Jurors, too, have to struggle against that tendency, and it is a struggle that all agree ought to be encouraged, fostered, and supported. Moreover, this principle is at the heart of the ideal that it is the prosecution's responsibility to prove guilt, not the defendant's responsibility to prove innocence. If, however, the jury intentionally ignores the judge's instruction not to take the defendant's refusal to testify as indicative of anything, then both the principles of the presumption of innocence and the right against self-incrimination would be compromised, if not altogether forfeit. Consider what the Court had to say on this issue in *People v. Smith*:[81]

> After all, if a jury is free to use its status as "representative of the community" or "the community's conscience" (or whatever else supporters of jury nullification claim gives the jury the prerogative to reject the trial court's instructions of law), then should the jury not be able to question *any* instruction that it finds questionable or archaic? For instance, why should a jury accept the trial court's admonition that the defendant's failure to testify should not be held against him? Clearly, this admonition is counterintuitive. Most jurors would expect in their daily lives that someone accused of criminal behavior would provide some defense or explanation. Most

---

play *some* role in their deliberative procedure. However, there is still a great deal of difference between deliberating upon a verdict while intentionally trying *not to* let a particular piece of testimony or evidence affect one's decision, and deliberating upon a verdict while intentionally trying *to* let a particular piece of testimony or evidence affect one's decision.

[81] 296 Ill. App. 3d 435 (Ill. App. Ct. 1998).

> jurors would also conclude that a person's failure to provide some explanation would indicate that he was guilty of the charge.[82]

Again, the problem here is that once it becomes clear to the jury that one judicial instruction can be safely ignored, it is a very small step to concluding (rightly or wrongly) that a great many others can as well, leading to *bad-faith* verdicts.

It seems obvious, therefore that the *nullification instruction* could encourage jurors to deliberate in *bad-faith* and thereby reject important judicial instructions regarding the procedural and substantive constraints embedded within the very notion of a fair trial. This is especially troubling, given that the particular elements of a fair trial that we have been looking at (fair rules of evidence, the presumption of innocence, and the burden of proof necessary for a conviction) are all safeguards put in place in an attempt to minimize the possibility of wrongful, unwarranted, and unjust convictions. The fact of the matter is, however, that such safeguards are, in a very real, *de facto* sense, discretionary. That is, the jury can ignore some or all of these procedural and substantive constraints with relative impunity – the principle of jury secrecy prevents the courts from inquiring into how and why a jury reached its verdict.[83] Given the fact that when juries ignore such judicial instructions and procedural constraints they can do so in a way that might guide their deliberations towards a guilty verdict, when a strict application of the law would otherwise demand a not guilty verdict, this is obviously some cause for concern *vis-à-vis* issues of justice and liberty. Thus, and given this danger, it seems reasonable and pragmatic to conclude that we ought not to give the *nullification instruction*. We ought not, in other words, institutionalize anything that might encourage jurors to convict in ways contrary to the law and evidence. While many proponents of jury nullification argue that the jury's *privilege* to behave in such a manner is more than simply an oversight (myself included), that it is, in fact, a design feature of the jury system, the same simply cannot be said about the 'privilege'[84] to ignore judicial instructions regarding the procedural and substantive elements of a fair trial. No one could possibly

---

[82] *Id.* at 442.

[83] See **CHAPTER 1** § 1.5.4: Jury Deliberations.

[84] If that's the proper way to describe it. The matter is really not relevant.

argue that this is either a design feature of the jury system or a positive element thereof. This type of jury discretion, unlike nullification, is nothing more than a malignant, *de facto*, emergent property of an otherwise efficacious and just means of procedural adjudication. My objection then is not that the practice of jury nullification itself will lead to more (and unjust) convictions. Nullification, by definition, can only result in acquittals. Rather, the fundamental claim at the heart of the *bad-faith-juror* objection is that the *nullification instruction* will lead to more unjust convictions by indirectly encouraging or licensing jurors to ignore or reject those judicial instructions specifically designed to guarantee a fair trial and minimize the risk of unjust convictions. Hence, the *bad-faith-juror* objection directly implicates the *nullification instruction* without thereby impugning the integrity of jury nullification. This is different than the objections we have been looking at heretofore, where the practice of jury nullification itself was seen to be the problem and the instruction was implicated only to the degree that it promoted instances of jury nullification. To my mind, the *bad-faith-juror* objection is the most successful objection to the *nullification instruction*. It both preserves the role and respect for jury nullification as "a fact of our jurisprudential process"[85] while at the same time explaining why, despite this fact, the jury ought not to receive judicial instructions regarding their *privilege*.

I want to be clear on what I am asserting here: my claim isn't merely that juries who receive the *nullification instruction* might thereby convict more often (though this would be worrisome enough). There is a more foundational concern at play here: that juries so informed will return guilty verdicts precisely in those cases where it is particularly important that all of the rules of a fair trial are maintained. I am referring to those cases where a high degree of moral opprobrium and revulsion is attached to the alleged crime. Consider a scenario where the defendant was accused of, say, pedophilia. Let us suppose that the evidence presented at trial was circumstantial at best, and that after the defense made its case it seemed unlikely that the prosecutorial burden of proof could be met. In these sorts of situations, the knee-jerk reactions that many of us might have of "where there's smoke there's fire," and "better safe than sorry," could very well

[85] *U.S. v. Powell*, 955 F.2d 1206, 1213 (9th Cir. 1992).

combine in the minds of the jurors so as to over-ride the judicial instructions regarding the burden of proof in a way that, I speculate, would not happen if the defendant was being accused of some more morally neutral crime, such as, say, fishing without a license. My worry with this example is that informed jurors might very well convict the defendant in a pedophilia case in circumstances where an uninformed jury would not. Less time, I speculate, will be spent during deliberations on the question of whether the evidence supports a guilty verdict when the crime alleged is of a morally heinous nature. While my claim in this respect is, admittedly, somewhat speculative in nature, it is a fairly well-established concern that has found voice in many of the procedural elements and constraints of the modern jury trial. This is why the bench issues orders to the jury cautioning them against being unduly influenced by the nature of the charge; this is why jurors are vetted during *voir dire* to ensure that they can evaluate the evidence free of prejudice (victims of sexual assault, for example, do not generally get to be jurors on cases involving sexual assault). While this sort of 'moral prejudice' attached to the crime alleged is perhaps unavoidable, giving the *nullification instruction*, I contend, will only exacerbate the problem. Jurors might very well feel free to give in to their moral prejudices and biases if they feel that they can do so with relative safety and impunity. And, as I mentioned above, it is a short logical leap from the realization that one judicial order can be safely ignored to the realization that a great many others can as well. If such an instruction is given, I claim, what we risk is a justice system whereby the type of crime a defendant is charged with will often end up playing a substantial and material role in the jury's decision to convict or acquit. And whatever this may be, it is certainly not justice. Again, this challenge to the *nullification instruction* is rather speculative in nature, and in order for it to be the least bit persuasive, it would help to have some evidence to confirm my suspicions.

Fortunately, there is empirical evidence that appears to directly confirm my conjectures regarding *bad-faith* deliberations. Irwin Horowitz, in *The Effect of Jury Nullification Instruction on Verdicts and Jury Functioning in Criminal Trials*,[86] conducted a study designed specifically to answer the following

[86] Horowitz, I. A., *The Effect of Jury Nullification Instruction on Verdicts and Jury Functioning in Criminal Trials*, Law and Human Behavior, 9(1), 25 (1985).

question: "will the jury operate in a manner which is different than its normal function if given explicit nullification instructions?"[87] His findings were surprising and prove ultimately to be detrimental to those who endorse the *nullification instruction*. Horowitz ran an experiment involving 45 mock juries, 270 jurors, and three different criminal cases. The mock juries were divided into three groups of 15 each with each group hearing a different criminal case (murder, drunk driving involving vehicular homicide, and euthanasia). Finally, each group was further divided into 3 groups of 5 mock juries, with each of these smaller groups hearing a different instruction from the bench regarding the proper purview of their authority in the case at hand. Two of these groups received standard pattern juror instructions; the third received explicit nullification instructions, or, as Horowitz labeled them, *Radical Nullification Instructions (RNI)*. Jurors were told that: i) "although they are a public body bound to give respectful attention to the laws, they have final authority to decide whether or not to apply a given law to the acts of the defendant on trial before them;"[88] ii) "they represent (the community) and that it is appropriate to bring into their deliberations the feelings of the community and their own feelings based on conscience;"[89] and, iii) "nothing would bar them from acquitting the defendant if they feel the law, as applied to the fact situation before them, would produce an inequitable or unjust result."[90]

After the juries heard their respective cases and related instructions, they retired to the jury-room to deliberate. These deliberations were recorded and later analyzed. This analysis yielded the following findings. RNI juries spent more time discussing the implications of the *nullification instruction* than did either of the other two jury types. This is not surprising, for obvious reasons. What is alarming is that RNI juries spent significantly less time considering the evidence against the accused than did either of the other two jury types. We can see exactly why this is alarming by looking at the verdicts these different juries returned. For the murder case there was no difference – all returned guilty verdicts (the evidence, states Horowitz,

[87] *Id.* at 25.
[88] *Id.* at 30
[89] *Id.* at 30-1.
[90] *Id.* at 31.

"clearly indicat[ed] the defendant's guilt").[91] There were, however, marked and substantial differences between all three juries in the euthanasia case. A full 80% of the RNI juries returned not guilty verdicts, whereas the number of not guilty verdicts for the other two juries was between 40% and 20%. This merciful response is in keeping, of course, with what proponents of the *nullification instruction* assume will occur. Euthanasia is certainly illegal, but many people are nonetheless sympathetic to its practice in some situations.[92]

The drunk driving case, however, is a different, and much more troubling story. Here, while both standard pattern jury types returned not guilty verdicts 40% of the time, the RNI juries voted to convict in *every instance* – a 100% conviction rate – despite hearing identical cases, arguments, and evidence. This is particularly distressing because these same RNI juries also spent less time deliberating upon the evidence than did either of the other jury types. Put plainly, the RNI jury was substantially more likely to condemn for drunk driving, regardless of the evidence, and spend less time deliberating on the evidence when doing so, than juries not so instructed. Why? Recall that these deliberations were monitored, and as Horowitz explains it:

> In the drunk driving case, RNI juries were more apt to convict the defendant of reckless vehicular homicide [than the other juries]… There was, however, at least a suggestive trend in the jury operating under RNI that the defendant, as [an alleged] drunk driver, was perceived quite unfavorably. Current campaigns aimed at curbing drunk driving have received a good deal of publicity… at the time this study took place.[93]

In other words, the jurors felt a certain amount of moral condemnation towards the accused, due, in great part, to his status as an alleged drunk driver, and while we can speculate that perhaps all of the jurors in all three jury sample cases felt this way, the fact remains that only the jurors who

[91] *Id.* at 31

[92] For instance, the jurors in the euthanasia case heard testimony from the deceased's wife that he had suffered great pain and had hoped for death to occur.

[93] Horowitz, *supra* note 86, at 33.

received the RNI *nullification instruction* were more apt to let their moral condemnation of the act alleged influence their verdict and were more apt to disregard or downplay the facts and law when returning a verdict.[94] Horowitz's study gives empirical credence to the *bad-faith-juror* objection and supports the conclusion that the *nullification instruction* leads to more unjust and unwarranted convictions in certain instances – convictions based, not on the evidence, but on the moral nature of alleged crime.

Because we have now established that giving the *nullification instruction* does, in fact, have negative associated consequences, these negative consequences must be weighed against the instruction's benefits. To begin with, the *nullification instruction* can certainly bring the standards of the community to bear on the administration of the criminal law, but as the *bad-faith-juror* objection illustrates, it can do so to the detriment of the accused, and not just to her benefit.[95] Secondly, while the *nullification instruction* can help ensure that the citizenry will not be victimized by unwarranted, arbitrary, and unjust state action, the *bad-faith-juror* objection shows that it cannot ensure that individual defendants will not be victimized by unwarranted, arbitrary, and unjust 'moral prejudice' on the part of the jury. As a matter of fact, giving the instruction is almost a guarantee that some defendants *will be* victimized in such a manner, and hence, will have their liberty unduly and unjustly constrained by unwarranted moral prejudice on the part of the jury. And while the *nullification instruction* can certainly add an element of mercy to the administration of the law, it is now equally clear that giving the instruction can also add an extra-legal element of malice to the administration of the law. Finally, while the *nullification instruction* can add an element of justice to situations where a strict adherence to the law might otherwise be unjust, it can also, as the *bad-faith-juror* objection explains, promote great injustices. Whatever a defendant's alleged crimes may be, the moral nature of said crimes ought never to be a factor in the determination of guilt or innocence. That is the very antithesis of justice. Whatever advantages to the administration of the law are realized by giving the *nullification instruction*, they are outweighed by the

---

[94] *Id.*

[95] It is important to bear in mind that the objection is not that jury nullification will work to the detriment of the accused. Rather, the complaint is that the *nullification instruction* will do so, albeit indirectly.

very real disadvantages that also accompany such an instruction. Or, as I put it, such an instruction encourages jurors to deliberate in *bad-faith* to the detriment of the accused, and hence ought not be given, lest we risk compromising a defendant's right to a fair and impartial trial.

While jury nullification can only act in a liberty enhancing way (i.e., can only result in acquittals), the *nullification instruction* has the unfortunate consequence of potentially limiting liberties unduly and unjustly. This last point illustrates perhaps one of the main rhetorical advantages of the *bad-faith-juror* objection, and what sets it apart from the prior three objections – it is not predicated on specious or irrationally counterfactual views about the purported dangers of jury nullification, nor does it impute a dissolute, vicious, or vengeful nature to jurors in order to condemn the instruction. The *nullification instruction* is, according to the *bad-faith-juror* objection, due to its practical consequences, contrary to justice, liberty, and the right to a fair trial.

To the degree that we embrace that fundamental principle of law and governance that "it is better for ten guilty persons to go free than to convict an innocent one,"[96] there are thereby compelling and conclusive reasons to reject the arguments offered in support of the *nullification instruction*. As the *bad-faith-juror* objection vividly demonstrates, it carries real and tangible risks to our cherished values of liberty, freedom, and the attainment of just, fair, and unbiased verdicts in the administration of the criminal law.

---

[96] *Bunnell v. Sullivan*, 947 F.2d 341, 352 (9th Cir. 1991). See, also, *United States v. Greer*, 538 F.2d 437, 441 (D.C. Cir. 1976): "It is a cardinal principle of Anglo-American jurisprudence that, in Blackstone's immortal words, better ten guilty persons should go free than one innocent person be convicted;" *United States v. Fips*, Case No.: 1:18 CR 722 *7-8 (N.D. Ohio Sep. 30, 2020): "the court emphasizes the fundamental principle that 'the law holds that it is better that ten guilty persons escape than that one innocent suffer;'" *Tucker v. Palmer*, 541 F.3d 652, 671 (6th Cir. 2008): "To conclude, I would like again to quote the sage words that '[b]etter that ten guilty persons escape than that one innocent suffer;'" *United States v. De Watson*, 792 F.3d 1174, 1183 (9th Cir. 2015): "No tradition is more firmly established in our system of law than assuring to the greatest extent that its inevitable errors are made in favor of the guilty rather than against the innocent. Our legal tradition has always followed Blackstone's principle that 'it is better that ten guilty persons escape than that one innocent suffer.'"

Conclusion

Jury nullification is a privilege. It has de jure status, and thus is a legitimate feature of the criminal jury system. Despite its de jure status, however, it is clearly not a legal right. Hence, nothing whatsoever follows from the jural legitimacy of jury nullification as regards the nullification instruction. We must look to wider policy-based considerations to resolve this issue. As the bad-faith-juror objection demonstrates, considerations of justice, fairness, truth, and liberty demand that we withhold such an instruction. The costs are too great; the risks are too high.

Let me review how I arrived at these findings/conclusions. I began this book with the bold claim that I would be providing clarity to the conceptual disarray currently plaguing the controversies surrounding the jurisprudence of jury nullification. Those controversies, recall, focused on two related but conceptually distinct questions: i) What is the legal status/jural nature of jury nullification? and, ii) Should jurors receive an in-court *nullification instruction*? While these two issues are often conflated, confused, and casually combined in much of the literature, neither of these questions can be properly addressed and answered, I posited, without a prior understanding of their unique nature and conceptual disparity. This monograph, then, is my attempt to clear the conceptual fog currently enveloping the jury nullification debate by demonstrating how, why, and in what ways these two questions and their respective answers are, indeed, conceptually distinct in nature, substance, and, most importantly, legal implication.

While Chapter 1 was purely an exegetical enterprise, its intent was to clearly demonstrate and elucidate how the history and current jurisprudence regarding the right to a jury trial in criminal cases have together traced a path that make jury nullification the structural inevitability that it is today. Chapter 2 expanded on the nature of this structurally inevitable and necessary character of jury nullification by showing how any practical methods of prevention or redress are ultimately in conflict with doctrine, statute, and constitutional law, as well as being antithetical to the foundational principles on which the jury system is based. Jury nullification is, I concluded, necessarily, an intrinsic part of the criminal jury system as it now exists. It was at this point that I turned my attention specifically to the issue of the *nullification instruction*.

In Chapter 3 I introduced, developed, and defended my *privilege* model of jury nullification as a way of addressing the current controversy around the *nullification instruction* question. This structural/conceptual analysis of nullification's jural nature was necessary, recall, as a response to those debates surrounding the *nullification instruction* that are predicated on jury nullification's status as either a *de jure* right or merely a *de facto* power. As my *privilege* account showed, the binary framework of this *rights/power* model of jury nullification is simply too narrow to properly explain nullification's role within the legal system. Jury nullification does indeed enjoy a *de jure* status; however, and most importantly, it status as such does not rise to the level of a *de jure* right. Jury nullification is, instead, a *de jure privilege*, and as such, nothing is implied structurally or constructively one way or the other *vis-à-vis* the *nullification instruction*. The major contribution of my *privilege* model of jury nullification, therefore, will be to hopefully forestall any and all future arguments either for or against the *nullification instruction* that rely on this conceptually unsound *rights/power* framework. Since we cannot solve the *nullification instruction* question through a conceptual analysis into the jural status of jury nullification itself, I concluded, we must look to *policy*-based, consequence-oriented reasons for or against doing so.

Chapter 4, therefore, began where Chapter 3 left off, with the search for *policy*-based reasons in favor of giving an in-court *nullification instruction*. While the *freedom from government oppression*, *community/democratic values*, and *mercy/justice* arguments all offered well-motivated reasons to view the *privilege* of jury nullification as a positive influence overall in the pursuit of a just and fair legal system, these arguments failed to establish the *necessity* of the *nullification instruction* as a means to realizing their ends. As such, they were all, I argued, vulnerable to the *damn-good-reason* objection as well as the *contextualist* account of juror deliberative behavior. I left off this chapter by remarking that, while these latter two objections to the *nullification instruction* were promising, neither of them provided significant reason, proof, or evidence for believing that the instruction was thereby unwarranted.

The search for a well-motivated objection to the *nullification instruction*, therefore, was the entire focus of Chapter 5. The *anarchy*, *racist-juror*, and *rule-of-law* objections, I established, simply proved insufficient to the task. To one degree or another, they relied on hyperbole, poor reasoning, or a fundamental misunderstanding of the jural and legal/political principles involved, respectively. Moreover – and this is the cardinal mistake that all such objections make – these three objections all focused on the purported ill-effects of jury nullification itself, and reasoned indirectly from there to the conclusion that the *nullification instruction* was thereby unwarranted. This is where the main advantage of my *bad-faith-juror* objection becomes most evident and apparent: I need not engage in specious or irrationally counterfactual reasoning about the supposed vices of jury nullification or the iniquitous nature of jurors in order to condemn the instruction. The *nullification instruction* is, on its own merits, unwarranted, unwise, and contrary to the fundamental principles of justice that our legal system is founded upon. And, as I demonstrated in that chapter, the *bad-faith-juror* objection not only benefits from its rhetorical strength, but also has the particular advantage of robust empirical confirmation.

Jury nullification is a fact. Juries have the discretionary ability to return a verdict "in the teeth of both law and facts,"[1] and the courts have absolutely no legitimate power or authority to prevent, punish, or otherwise respond to such behavior. But whether jury nullification is a *de jure* fact, or a *de facto* fact is, I have demonstrated, ultimately irrelevant to the issue of the *nullification instruction*. Does jury nullification have *de jure* status? Yes – but it is a *privilege*, and as such implies nothing whatsoever about the *nullification instruction*. Should the jury receive a *nullification instruction*? No – because doing so thereby increases the likelihood of unjust and unwarranted convictions of otherwise innocent defendants.

If I have contributed anything of value to the jury nullification debate, I hope that, at the very least, I have shown that questions about the jural

[1] *Horning v. District of Columbia*, 41 S.Ct. 53 (1920).

nature of, legal status regarding, benefits realized by, or harms incurred through, the jury's *privilege* to nullify are conceptually distinct in scope and implication from similar questions regarding the *nullification instruction*. This leads me to my next major insight and contribution to the debate: because of their fundamental conceptual dissimilarity, what we say about the *privilege* to nullify does not necessarily imply anything of substance regarding what we are committed to saying about the *nullification instruction* – and *vice versa*. I believe my own views on the issue reflect this.

As Kadish and Kadish argued, we can count on jurors to *legitimately* nullify – that is, to nullify in a manner consistent with the overall principles of justice that the legal system is based upon – where there are *damn-good-reasons* to do so, even in the absence of any *nullification instruction*. This seems unambiguously correct, and is certainly backed by substantial historical evidence.[2] Moreover, the *damn-good-reason* account of nullificatory behavior is, in this respect, entirely consistent with the virtues of jury nullification posited by the advocates of the *freedom from government oppression, community/democratic values,* and *mercy/justice* arguments. To that degree, I take the *privilege* of jury nullification to be a positive and valuable aspect of our criminal justice system. Moreover, I take the dangers of state oppression, undemocratic enforcement, and unjust application of the law to be real and significant threats to individual liberty and freedom; occasional recourse to equitable resolution of the law through jury nullification is therefore fundamentally necessary in certain contexts to preserve justice within an otherwise overall just and fair legal system. Jury nullification, to quote one jurist, injects "a slack into the enforcement of law, tempering its rigor by the mollifying influence of current ethical conventions."[3] It provides the legal system with "'play in the joints'… with the jury acting as a 'safety valve' for exceptional cases."[4] It is, in the words of Roscoe Pound, "the great corrective of law in its actual administration."[5] I celebrate and defend the *privilege* of jury nullification as a positive

[2] See, for instance, CHAPTER 4, notes 59, 60, and 61.
[3] *United States v. Adams*, 126 F.2d 774, 776 (2d Cir. 1942).
[4] *U. S. v. Dougherty*, 473 F.2d 1113, 1134 (D.C. Cir. 1972).
[5] Pound, Roscoe, *Law in Books and Law in Action*, 44 Am. L. Rev. 12, 18 (1910).

reflection of the State's commitment to the just, democratic, and liberty-enhancing administration of the criminal justice system.

I condemn, however, any attempt to educate, instruct, or otherwise inform the jury of their nullificatory *privilege* within the courtroom setting.[6] As my *bad-faith-juror* objection to the instruction has demonstrated, any move by the court to promote jury nullification is a concomitant move to thereby promote unjust, unwarranted, and unsupportable verdicts of guilty – to the detriment of those defendants who, by the law and evidence are, in fact, innocent. Our commitment to justice, liberty, truth, and fairness in the law simply cannot tolerate this. All things being equal, we ought to withhold from the jury any and all in-court instructions or information regarding their *privilege* to nullify, regardless and in spite of, any and all inherent virtues of the *privilege* itself. To the degree that we view unjust convictions as anathema to the overall goals and foundational principles of our criminal justice system, we are thereby committed to rejecting the *nullification instruction*.

[6] I am quite ambivalent, actually, about extra-legal attempts to so inform the jury, and, in fact, am even somewhat sympathetic to Dr. Butler's strategy of community-based educational initiatives.

Bibliography

Books

Berlin, Isaiah, *Four Essays on Liberty* (Oxford University Press, 1969).

Black's Law Dictionary (11th ed., 2019).

Blackstone, W., *Commentaries on the Laws of England, Book the Third* (1768).

Bothe, L.; Esders, S.; and Nijdam, J. A. (Eds.), *Wergild, Compensation and Penance. The Monetary Logic of Early Medieval Conflict Resolution* (Medieval Law and Its Practice; Vol. 31) (2021).

Conrad, Clay S., *Jury Nullification: Evolution of a Doctrine* (Carolina Academic Press, 1998).

Devlin, P., *Trial by Jury* (3rd ed., Stevens, London, 1966).

Dicey, A. V., *Introduction to the Study of the Law of the Constitution* (Liberty Fund, 1982).

Finkel, Norman, *Common Sense Justice: Jurors' Notions of the Law* (Harvard University Press, 1995).

Finnis, John, *Natural Law and Natural Rights* (Oxford University Press, 1979).

Forsyth, W., *History of Trial by Jury* (2nd ed., Frederick D. Linn, 1875).

Fuller, Lon, *The Morality of Law* (Yale University Press, 1969).

Gertner, Nancy; Mizner, Judith H.; and Dubin, Joshua, *The Law of Juries* (Thomson Reuters, 2018).

Granger, Christopher, *The Criminal Jury Trial in Canada* (2nd ed., Carswell Press, 1996).

Green, Thomas A., *Verdict According to Conscience: Perspectives on the English Criminal Trial Jury, 1200-1800* (Chicago: University of Chicago Press, 1985).

Groot, Roger D., *The Early-Thirteenth Century Criminal Jury* (Princeton University Press, 1988).

Hale, Dennis. *The Jury in America: Triumph and Decline* (University Press of Kansas, 2016).

Hart, H.L.A., *The Concept of Law* (Oxford University Press, 1961).

Hayek, Friedrich, *The Political Ideal of the Rule of Law, lecture III* (N.B.E. Press, 1955).

Holmes, Stephen, *Passions and Constraint: On the Theory of Liberal Democracy* (University of Chicago Press, 1995).

Kadish, Sanford H. and Kadish, Mortimer R., *Discretion to Disobey: A Study of Lawful Departures from Legal Rules* (Stanford University Press, 1973).

Kalven, Harry and Zeisel, Hans, *The American Jury* (Little Brown Co., 1966).

Kipnis, Kenneth, *Philosophical Issues in Law: Cases and Materials* (Prentice-Hall, 1977).

Levy, Leonard W., *The Palladium of Justice: Origins of Trial by Jury* (Ivan R. Dee, 1999).

Marcus, Paul; Duncan, David K.; Miller, Tommy; and Moreno, Joëlle Anne, *The Rights of the Accused under the Sixth Amendment: Trials, Presentation of Evidence, and Confrontation, Second Edition* (Faculty Books, 2016).

Rawls, John, *A Theory of Justice* (Harvard University Press, 1971).

Raz, Joseph, *The Authority of Law: Essays on Law and Morality* (Oxford University Press, 1979).

Weber, Max, *Economy and Society*, ed. G. Roth and R. Wittich (University of California Press, 1978).

Articles

Abramson, Jeffery, *Two Ideals of Jury Deliberations*, 1998 U. Chi. Legal F. 125 (1998).

Black, Robert C., *FIJA: Monkeywrenching the Justice System*, 66 UMKC L. Rev. 11 (1997).

Butler, Paul D., *Race-Based Jury Nullification: Case-in-Chief*, 30 J. Marshall L. Rev. 911 (1997).

Butler, Paul, *Racially Based Jury Nullification: Black Power in the Criminal Justice System*, 105 Yale Law Journal 677 (1995).

Carroll, Jenny E., *The Jury as Democracy*, 66 Ala. L. Rev. 825 (2015).

Christie, George C., *Lawful Departures from Legal Rules: 'Jury Nullification' and Legitimated Disobedience* 62 California Law Review 1289 (1974).

Corbin, Arthur L., *Jural Relations and Their Classification*, 30 Yale Law Journal 226 (1921).

Crispo, Lawrence W.; Slansky, Jill M.; and Yriarte, Geanene M., *Jury Nullification: Law Versus Anarchy*, 31 Loy. L.A. L. Rev. 1 (1997).

Dershowitz, Alan, *Editorial - Barry Employs a Redneck Trick: Jury Nullification Play Appeals to Racist Instincts*, Buffalo News C3 (June 9, 1990).

Eisen, Mitchell; Dotson, Brenna; and Olaguez, Alma, *Exploring the Prejudicial Effect of Gang Evidence: Under What Conditions Will Jurors Ignore Reasonable Doubt*, 2 Crim. L. Prac. 41 (2014).

Epps, D. and Ortman, W., *The Informed Jury*, 75 Vand. L. Rev. 823 (2022).

Green, Thomas A., *The Jury and the English Law of Homicide, 1200-1600*, 74 Michigan Law Review 413 (1976).

Heller, Michael, *The Boundaries of Private Property*, 108 Yale Law Journal 1163 (1999).

Hoffman, Paul, *Double Jeopardy Wars: The Case for a Civil Rights 'Exception,'* 41 UCLA Law Review 649 (1994).

Hohfeld, Wesley N., *Fundamental Legal Conceptions as Applied in Judicial Reasoning*, 23 Yale Law Journal 16 (1913).

Holmes, O.W., *Law in Science and Science in Law*, 12 Harv. L. Rev. 443 (1899).

Horowitz, I. A., *The Effect of Jury Nullification Instruction on Verdicts and Jury Functioning in Criminal Trials*, 9(1) Law and Human Behavior 25 (1985).

Hreno, Travis, *Jury Nullification and the Bad-Faith Juror*, vol. 1, no. 1 LEAP: The Journal of Legal Ethics and Philosophy 53 (Spring 2013).

Hreno, Travis, *Necessity and Jury Nullification*, vol. 20, no. 20 Can. J. L. & Juris. 351 (2007).

Hreno, Travis, *The Jury Nullification Instruction and the De Jure / De Facto Debate: A Hohfeldian Analysis*, vol. 22, no. 3 Public Affairs Quarterly 231 (July 2008).

Hreno, Travis, *The Rule of Law and Jury Nullification*, vol. 34, no. 2 The Commonwealth Law Bulletin 297 (June 2008).

Jefferson, Thomas, *Letter to Thomas Paine*, ME 7:408, Papers 15:269 (1789).

Johnson, Julie, *The Jury Nullification Debate*, 5 U.S. A.F. Acad. J. Legal Stud. 139 (1994-1995).

Jolly, Richard L., *Jury Nullification as a Spectrum*, Pepperdine Law Review 49 (2022).

Kennedy, Duncan, *Legal Formality*, 2 J. Legal Stud. 31-2 (June 1973).

Kerr, Margaret H.; Forsyth, Richard D.; and Plyley, Michael J., *Cold Water and Hot Iron: Trial by Ordeal in England*, Vol. 22, No. 4 The Journal of Interdisciplinary History 573 (Spring, 1992).

Leipold, Andrew D., *Race-Based Jury Nullification: Rebuttal (Part A)*, 30 J. Marshall L. Rev. 923 (1997).

Levine, James, *Review Essay/Jury Wisdom*, 8 Crim. Just. Ethics 49 (1997).

Liu, Yingxi, *Does the Modern Jury Represent a Successful Exercise in Democracy?*, vol. 5, issue 13 Academic Journal of Humanities & Social Sciences 4 (2021).

Loesch, Martin C., *Motive Testimony and a Civil Disobedience Justification* 5 Notre Dame Journal of Law, Ethics, and Public Policy 1069 (1991).

Nepveu, Kate H., *Beyond 'Guilty' or 'Not Guilty': Giving Special Verdicts in Criminal Jury Trials*, vol. 21, no. 1 Yale Law & Policy Review 263 (2003).

Note: Jury Nullification: The Forgotten Right, New Eng. L. Rev. 105 (1971).

Note: The Case for Black Juries, 79 Yale Law Journal 531 (1970).

Note: Toward Principles of Jury Equity, 83 Yale Law Journal 1023 (1974).

Palmer, Robert C., *Review - Conscience and the Law: The English Criminal Jury - Green's Verdict According to Conscience*, 84 Michigan Law Review 787 (1986).

Pew Research Center, *Report: Most Americans Favor the Death Penalty Despite Concerns About Its Administration* (June 2021).

Pound, Roscoe, *Law in Books and Law in Action*, 44 Am. L. Rev. 12 (1910).

Royer, Caisa E., *The Disobedient Jury: Why Lawmakers Should Codify Jury Nullification*, 102 Cornell L. Rev. 1401 (2017).

Scheflin, Alan W., *Jury Nullification: The Right to Say No*, 45 Southern California Law Review 168 (1972).

Scheflin, Alan W. and Van Dyke, Jon M. *Jury Nullification: The Contours of a Controversy*, 43 Law & Contemp. Probs. 51 (1980).

Scheflin, Alan W. and Van Dyke, Jon M., *Merciful Juries: The Resilience of Jury Nullification*, 48 Wash. & Lee L. Rev. 165 (1991).

Schlag, Pierre, *How to Do Things with Hohfeld*, 78, Law & Contemp. Probs. 185 (2015).

Schmidt, Jr., Benno C., *Juries, Jurisdiction, and Race Discrimination: The Lost Promise of Strauder v. West Virginia*, 61 Texas Law Review 1401 (1983).

Schulhofer, Stephen J., *[Book Review] - Just Punishment in an Imperfect World - Bazelon's Questioning Authority*, 87 Michigan Law Review 1263 (1989).

Scott, Philip B., *Jury Nullification: An Historical Perspective on a Modern Debate*, 91 West Virginia Law Review 389 (1989).

Simson, Gary J., *Jury Nullification in the American System: A Skeptical View*, 54 Texas Law Review 488 (1976).

Yorke, Susan, *Jury Nullification Instructions as Structural Error*, 95 Wash. L. Rev. 1441 (2020).

Cases

Alden v. Maine, 527 U.S. 706 (1999).

Annas v. State, 726 P.2d 552 (Alaska App. 1986).

Apprendi v. New Jersey, 530 U.S. 466 (2000).

Arshack v. United States, 321 A.2d 845 (D.C. 1974).

Babson v. United States, 330 F.2d 662 (9th Cir. 1964).

Baldwin v. New York, 399 U.S. 66 (1970).

Ballew v. Georgia, 435 U.S. 223 (1978).

Bartholomew v. Clark, 1 Conn. 472 (1816).

Batson v. Kentucky, 476 U.S. 79 (1986).

Beavers v. State, 236 N.E. 2d 549 (Ind., 1975).

Beckwith v. State, 386 So. 2d 836 (Fla. Dist. Ct. App. 1980).

Benton v. Maryland, 395 U.S. 784 (1969).

Berra v. United States, 351 U.S. 131 (1956).

Bivins v. State, 642 N.E.2d 928 (Ind. 1995).

Britt v. State, 334 Ark. 142 (Ark. 1998).

Bryant v. State, 163 Ga. App. 872 (Ga. Ct. App. 1982).

Bunnell v. Sullivan, 947 F.2d 341 (9th Cir. 1991).

Burns v. PA Department of Correction, 544 F.3d 279 (3d Cir. 2008).

Bushel's Case, 124 Eng. Rep. 1006 (1670).

C 260/68, no. 20 (1357); Pardon: C.P.R., May 3, 1357, 530.

C. 260/50, no. 61 (1339).

Cargill v. State, 255 Ga. 616 (Ga. 1986).

Clark v. United States, 289 U.S. 1 (1933).

Commonwealth v. Fernette, 398 Mass. 658 N.E.2d 1290 (1986).

Cooley v. United States, 501 F.2d 1249 (9th Cir. 1974).

Corson v. United States, 147 F.2d 437, 438 (9th Cir. 1945).

Craigmire v. State, C.C.A. No. 03C01-9710-CR-00440, (Tenn. Crim. App. July 20, 1999).

Davis v. State, 520 So. 2d 493 (Miss. 1988).

Duncan v. Louisiana, 391 U.S. 145 (1968).

Dupont de Nemours v. Vance, 60 U.S. 162 (1856).

Elonis v. United States, 135 S. Ct. 2001 (2014).

Fauvre v. Roberts, 309 Or. 691 (Or. 1990).

Fenwick v. Chapman, 34 U.S. 461 (1835).

Flast v. Cohen, 392 U.S. 83 (1968).

Fong Foo v. United States, 369 U.S. 141 (1962).

Furman v. Georgia, 408 U.S. 238, 313 (1972)

Georgia v. Brailsford, 3 U.S. 1 (1794).

Garcia v. State, 480 Md. 467 (Md. 2022).

Golden State Transit Corp. v. Los Angeles, 493 U.S. 103 (1989).

Green v. United States, 356 U.S. 165 (1958).

Hamilton and Fletcher v. State, 12 Md. App. 91 (Md. Ct. Spec. App. 1971).

Horning v. District of Columbia, 41 S. Ct. 53 (1920).

Horning v. District of Columbia, 254 U.S. 135 (1920).

Hudyih v. Smith, 12-CV-1761 (SAS) (S.D.N.Y. July 1, 2015).

In re Stankewitz, 40 Cal.3d 391 (Cal. 1985).

In re Zuhone, 88 F.3d 469 (7th Cir. 1996).

JUST 2/18, m.41d/2: 1356.

Jackson v. Virginia, 443 U.S. 307 (1979).

Johnson v. State, 150 Ga. App. 405 (Ga. Ct. App. 1979).

Jurek v. State, 522 S.W.2d 934, 940 (Tex. Crim. App. 1975)

Kane v. Commonwealth, 89 Pa. 522 (1879).

Keenan v. State, 379 So.2d 147 (Fla.App. 1980).

Khan v. United States, 928 F.3d 1264, (11th Cir. 2019).

Kimbrell v. State, 148 Ga. App. 302 (Ga. Ct. App. 1978).

Kratz v. Newsom, 251 So. 2d 539 (Fla. Dist. Ct. App. 1971).

Lee v. State, 743 P.2d 296 (Wyo. 1987).

Leech's Case, 83 Eng. Rep. 53 (1664).

London Coroners' Rolls, Roll H, no. 9.

Losey v. Frank, No. 02-C-1252 (E.D. Wis. June 16, 2003).

Mabry v. Superior Court, 185 Cal.App.4th 208 (Cal. Ct. App. 2010).

Martinez v. Court of Appeal of Cal., Fourth App. Dist, 528 U.S. 152 (2000).

Mattox v. United States, 146 U.S. 140 (1892).

McCullough v. State, 351 Ga. App. 385 (Ga. Ct. App. 2019).

McDonald v. Pless, 238 U.S. 264 (1915).

McDonough Power Equipment, Inc. v. Greenwood, 464 U.S. 548 (1984).

Meeks v. State, 759 N.E.2d 1126 (Ind. Ct. App. 2001).

Merced v. McGrath, 426 F.3d 1076 (9th Cir. 2005).

Merced v. McGrath, No. C 03-1904 CRB (N.D. Cal. Feb. 10, 2004).

Merriam v. Kunzig, 476 F.2d 1233 (3d Cir. 1973).

Mills v. State, 310 Md. 33 (Md. 1987).

Mitchell v. Harmony, 54 U.S. 115 (1851).

Morissette v. United States, 342 U.S. 246 (1952).

Neder v. United States, 527 U.S. 1 (1999).

New v. State 19 Ala. App. 140, 96 So. 720.

Pena-Rodriguez v. Colorado, 137 S. Ct. 855 (2017).

Penn & Meads' Case, (22 Charles II 1670).

People v. Alford, 2d Crim. No B312837 (Cal. Ct. App. July 26, 2022).

People v. Boyd, 31 N.Y.3d 953 (N.Y. 2018).

People v. Childs, 159 Ill. 2d 217 (Ill. 1994).

People v. Croswell, 3 Johns. Cas. 337 (N.Y. Sup. Ct. 1804).

People v. Dillon, 34 Cal.3d 441 (Cal. 1983).

People v. Douglas, 178 Misc. 2d 918 (N.Y. Sup. Ct. 1998).

People v. Frazier, 123 Ill. App. 3d 563 (Ill. App. Ct. 1984).

People v. Kriho, 996 P.2d 158 (Colo. App. 1999).

People v. Lem You, 97 Cal. 224, 228 (Cal. 1893).

People v. Mesik, 775 N.W.2d 857 (Mich. Ct. App. 2009).

People v. Mina, No. F074901 (Cal. Ct. App. Dec. 13, 2018).

People v. Nicolas, G054672 (Cal. Ct. App. Oct. 5, 2018).

People v. Rendon, G054006, (Cal. Ct. App. June 26, 2018).

People v. Rodriguez, 508 P.3d 276 (Colo. App. 2022).

People v. Senter, B225495 (Cal. Ct. App. Feb. 21, 2012).

People v. Smith, 79 N.Y.2d 309 (N.Y. 1992).

People v. Smith, 296 Ill. App. 3d 435 (Ill. App. Ct. 1998).

Perlot v. Green, 609 F. Supp. 3d 1106 (D. Idaho 2022).

Poyner v. Commonwealth, 229 Va. 401 (Va. 1985).

Pyburn v. State, 301 Ga. App. 372, (Ga. Ct. App. 2009).

R. v. Bryant, 42 C.R. (3d) 312 (1984).

R. v. Krieger, [2006] 2 S.C.R. 501, 2006 SCC 47.

Ramos v. Louisiana, 140 S. Ct. 1390 (2020).

re Globe Newspaper Co., 920 F.2d 88 (1st Cir. 1990).

Reid v. Covert, 354 U.S. 1 (1956).

Remmer v. United States, 350 U.S. 377 (1956).

Rex v. Arnold, 16 How. St. Tr. 695 (1724).

Rex v. Selby, 1 Keble 769, 83 Eng. Rep. 1223 (1664).

Rex. v. Wagstaffe, 1 Keble 934, 1 Sid. 237, 82 Eng. Rep. 1101 (1665).

Richardson v. State, 403 So. 2d 293 (Ala. Crim. App. 1981).

Sapir v. United States, 216 F.2d 722 (10th Cir. 1954).

Sparf and Hansen v. United States, 156 U.S. 51 (1895).

Spaziano v. Florida, 468 U.S. 447, 462 (1984).

State ex Rel. Kincaid v. Parsons, 191 W. Va. 608 (W. Va. 1994).

State v. Allie, 147 Ariz. 320, 710 P.2d 430 (1985).

State v. Carlin, 40 Wn. App. 698 (Wash. Ct. App. 1985).

State v. Charboneau, 116 Idaho 129 (Idaho 1989).

State v. Cote, 129 N.H. 358 A.2d 775 (1987).

State v. Croteau, 23 Vt. 14 (1849).

State v. Grey, 147 N.J. 4 (N.J. 1996).

State v. Hooks, 752 N.W.2d 79 (Minn. Ct. App. 2008).

State v. Hudson, 152 Ariz. 121 (Ariz. 1986).

State v. Hunter, 586 S.W.2d 345 (Mo. 1979).

State v. Kebbie, SUPREME COURT DOCKET NO. 2018-064, 2 (Vt. Nov. 21, 2018).

State v. Kills on Top, 241 Mont. 378 (Mont. 1990).

State v. Kirkman, 159 Wn. 2d 918 (Wash. 2007).

State v. LaMere, 298 Mont. 358, (Mont. 2000).

State v. Lang, 46 N.C. App. 138, 264 S.E.2d 821 (1980).

State v. Lang, 458 P.3d 791 (Wash. Ct. App. 2020).

State v. Lankford, 116 Idaho 860 (Idaho 1989).

State v. Lawson, 144 Ariz. 547 (Ariz. 1985).

State v. Lum, I.D. No. 1408022157 A&B (Del. Super. Ct. June 29, 2016).

State v. McClanahan, 212 Kan. 208, 510 P.2d 153 (1973).

State v. Nicholas, 185 Wash. App. 298 (Wash. Ct. App. 2014).

State v. Paredes-Solano, 223 Ariz. 284 (Ariz. Ct. App. 2009).

State v. Peeler, 2007 Ct. Sup. 12157 (Conn. Super. Ct. 2007).

State v. Perkins, 353 N.W.2d 557 (Minn. 1984).

State v. Ragland, 105 N.J. 189, (N.J. 1986).

State v. Revey, 134 Wn. App. 1028 (Wash. Ct. App. 2006).

State v. Saintcalle, 178 Wash. 2d 34 (Wash. 2013).

State v. Sayles, 2021 WL 302807 (Md. 2021).

State v. Scott, 314 N.C. 309 (N.C. 1985).

State v. Showell, No. A-1981-12T1 (App. Div. Aug. 12, 2014).

State v. Silcox, 103 Idaho 483 (Idaho 1982).

State v. Simon, 79 N.J. 199 (N.J. 1979).

State v. Steenhard, 9 Wn. App. 2d 1072 (Wash. Ct. App. 2019).

State v. Vigna, 260 N.W.2d 506 (S.D. 1977).

State v. Wilkinson, 2 Vt. 480 (1829).

State v. Willis, 218 N.W.2d 921 (Iowa 1974).

Stepney v. Lopes, 592 F. Supp. 1538 (D. Conn. 1984).

Stow v. Murashige, 389 F.3d 880 (9th Cir. 2004).

Strickland v. Washington, 466 U.S. 668 (1984).

Sutton v. State, 262 Ga. 181 (Ga. 1992) (dissenting opinion).

Tanner v. United States, 483 U.S. 107 (1987).

Taylor v. Louisiana, 419 U.S. 522 (1975).

Thornburgh v. American College of Obstetricians & Gynecologists, 476 U.S. 747 (1986).

Tucker v. Palmer, 541 F.3d 652 (6th Cir. 2008).

U.S. v. Battiste, 24 F. Cas. 1042 (C.C.D. Mass., 1835).

U.S. v. Buffington, 815 F.2d 1292 (9th Cir. 1987).

U.S. v. Boone, 458 F.3d 321 (3d Cir. 2006).

U.S. v. Doherty, 675 F. Supp. 726 (D. Mass. 1987).

U.S. v. Dougherty, 473 F.2d 1113 (D.C. Cir., 1972).

U.S. v. Gilliam, 994 F.2d 97 (2d Cir. 1993).

U.S. v. Green, 346 F. Supp. 2d 259 (D. Mass. 2004).

U.S. v. Kerley, 838 F.2d 932 (7th Cir. 1988).

U.S. v. Krzyske, 836 F.2d 1013 (6th Cir. 1988).

U.S. v. Lucero, 895 F. Supp. 1421 (D. Kan. 1995).

U.S. v. Lynch, 181 F.3d 330 (2d Cir. 1999).

U.S. v. Manning, 79 F.3d 212 (1st Cir. 1996).

U.S. v. Moloian, No. 10-CR-20666 (E.D. Mich. Aug. 19, 2011).

U.S. v. Monea, 376 F. App'x 531 (6th Cir. 2010).

U.S. v. Polizzi, 549 F. Supp. 2d 308 (E.D.N.Y. 2008).

U.S. v. Powell, 955 F.2d 1206 (9th Cir. 1992).

U.S. v. Robertson, 74 F.3d 1247 (9th Cir. 1996).

U.S. v. Sepulveda, 15 F.3d 1161 (1st Cir. 1993).

U.S. v. Siegelman, 640 F.3d 1159 (11th Cir. 2011).

U.S. v. Thomas, 116 F.3d 606 (2d Cir. 1997).

U.S. v. Unruh, 855 F.2d 1363 (9th Cir. 1987).

U.S. v. West, 552 F. Supp. 2d 74 (D. Mass. 2008).

United States v. Adams, 126 F.2d 774 (2d Cir. 1942).

United States v. Baker, 342 F. Supp. 3d 1189 (D.N.M. 2018).

United States v. Ball, 163 U.S. 662 (1896).

United States v. Boardman, 1970 419 F.2d 110 (1st Cir. 1970).

United States v. Burton, 575 F. Supp. 1320 (E.D. Tex. 1983).

United States v. Datcher, 830 F. Supp. 411 (M.D. Tenn. 1993).

United States v. De Watson, 792 F.3d 1174 (9th Cir. 2015).

United States v. Dellinger, 472 F.2d 340 (7th Cir. 1972).

United States v. Diaz, 820 F. Supp. 2d 301 (D.P.R. 2011).

United States v. Edwards, 266 F. Supp. 3d 1290 (D.N.M. 2017).

United States v. Ehrens, No. CR-15-200-C (W.D. Okla. Dec. 1, 2015).

United States v. Fips, Case No.: 1:18 CR 722 (N.D. Ohio Sep. 30, 2020).

United States v. Folse, No. CR 15-2485 JB (D.N.M. Nov. 9, 2015).

United States v. Funches, 135 F.3d 1405 (11th Cir. 1998).

United States v. Gaudin, 515 U.S. 506 (1995).

United States v. Gleason, 726 F.2d 385 (8th Cir. 1984).

United States v. Gonzales, 841 F.3d 339 (5th Cir. 2016).

United States v. Greer, 538 F.2d 437 (D.C. Cir. 1976).

United States v. Heicklen, 858 F. Supp. 2d 256 (S.D.N.Y. 2012).

United States v. Johnson, 432 F.2d 626 (D.C. Cir. 1970).

United States v. Jones, No. 3:16-cr-059 (S.D. Ohio Jan. 30, 2021).

United States v. Kirk, 1:20-cr-0079 KWR (D.N.M. May 27, 2020).

United States v. Kleinman, 880 F.3d 1020 (9th Cir. 2017).

United States v. Little, CASE NO.: 2:19-cr-43 (S.D. Ga. May 7, 2020).

United States v. Lynch, 903 F.3d 1061 (9th Cir. 2018).

United States v. Laffitte, CRIMINAL ACTION 9:22-00658-RMG (D.S.C. Mar. 6, 2023).

United States v. Manzano (In re United States), 945 F.3d 616 (2d Cir. 2019).

United States v. Martin Linens Supply Co., 430 U.S. 564 (1977).

United States v. Miller, 284 F. Supp. 220 (D. Conn. 1968).

United States v. Moten, 582 F.2d 654 (2d Cir. 1978).

United States v. Molt, 589 F.2d 1247 (3d Cir. 1978).

United States v. Moylan, 417 F.2d 1002 (4th Cir. 1969).

United States v. Nixon, 418 US 683 (1974).

United States v. Olano, 507 U.S. 725 (1993).

United States v. Patterson, 587 F. App'x 878, 24 (6th Cir. 2014).

United States v. Penn, 969 F.3d 450 (5th Cir. 2020).

United States v. Pimentel, 654 F.2d 538 (9th Cir. 1981).

United States v. Renfroe, 634 F. Supp. 1536 (W.D. Pa. 1986).

United States v. Richardson, 418 U.S. 166 (1974).

United States v. Roy, 855 F.3d 1133 (11th Cir. 2017).

United States v. Scott, 437 U.S. 82 (1978).

United States v. Shelton, 588 F.2d 1242 (9th Cir. 1978).

United States v. Simpson, 460 F.2d 515 (9th Cir. 1972).

United States v. Spock, 416 F.2d 165 (1st Cir. 1969).

United States v. Stevenson, 215 U.S. 190 (1909).

United States v. Trujillo, 714 F.2d 102 (11th Cir. 1983).

United States v. Warwick, No. 16-CR-4572 MCA (D.N.M. Oct. 30, 2017).

United States v. West Coast News Company, 228 F. Supp. 171 (W.D. Mich. 1964).

United States v. Wiley, 503 F.2d 106 (8th Cir. 1974).

United States v. Young, 403 F. Supp. 3d 1131 (D.N.M. 2019).

United States v. Zipkin, 729 F.2d 384 (6th Cir. 1984).

United States v. Zubaydah, 142 S. Ct. 959 (2022).

Vaise v. Delaval, (1785).

Walker v. State, 445 N.E.2d 571 (Ind. 1983).

Walker v. State, 723 P.2d 273 (Okla. 1986).

Washington v. Watkins, 655 F.2d 1346 (5th Cir. 1981).

Watkins v. State, 265 Ga. App. 54 (Ga. Ct. App. 2004).

Williams v. Commonwealth, 644 S.W.2d 335 (Ky. 1983).

Williams v. Florida, 399 U.S. 78 (1970).

Witherspoon v. Illinois, 391 U.S. 510 (1968).

Wofford v. Woods, 969 F.3d 685 (6th Cir. 2020).

Yu v. Paperchase Partnership, 114 N.M. 635 (N.M. 1992).

www.ingramcontent.com/pod-product-compliance
Lightning Source LLC
LaVergne TN
LVHW101504200926
848483LV00001B/227
* 9 7 8 1 8 0 4 4 1 0 9 0 5 *